PUBLIC WELFARE, SCIENCE, AND PROPAGANDA IN SEVENTEENTH CENTURY FRANCE

The Innovations of Théophraste Renaudot

PUBLIC WELFARE, SCIENCE, AND PROPAGANDA IN SEVENTEENTH CENTURY FRANCE

THE INNOVATIONS OF THÉOPHRASTE RENAUDOT

Howard M. Solomon

PRINCETON UNIVERSITY PRESS

PRINCETON, NEW JERSEY

Publication of this book has been aided
by a grant from the
Whitney Darrow Publication Reserve Fund
of Princeton University Press

This book has been set in Linotype Granjon
Printed in the United States of America by
Princeton University Press, Princeton, New Jersey

To My Parents

Contents

Acknowledgments

SINCE the summer of 1966, when I began the study which is the basis of this book, a number of people have patiently let me share Renaudot with them. My two mentors at Northwestern University deserve particular mention. E. William Monter, who supervised my dissertation, had confidence in my approach to early modern history even when I had reason to doubt it (as did others). He has been a rigorous and imaginative critic. George T. Romani has long been a source of wise counsel and healthy skepticism, and his kindness has taken many forms. I hope this book reflects well upon the scholarship and humanity I have gained from these two scholars.

Several historians read the manuscript at various stages of its development, and unselfishly shared their expertise with me. In particular, I wish to thank Robert Bezucha, Northwestern University; Raymond Birn, University of Oregon; William F. Church, Brown University; Natalie Z. Davis, University of California at Berkeley; and Orest Ranum, The Johns Hopkins University. My former chairman, John W. Wilkes, and his colleagues at University College, New York University, provided a congenial environment in which to write and rewrite. Wendy Deutelbaum and Jo McNally cheerfully typed the manuscript. To these friends and colleagues, and many others, my gratitude for enduring the constant presence of Renaudot in my life since 1966. In no small measure, these friendships make it easier for me to accept the faults this book may still have.

Institutional support has generously aided the completion of this project. A Dissertation Year Fellowship, as well as a History Department Travel Grant from Northwestern University supported research in Paris during the period from June 1967 to August 1968. Grants from New York University's Arts and Sciences Research Fund permitted me to return to France during the summers of 1969 and 1970; this aid also covered duplication and typing costs. Most of my research was done in Paris at the Bibliothèque Nationale, Bibliothèque de l'Arsenal, and the Faculté de Médecine, but I have also used the excellent resources of several American libraries. These include the John Crerar Library and Newberry Library in Chicago, the New York Public Library, and the libraries of Northwestern, New York, Princeton, and Columbia Universities.

My final gratitude is to my parents. As only my brothers and I can know, this is their book.

Tufts University   H.M.S.
September 1971

Preface

IN THE second act of Edmond Rostand's *Cyrano de Bergerac* a man with a pen, grasping a bundle of notebooks under his arm, rushes onto the scene. Cyrano learns

> C'est Théophraste Renaudot! l'inventeur de la *Gazette* . . .
> Cette feuille où l'on fait tant de choses tenir!
> On dit que cette idée a beaucoup d'avenir!

Written at the very end of the nineteenth century, these lines were well founded; the French press did have "beaucoup d'avenir." The same, it would seem, was true of the memory of Théophraste Renaudot himself. In June 1893 a large statue in his honor had been erected in Paris on the rue de Lutèce, between the Palais de Justice and the Hôtel Dieu. Along with dignitaries of the nation and city, representatives of the institutions which felt a debt to Renaudot were there to pay homage; the hospitals of Paris, the *mont-de-piété*, the press, and, amicably side by side, the medical faculties of Paris and of Montpellier.[1] Renaudot was finally in the best of company. The only other statues on the Île de la Cité were of Henry IV and Charlemagne.

Two full-length biographies of this man had appeared.

---

[1] The statue, done by Alfred Boucher, portrayed Renaudot sitting at a writing table, alertly turning his head as if to receive a bit of news. Boucher decorated the marble base with Renaudot's favorite device, a crowing cock. After the dedication, Georges Gilles de la Tourette, Renaudot's biographer, was awarded the Legion d'Honneur for his efforts in erecting the statue. *Inauguration de la statue de Théophraste Renaudot, fondateur de journalisme et des consultations charitables pour les pauvres malades, 4 juin 1893* (Paris: 1893), 48 pp. Even though this statue was destroyed, a plaque on a building on the Quai Marché Neuf still marks the approximate location of Renaudot's Maison du Grand Coq.

xi

Eugène Hatin, bibliographer and historian of the French press, published *Théophraste Renaudot et ses 'innocentes inventions'* in 1883. A year later, Georges Gilles de la Tourette, a young graduate of the Parisian medical faculty, published *Théophraste Renaudot, d'après des documents inédits*. This work is less panegyrical than Hatin's but its medical orientation is as one-dimensional as the earlier study done by the journalist. Contemporaries, affected by their zeal, likewise took up the pen in a long-delayed effort to restore Renaudot's reputation. With the exception of a thesis on Renaudot's medical ideas,[2] these are just poorly rehashed versions of Hatin and Gilles de la Tourette. Scholarly interest flourished long enough to erect the statue, and then faded as quickly as did the music of that June ceremony. The *fin de siècle* enthusiasm was long dead in 1941, when the statue was melted down during the German occupation.

Time has been as ungenerous to Renaudot as was the German occupation. He usually earns a few paragraphs in popular French accounts of the history of journalism or of medicine in the ancien régime, his name appears in bookshop windows displaying the yearly winner of the *Prix Renaudot*, he is categorized as founder of the *Gazette de France* by students at the lyceums cramming for the *baccalauréat*, and that is all. No new treatments of his life have emerged, even though there has been renewed interest in several areas in which Renaudot distinguished himself. Swedish and French scholars have established that his *Gazette* was not the first to appear in Paris,[3] yet there has been no serious attempt to analyze Renaudot's work as a journalist. A recent French thesis has examined Richelieu's publicists, but hardly mentions Renau-

[2] Michel Émery, *Renaudot et l'introduction de la médication chimique* (Montpellier: 1888).

[3] Folke Dahl, Fanny Petibon, Marguerite Boulet, "Les débuts de la presse française," *Acta Bibliothecae Gotoburgensis* (Goteburg and Paris: 1951).

dot's important contributions.[4] Another gives a definitive
treatment of book publishing in seventeenth century Paris,
but does not discuss the gazettes and *pièces volantes* with
which Renaudot was involved.[5] Several recent studies have
examined social welfare in sixteenth and seventeenth century
France, yet none has considered Renaudot's public welfare
schemes.[6] Interest in the erudite libertines has been paralleled
by scholarly interest in the more chimerical realm of *culture
populaire*; the work of Robert Mandrou comes to mind. Yet
Renaudot's academy and medical ideas straddle both the
libertine salons and the world of the Pont Neuf and *bibliothèque bleue* at the same time. A definitive study of the nine-
year career of Renaudot's academy would be in effect an

[4] Étienne Thuau, *Raison d'État et pensée politique à l'époque de
Richelieu* (Paris: 1966).
[5] Henri-Jean Martin, *Livre, pouvoirs et société à Paris au XVIIe siècle
(1598-1701)* (Geneva: 1969).
[6] Natalie Zemon Davis, "Poor Relief, Humanism, and Heresy: the
Case of Lyon," *Studies in Medieval and Renaissance History*, v (1968),
217-75; R. M. Kingdon, "Social Welfare in Calvin's Geneva," *American
Historical Review*, LXXVI (1971), 50-69; Jean Imbert, "Les prescriptions
hospitalières du Concile de Trent et leur diffusion en France," *Revue
d'histoire de l'Église de France*, XLII (1956), 5-28; Michel Mollat, "La
notion de pauvreté au moyen âge: position de problèmes," *Revue
d'histoire de l'Église de France*, LII (1966), 6-24; R. Stauffenegger,
"Réforme, richesse, et pauvreté," *Revue d'histoire de l'Église de France*,
LII (1966), 47-58; Marc Venard, "Catholicisme et usure au XVIe siècle,"
Revue d'histoire de l'Église de France, LII (1966), 59-74; Emanuel Chill,
"Religion and Mendicity in Seventeenth Century France," *International
Review of Social History*, VII (1962), 400-25; Pierre Deyon, "À propos
du pauperisme au milieu du XVIIe siècle: peinture et charité chré-
tienne," *Annales*, XIII (1967), 137-53; J-P. Gutton, "À l'aube de XVIIe
siècle: idées nouvelles sur les pauvres," *Cahiers d'histoire*, x (1965), 87-
97. Gutton is including a discussion of Renaudot in his forthcoming
La société et les pauvres dans la France d'ancien régime. A recent edition of *Dix-septième siècle* (Nos. 90-91, 1971) is devoted to "Les oeuvres
de charité en France au XVIIe siècle." In particular see the articles by
R. P. Chalumeau, "l'Assistance aux malades pauvres au XVIIe siècle,"
75-86; and R. Darricou, "l'Action charitable d'une reine de France:
Anne d'Autriche," 111-25.

analysis of the intellectual world of the mid-seventeenth century: my efforts have simply been to outline the major concerns of the academy, while considering its institutional role in Paris.

Much attention has been devoted to Renaudot's fellow projectors in England of the first half of the seventeenth century. Ranging from Henry Robinson's hardheaded practicality to Jan Amos Comenius' pansophic idealism, their projects have had their historians.[7] Educational reform, social application of accumulated knowledge, state direction of social and economic reform, improvement of communication and social intercourse—these hopes drew upon a mixture of Baconian, mercantilist, and Renaissance academic sources. But such sources were hardly limited to England, and Renaudot borrowed as widely and deeply as they. Unlike his contemporaries in England, however, he succeeded in putting all of his projects into practice. During the 1630's and early 1640's, with the active support and encouragement of Richelieu and Louis XIII, all of his disparate activities at the Bureau d'Adresse thrived as an organic whole. Renaudot was the most successful projector of his era, yet no one has studied his schemes in such a context.

Throughout this book I have been struck by the corporate entanglements within which Renaudot, as a physician, journalist, and philanthropist, was forced to operate. Corporate life, its

[7] H. R. Trevor-Roper, "Three Foreigners: the Philosophers of the Puritan Revolution," *The Crisis of the Seventeenth Century* (New York: 1968), pp. 237-93; G. H. Turnbull, *Samuel Hartlib* (London: 1920); G. H. Turnbull, *Hartlib, Dury and Comenius* (London: 1947); Matthew Spinka, *John Amos Comenius* (Chicago: 1943); Grace A. Hawley, *John Evelyn and the Advancement of Learning* (New York: 1962); W. K. Jordan, *Men of Substance: A Study of the Thought of Two English Revolutionaries, Henry Parker and Henry Robinson* (Chicago: 1942); W. K. Jordan, *Philanthropy in England 1480-1660* (London: 1959), pp. 174-240; Richard F. Jones, *Ancients and Moderns* (Berkeley: 1965); W. E. Houghton, Jr., "The History of Trades," *Journal of the History of Ideas*, II (1941), 33-60.

attitudes and psychological outlook, remain a major elusive factor in studying early modern urban society. Its presence confronts and confounds the student of this period and this city at every turn. Regardless of his unique experiences and experiments, Renaudot was a man of his epoch, and as such had no choice but to operate within that world. His relations to a corporate society color his public welfare, journalistic, and medical careers; these relations provide a lifelong constant which help to focus his seemingly disparate activities.

PUBLIC WELFARE, SCIENCE, AND PROPAGANDA IN SEVENTEENTH CENTURY FRANCE

The Innovations of Théophraste Renaudot

NOTE ON MECHANICS

Citations in sixteenth and seventeenth century French reproduce the spelling, accents, and punctuation of the original sources. References to the *Gazette* and the Conferences of the Bureau d'Adresse are by date rather than by page. All citations from Guy Patin's correspondence refer to the Reveillé-Parise edition, unless otherwise indicated.

CHAPTER I

Early Career: 1586-1630

IN HIS 1626 *Abrégé des antiquitez de Loudun*, Louis Trincant, Loudun's public prosecutor, boasted that his birthplace had been as fertile in great men and events as it was in beautiful buildings and crops.[1] Permitting a certain amount of home-town bias, Trincant's zeal was still labored and excessive. Except for its relatively large population (14,000) there had been little to distinguish Loudun from similar regional centers: a decaying medieval donjon, an old wall which, in local legend at least, dated from the Roman era when the town was supposedly known as Juliodunum.[2] Undisturbed by history, resigned to the periodic cruelties of famine and plague, Loudun had been left alone to enjoy the moderate prosperity and tranquility of the Poitevan countryside. Physically, economically, historically, Loudun was a nondescript town.

The religious wars of the sixteenth century would change all of this. In 1563 Loudun's Protestants received permission from Charles IX to hold public worship. Protestants represented a sizable part of the population, and by the 1570's were in the majority. By the mid-1580's the town was staunchly loyal to the armies and ideas of Henry of Navarre, the *politique* leader of French Protestantism. Religious antagonisms in Loudun heated during the decade, and intensified in 1586-1587 when the town was threatened with destruction by the troops of the Catholic monarch Henry III.[3] The 1598

---

[1] *Abrégé des antiquitez de Loudun et pais du Loudunois* (1626), ed., Roger Drouault (Loudun: 1894), pp. 41ff.

[2] Dumoustier de la Fond, *Essais sur l'histoire de Loudun* (Poitiers: 1778), Chapter 1. The early chapters of A. Huxley's *Devils of Loudun* (New York: 1965), describe Renaudot's Loudun well.

[3] A. Lerosey, *Loudun, histoire civile et religieuse* (Loudun: 1908), pp. 63-70.

Edict of Nantes recognized the political rights of Loudun as a Protestant city, but religious enmities would long cloud town life. It was an exciting and challenging time to be born a Protestant.

Théophraste Renaudot was born at Loudun in 1586. This information comes from Renaudot himself; town records for the period are missing. The family name first appeared in a 1590 register, testifying that a Jehan Renaudot had attended a town meeting. This Jehan Renaudot, Théophraste's father, was originally from Burgundy or Anjou, and was Protestant. Records cite a baptism of his son Jehan, Théophraste's younger brother, in 1591.[4] We do not know what the elder Renaudot's profession was, although he was successful enough to leave a solid patrimony when he died. The family home in which Théophraste was born still stands, and by sixteenth century bourgeois standards, appears comfortable and perhaps even large. Nowhere did Renaudot speak of his parents.

Renaudot wrote little about his childhood and schooling. By the 1590's Benedictines had established a public school at Loudun, but not until 1598, when Renaudot was twelve, could young Protestants attend their own public classes. Until then the Protestant community was served by independent schoolmasters. Renaudot was lucky: his parents sent him to take

---

[4] R. Drouault, "Notes inédites sur la famille de Théophraste Renaudot," *Revue poitevine*, 1892, p. 6. Renaudot offered this information in *Response . . . au libelles fait contre les consultations charitables* (Paris: 1641). It is also corroborated by an engraving of Renaudot appearing in the Bibliothèque Nationale's copy of *Recueil des Gazettes de l'année 1631*. The caption of the engraving (which was later glued to the frontispiece of the volume) reads: "Théophrastus Renaudot Juliodunensis, Medicus et Historiographus Regius, aetatis ano 58: salutis 1644." His 1 November 1653 obituary in the *Gazette* said he was 70 years old when he died. His son Eusèbe, who probably wrote the obituary, recorded in his *Journal des principalles affaires de ma vie* that his father "mourut en sa 69 année ou environ." B.N. mss. f.fr. 14348, f. 9r. (Republished in *Mémoires de la Société de l'histoire de Paris* [1878], IV, pp. 239-69.)

lessons from Daniel Boulenger, whose father had "occupied a notable place among the greatest teachers of his century."[5] Renaudot received a thorough grounding in the traditional classical subjects, all of which would serve him well in his future career. It is likely that Renaudot left Loudun to attend a university, probably Poitiers, at the age of twelve or thirteen. His father could afford to send him, and his subsequent sophistication suggests that he would have exhausted the limits of the town's Protestant school. Moreover, his rapid progress at the University of Medicine of Montpellier suggests that he had already attended a university before matriculating at Montpellier.

Once he had finished his schooling, Renaudot found his career alternatives well defined. He was bourgeois and Protestant. A military or a clerical career was immediately out of the question, and commerce would be a waste of his talents. He decided to study medicine.

Most seventeenth century medical students wanted to study at the Faculty of Medicine of the University of Paris, the most prestigious, influential, and ancient faculty in the realm. This was not true, however, if the student were Protestant; the reformed statutes of 1600 required proof of *la foi catholique apostolique et Romaine* of all students and faculty.[6] There were, however, other alternatives. One could study with a college of surgeons. While this training was often more sound than the formalism followed at the University of Paris, the best of surgeons, according to law and tradition, was still a handmaiden to the faculty-trained physician.

He could follow the route taken by thousands of subse-

[5] Scévole Sainte-Marthe, *Éloges des hommes illustres* (Paris: 1644), p. 370.
[6] By these statutes, Protestant day students could remain aloof from the college system, but so few dared that their rights had to be defended by parlementary action. M. Pattison, *Isaac Casaubon* (Oxford: 1892), p. 164.

5

quently forgotten country doctors, and attach himself to a
provincial faculty. The nearest of these to Loudun was at
Poitiers. Medical education in the seventeenth century presented few of the technical and financial problems that confront medical faculties today. Laboratories, anatomical the-
aters, and extensive libraries were rare, and within the
traditional confines of accepted medical theory, often anathema.[7] Medical education was much more literarily than
technically oriented. Such a school could easily furnish versions of the Galen and Hippocrates taught at Paris. We know
from Renaudot himself that the Faculty of Medicine at Poitiers,
as was true of the better of these provincial faculties, established standards of licensing and practice within the province's
medical community.[8]

He could attend a provincial academy where, for a few
sous, he would be "licensed" to practice medicine. Speaking
for his fellow physicians, Renaudot wrote to the faculty at
Poitiers complaining of one of these graduates (in this case,
of an academy at Cahors) who was practicing at Loudun;
the fellow had presented baccalaureate, licentiate, and doctorate certificates, all of them granted on the same day![9] It
is no wonder that degree-mills were so numerous. The principles of medical theory were simple, well defined, and
readily understood by everyone. Medical practice was equally
formalized and ritualized, and the person who knew a few
"simples" and prescriptions and could quote his authorities
with sufficient flourish—who knew if the Latin were correct?
—needed only an impressive parchment to attest to his
knowledge.

Finally, the bright and ambitious student could attend the
University of Medicine of Montpellier. Its fame south of the

[7] See Chapters III and VI.
[8] M. de la Bouralière, "Une lettre inédite de Théophraste Renaudot,"
Bulletin de la Société des Antiquaires de l'Ouest (1884), pp. 307-12.
[9] *Ibid.*, p. 310.

Loire rivaled that of the University of Paris, and a degree from Montpellier was nearly as prestigious and politically influential. More important in Renaudot's case, the Montpellier faculty not only tolerated but even seemed to welcome Protestant students. Ever since the Cathari and Albigensian heresies, Languedoc had a reputation for tolerating strange religious opinions. Montpellier was one of four university or academy towns left to the Protestants by the Edict of Nantes, and as Louis XIII and Richelieu would learn, the remnants of such independent particularism were still strong.

No less extraordinary was the reputation of Montpellier as a bastion of novel medical ideas. As early as the twelfth century, Montpellier was providing medical training. For centuries, in spite of the protests of the Paris faculty, many royal physicians were Montpellier graduates. The faculty placed greater emphasis on practice and experimentation than did its sister faculty to the north. It had its own anatomical theater in 1556, a chair in anatomy and botany in 1593, a chair in surgery and pharmacy in 1597, a botanical garden and an official anatomist in 1595—all before the University of Paris.[10] This gave to Montpellier an alluring reputation, and it was to Montpellier that the 19 year old Renaudot came in 1605.

Renaudot matriculated on 14 November 1605; was received Bachelor of Medicine on 16 January 1606; received his licentiate from the Dean on 5 April; and, finally, passed the *Actus Triumphalis* on 12 July 1606.[11] Eight months only, from matriculation to final graduation as doctor of medicine, with all of the rights and honors pertaining thereto. The reaction of a twentieth century medical student to this academic record

[10] A. Germain, *l'Université de Montpellier* (Montpellier: 1879-1886), passim. This is a collection of 12 different articles.

[11] These documents are reproduced in the appendix of M. Émery, *Renaudot et l'introduction de la médication chimique* (Montpellier: 1888).

7

would probably be similar to that of the Parisian faculty; Montpellier was a degree-mill, and Renaudot had bought his doctorate.

Their suspicion was understandable. The University of Medicine of Montpellier had long enjoyed the papal license of *hic et ubique terrarum*. In other words, its graduates could practice in Montpellier and throughout the realm. Unlike the Faculty of Medicine of the University of Paris, which claimed the same *hic et ubique terrarum* privilege, the Montpellier faculty seemed to have two different standards. Its demands were more rigorous upon those who would remain in Montpellier than upon those who, trained *à la petite mode*, would leave the city after graduation.[12]

This does not necessarily mean that Renaudot received a watered-down education intended for those *à la petite mode*. Most likely, the faculty ignored certain technical requirements in special cases. The faculty had waived the waiting period between examinations before, and such rapid progress was not unknown in cases of precocious students.[13] And Renaudot was certainly that: his professors had thought enough of his abilities to have him serve on examination committees with them even before he received his doctorate.[14] It is possible that Renaudot had already studied at a provincial university, most probably Poitiers, or with the surgeons of the College of St. Côme in Paris, before he went to Montpellier.[15] In any case, his progress was rapid and remarkable.

Renaudot could have practiced medicine with the licentiate, but since defending a thesis was not necessary, he decided

[12] M. Raynaud, *Les médecins au temps de Molière* (Paris: 1862), p. 260.

[13] There are many examples in the 4,000 dossiers reproduced by M. Gouron in his edition of *Matricule de l'Université de Médecine de Montpellier 1503-1599* (Geneva: 1957).

[14] F. Granel, "l'Empreinte montpellieraine de Théophraste Renaudot," *Monspelliensis Hippocrates* (1963), p. 16.

[15] *Ibid.*, p. 14.

to attain the more prestigious doctorate. He was then entitled to celebrate the supplementary *Actus Triumphalis*, the public ceremony by which he was named Doctor of Medicine. The austerities imposed by the Wars of Religion had dulled some of its splendor, but Renaudot's *Actus Triumphalis* must have been similar, at least in essence, to that defined in the University's 1534 statutes. The entire university community would have been present at the Church of St. Firmin, seated according to rank, all resplendent in their robes of station. The candidate first rendered homage in Latin to the university, the faculty, and the noble art to which he was dedicating himself. Then the presiding officer of the session (usually the student's master) crowned him with the red-tufted, gold-bordered black bonnet. Finally, magnanimously, the new doctor was seated in honor at his master's side. After receiving the praise and congratulation of the assembled guests, the new doctor returned their compliments in the form of gifts (gloves, condiments, etc., but the 1534 statutes urged restraint).[16] The *Actus Triumphalis* was complete: Alma Mater had sent forth another son, with all the blessings she could muster.

Renaudot was now 20 years old, and a Doctor of Medicine of Montpellier. "Knowing that age is necessary to authorize a physician, I spent a few years traveling both within and outside this Kingdom, to take in what I found best in the practice of this art."[17] He did not say where, or how long. Some have suggested that he traveled to Italy and to England, that he went to Germany where he became even more familiar with the Paracelsian ideas he may have first imbibed

---

[16] A. Germain, "l'École de Médecine de Montpellier," *l'Université de Montpellier* (1880), p. 23. John Locke attended a similar ceremony when he visited Montpellier in 1675, and he described it in his journal. See K. Dewhurst, *John Locke: Physician and Philosophy* (London: 1963), pp. 65-66.

[17] *Response . . . au libelles*, p. 41.

9

at Montpellier.[18] It is possible that he went to Paris and continued his studies with a barber-surgeon, perhaps he practiced in some obscure village, but this too is conjectural. Such a *wanderjahr* was by no means rare for young physicians, formal medical education being so bookish that additional experience was a virtual necessity. Part of the time was spent in practice. For the Platter family, three of whom have left accounts of their education at Montpellier in the sixteenth century, the custom was *de rigeur*. Thomas the younger, for example, practiced in a tiny Languedoc town for 18 months before setting out on his travels and returning to practice in Basel.[19] Jerome Cardan describes doing much the same thing in the little town of Sacco, near Padua, in the 1530's.[20] It could be that a lot of medical professors advised their students to make their mistakes early and in obscurity before returning to their hometowns to practice, since no intern system existed.

Eventually Renaudot returned to Loudun. He was established there by 1609, when at the age of 23 he married Marthe Dumoustier, of one of Loudun's most prosperous Protestant families. Théophraste *fils* was born in 1610, Isaac in 1611, Eusèbe in 1613. At least two daughters (Marie and Jacqueline) and perhaps another son came from this marriage.[21] Surrounded by a growing family, encouraged by a growing practice, the young doctor could look forward to a comfortable and secure future.

Renaudot was a graduate of a renowned university, a traveler who had returned to his *pays* from study and adventure in strange and distant places. Only a handful of townsmen had ever ventured beyond the neighboring towns of Saumur,

[18] G. Gilles de la Tourette, *Théophraste Renaudot* (Paris: 1884), pp. 11-12; Granel, p. 18. All of this is conjectural.

[19] R. Keiser, ed., *Thomas Platter d.J.: Beschreibung der Reisen durch Frankreich, Spanien, England und die Niederlande (1559-1600)* (Basel: 1968).

[20] *Book of My Life* (New York: 1930), p. 13.

[21] Drouault, "Notes inédites," p. 7.

Tours, or Poitiers, two days journey to the south. To his neighbors, Renaudot had exciting credentials. His opinions would be solicited on all civic matters, his advice taken seriously by men in awe of his experience. By the age of 25 Renaudot had become a town father.

At some point, Renaudot became concerned with Loudun's mendicity and public welfare problems. He was investigating different welfare schemes, and considered writing a treatise on the subject.[22] The problems of Loudun's sick and poor were extreme, but little different from those elsewhere in France. Before 1647, when Loudun erected a Maison de Charité, there were several independent charitable institutions with overlapping functions. There was a leprosarium, without much revenue or very many patients. But leprosy was hardly a problem in Loudun. Throughout the fifteenth and sixteenth centuries, there had been a sharp decline in Europe's leper population, and Loudun buried the last inmate of her leprosarium in 1626.[23] A greater problem was the poor.

Typical of most towns, Loudun had a Maison Dieu, where the poor could find food, shelter, and spiritual nourishment. It had been founded in 1272, with benefices to support six monks and a prior charged with the care of the sick and the poor. But by the middle of the sixteenth century, it was so destitute that it could barely support the single prior. He was expected to keep a 9-bed hospital (5 beds for general use, but each one of the others reserved for priests, pregnant women, lepers, and stroke victims), as well as bury the dead, care for foundling children, clean and heat the rooms where the poor slept. The prior constantly complained to the town fathers about shortages of fuel, food, and donations. Civil war and famines virtually killed the dying institution. Its hospitals, almonry, and chapel were destroyed, its last rents alienated,

[22] B.N. mss. f.fr. 18605, ff. 19-20.
[23] R. Drouault, *Recherches sur les établissements hospitalières du Loudunais* (Loudun: 1897), pp. 8-9.

its prior resigned in desperation. Beggars and vagabonds hiding within its walls gave it a reputation as a veritable *cour des miracles.*[24]

Loudun was no stranger to plague and famine. In 1563 plague had taken 3,623 lives, and equally severe attacks followed in 1597 and 1603. In 1603 the town fathers established a commission, or Sanitat, to care for plague victims. In addition to traditional plague control methods—public prayers, banning all markets, meetings, and funerals, burning bonfires and shooting cannons to disperse the diseased air— it also built a hospital for plague sufferers. Above the entrance was emblazoned

> On a basty ce lieu
> Aux despens de la ville,
> Mais y fault prier Dieu
> Qu'il demuer inutille.

By 1607 the immediate threat of plague had disappeared, and the Sanitat's hospital was closed.[25]

But what about aid to poor people who were not victims of plague or famine, who were healthy enough to work but had no jobs? There were a number of almonries in the countryside, but they were impoverished by the same fates which had nearly killed the Maison Dieu. The city periodically chased the foreign beggars outside its gates, but this did substantially little to aid Loudun's own poor. Until new religious houses were established in Loudun (Jesuits, 1610; Capuchins, 1616; Sisters of Calvary, 1624; Ursulines, 1626), the only refuge for the poor was the crumbling Maison Dieu.[26]

Loudun, then, had old institutions ill-suited to new pres-

[24] Drouault, *Établissements hospitalières,* pp. 23-39.
[25] *Ibid.,* pp. 48-53. Also see P. Delaroche, *Une epidemie de peste à Loudun en 1632* (Bordeaux: 1936).
[26] Drouault, *Établissements hospitalières,* pp. 55-62.

sures of chronic unemployment and civil chaos. During crises, such as the plague, new institutions had to be established, and then were disbanded as soon as the immediate crisis had passed. New religious houses aided the poor, but under the aegis of Counter Reformation Catholicism in a city still strongly Protestant.

For Renaudot, several issues had to be resolved. Aid to the poor, as a civic and economic problem, had to cut across devotional lines, for the Protestant poor were as helpless as their Catholic neighbors. The chronic unemployed needed adequate jobs to lessen pressures on financially desperate institutions. Renaudot had seen beggars and unemployed journeymen, cripples of war and plague victims everywhere during his travels; conditions in his hometown were unfortunately not at all unique. Loudun's problems were not local, but regional and even national in scope.

Renaudot's opinions made the rounds of Loudun's intellectual and social circles. Such ideas might well have stayed within Loudun, were it not for a fortuitous acquaintance with François Leclerc du Tremblay, better known as Père Joseph. In 1611 Père Joseph was on an inspection tour of religious houses near Loudun. Perhaps Renaudot's theories preceded him; perhaps he was presented at a social gathering; perhaps, more prosaically, the Capuchin needed medical attention and Renaudot was called to his aid. In any case, the acquaintance would serve Renaudot well, for it was Père Joseph who introduced Renaudot to the young bishop of Luçon, in whose diocese Loudun was located. The bishop was Armand-Jean du Plessis de Richelieu.

Richelieu and Père Joseph themselves had just met, and at this point in their careers Père Joseph was the more prominent in court circles.[27] He introduced the bishop to Marie de Medici, the Queen Regent, and soon she was aware of

[27] It was Marie de Medici who had sent Père Joseph on the inspection tour which brought him into Richelieu's diocese.

Richelieu's considerable abilities. His diocese, so poor that he considered it "the vilest in France, the most wretched and disagreeable,"[28] was responding to his direction. Revenues had increased, a seminary was established, and even the most independent parish priest felt the tightened control from the episcopal seat at Luçon. Richelieu's entrance into royal power was slow and cautious, but no less sure.

In 1612 Richelieu suggested that the conference on mendicity meeting in Paris might learn something from his new acquaintance. As a result, Renaudot was called from Loudun to present his ideas before the assembly. The court paid the expenses of Renaudot's journey, and more important, rewarded him with a title of royal physician, with a yearly stipend of 800 *livres*.[29] Renaudot's title was confirmed on 30 October 1617, and on 3 February 1618 he was named *Commissaire Général des Pauvres du Royaume*.[30]

At first glance, Richelieu's patronage of this young and obscure Huguenot is rather baffling, considering that this was the most "Catholic Reformation" part of Richelieu's career. There is little to indicate that Renaudot possessed a unique, arresting personality. Physically, Renaudot was not at all striking. There are two anonymous engravings of him, a 1631 allegory showing him seated at a writing table surrounded by Truth, Gazette, etc., and a conventional portrait, done in 1644 when he was 58 years old.[31] Both portray him a man of medium stature, with deep-set eyes and a short beard, his face distinguished only by a broad, flat nose. Guy Patin,

[28] Quoted by G. Hanotaux, *Histoire du Cardinal de Richelieu* (Paris: 1896), I, 92.

[29] B.N. mss. f.fr. 18605, ff. 19-20. He took the oath of *Médecin du Roi* on 14 October 1612 from Heroard, Louis XIII's physician. *Factum du procez d'entre Théophraste Renaudot* . . . (s.l.n.d.).

[30] B.N. mss. f.fr. 18605, f. 19v.

[31] Bibliothèque Nationale, Cabinet des Estampes, "Pièce allegorique de la Gazette," Histoire. Qb. 1630-1639; frontispiece to *Recueil des Gazettes de l'année 1631* (4°Lc2.1).

Renaudot's most vociferous enemy, considered him downright ugly. The two portraits, which presumably sought to flatter Renaudot, confirm Patin's opinion. In his later years, Renaudot was afflicted by syphilitic sores, and his *camus* nose was considerably worn away.

His personality was equally nondescript. Never did a man write more and reveal less of his family, personality, or life style. Traces of a private Renaudot hardly exist. Except for occasional bouts of self-righteousness, Renaudot's writing was even tempered and devoid of passion, assets for a man selling his pen to a patron. Given the complexity of his activities, Renaudot was analytic and meticulous, attentive to detail and organization. He may have called for revolutions in medical practice, public welfare, and pedagogy, but his hopes were always tempered by the real world of balance-sheets, profits, and political power. For all his vision, Renaudot was a patient pragmatist. In addition to supporting Renaudot's poor relief schemes, Richelieu and Renaudot shared ideas on the French economy, the uses of propaganda, and the revitalization of the nobility. In Renaudot the cardinal-minister found a like-minded compatriot.

Richelieu and Renaudot, both of Poitou, shared a common regional origin. In early modern French society, this was no minor matter. Men of the same region spoke with a common vocabulary and accent, enjoyed the same regional customs and traditions, understood the realities of political power within their *pays*. Trust was shared when countrymen confronted outsiders, *étrangers*, strengthening the bonds of mutual dependence and service. Richelieu would feel these obligations throughout his life not only to Renaudot, but to countless other fellow countrymen. Renaudot felt similar obligations, and one can imagine boys from Loudun, newly arrived in Paris, seeking out Renaudot's aid. For men who had exchanged the *pays* for Paris, the creator-creature relationship helped to combat the disorientation of urban life.

15

Servility and self-seeking may be present in any patronage relationship, but the role of shared common regional origins cannot be denied.

Renaudot was part of a large and complex patron-client system, and gladly served others who considered themselves creatures of Richelieu. These ranged from people of the first rank of power, such as Père Joseph and the Secretary of State Chavigny, to people such as the Abbé de Masles and Richelieu's personal physician Citoys. All of Richelieu's creatures benefited from the cardinal's power. All identified their fortunes with his; all shared his glory; all suffered when he died. Renaudot exploited and was exploited by Richelieu's other creatures, but without Richelieu's existence, he was nothing.

Renaudot traveled to Paris occasionally to attempt to confirm his patents and to implement the ideas he had presented in 1612, but without success. Otherwise he stayed at Loudun. His life continued to be that of a moderately prosperous and respected provincial physician.

He occupied himself with his medical practice. As we have seen, he spoke for the physicians of Loudun concerning an improperly certified practitioner.[32] He was known, again according to his own testimony, as one of the most famous physicians of Poitou.[33] He wrote several works on medical theory and practice, and at least two of them are still extant.[34] There were a few administrators, lawyers, and fellow physicians with whom an educated man could discuss the classics, or share the intellectual gossip which might drift into town with a clandestine copy of Vanini or Sarpi. And certainly Renaudot would find polite reception of his ideas on treatment of the poor. This was hardly the heady intellectual

[32] Bouralière, passim.   [33] *Response . . . au libelles*, p. 40.
[34] *Description d'un médicament appelé Polychreston* (Loudun: 1619); *Discours sur le scelet* (Loudun: 1629). For a long time, the *Discours sur le scelet* was unknown; perhaps the only extant copy of it is in the Northwestern University Medical Library.

atmosphere Renaudot would find a few years later in Paris, but at least it could permit one to while away the years without complete boredom.

Things took a turn for the better in 1619. Scévole de Sainte Marthe, considered the greatest grammarian of his age, returned to his family home in Loudun. Sainte Marthe had served Henry III and Henry IV as Treasurer of France, and Ronsard described his Latin and French verses as "The muses themselves . . . I much prefer the author of these verses to all the poets of our century."[35] A steady stream of well-wishers came to Loudun to pay him homage, including de Thou and Charles I of England. His home became "a meeting place for a brilliant and literate society."[36] The relations between Renaudot and Sainte Marthe were quite warm, and only three months before his death he read the treatise on poor relief which Renaudot had dedicated to him.[37]

Another habitué of Sainte-Marthe's circle was Urbain Grandier, fiery curé of St. Pierre du Marché. He and Renaudot became friends. Much later, when Grandier had become the most notorious cleric in France and Loudun the most bewitched town in Christendom, this friendship would provide grist for Renaudot's enemies.[38] But all of this was far in the future. The cavalier priest and the retiring Protestant physician were regular pillars of Sainte Marthe's salon. After the great man's death on 29 March 1623, Grandier conducted the funeral service in the church of St. Pierre du Marché and Renaudot delivered a public elegy at the Palais.[39] Grandier

---

[35] Quoted by A. Huxley, p. 17.

[36] G. Legué, *Urbain Grandier* (Paris: 1880), p. 22.

[37] Renaudot, *Oraison funebre pour monsieur Sainte-Marthe* (Samur: 1623), p. 15.

[38] In addition to A. Huxley's excellent *Devils of Loudun*, also see R. Mandrou, *Magistrats et sorciers en France au XVIIᵉ siècle* (Paris: 1968), esp. pp. 210-19.

[39] Dumoustier de la Fond, p. 108.

and Louis Trincant, the public prosecutor, then became main-stays of Loudun's intellectual set.

Renaudot was one of the most influential and high-placed members of Loudun's Protestant community. Several members of his family served in the ministry,[40] and Renaudot twice addressed the national Protestant assembly meeting in Loudun in 1619-1620, on medical topics.[41] This was a high honor for any man, physician or Protestant, to receive. Nevertheless, Renaudot certainly knew that his religion was a political liability. The obstinacy of the Parlement of Paris in registering his patents was a sure sign, and in Loudun tensions between Protestant and Catholic had increased. To be a Protestant in the early 1620's was not a simple thing. Louis XIII was the most devout Catholic of all the Bourbons, and his political energies during this time were directed in a crusade against French Protestantism. In May 1621 royal armies swept through Poitou, one of the strongest Protestant regions, and Loudun was one of many towns which did not dare oppose their presence.[42] With the royal troops came Catholic preachers, using the weapons of persuasion and pressure on Loudun's Protestants. There was nothing in Renaudot's career to indicate that he was a zealous Protestant. On the contrary, religious conviction always seemed to be beyond his concern as a social thinker. Had he lived a generation earlier, he might have called himself a *politique*. The arguments of Catholic preachers, the encouragement of Richelieu, and the realities of political power in an increasingly Catholic age all had their effect upon him.

Renaudot must have become a Catholic prior to 1626. His first wife, Marthe Dumoustier, had died in 1623 or 1624, and

[40] Drouault, "Notes inédites," pp. 14-15.

[41] Both addresses were published. See note 34.

[42] D. Ligou, *Le Protestantisme en France de 1598 à 1715* (Paris: 1968), pp. 70-81.

18

he then married Jehanne Baudot.[43] They baptized a daughter in 1626, shortly after moving from Loudun to Paris. Three years later, his sons renounced their Protestantism.[44] Renaudot's baptism and settlement in Paris were not simply coincidental. By these two acts, he renounced his past and declared his active service to Richelieu.

Renaudot practiced medicine during his first years in Paris. Even though a Montpellier graduate, his title as royal physician exempted him from the ban on foreign trained physicians in Paris. He served as the personal physician of the Abbé de Masle, Sieur de Roches, Richelieu's confidant and life-long secretary, as well as developing a large practice based upon his use of chemical medication.[45] But his primary energy was spent in advancing his public welfare schemes. He made the rounds of members of Parlement, the royal councilors, as well as urging Richelieu's aid whenever the moment presented itself. He wrote two pamphlets in 1627, *Éloge d'Armand Jean du Plessis, Cardinal de Richelieu*, praising Richelieu as "the Gallic Hercules," and *Stances pour la Santé du Roy*, dedicated to Richelieu.[46] Renaudot knew that all his fortunes depended upon the growing power of his patron.

[43] *Examen de la requeste présentée à la Reine* (4 Nov. 1643), pp. 27, 35. Renaudot said that his first wife, Marthe Dumoustier, accepted Catholicism on her deathbed, and died within the Church. *Response à l'examen de la requeste présentée à la Reine par Théophraste Renaudot portée . . . par Machurat* (Paris: 1644), p. 53.

[44] "J'ai trouvé dans mes papiers" wrote Eusèbe in *Journal des principalles affaires de ma famille*, "que moy, Eusèbe Renaudot, suis né à Loudun le 21 febvrier 1613 à six heures du matin, et que j'ay été baptizé le matin au temple du dit lieu par un ministre de la religion huguenote que mon père professoit et que nous avons renouncée en 1629 par la grace de Dieu." B.N. mss. f.fr. 14348. Even though the Parisian branch of the Renaudot family became Catholic and produced notable Church figures, the Loudun-based branch remained Huguenot. Drouault, "Notes inédites," pp. 14-15.

[45] See p. 152, n. 100.

[46] *Éloge* . . . , p. 3. Both were published in Paris.

Renaudot's 13 October 1612 patents were reconfirmed by royal council on 24 February and 22 March 1624. They remained without effect, patents on paper only. Finally, on 31 March 1628 all of his previous patents were confirmed. In addition Louis XIII granted Renaudot permission to establish his Bureau d'Adresse.[47] At the age of 42, after a life of provincial obscurity, Renaudot was firmly installed in Paris. Through the influence of Richelieu, he had been granted royal patents and privilege, and could now execute the plans he had suggested 16 years earlier.

[47] Published with *Table des choses dont on peut donner & recevoir advis au Bureau d'Adresse* (Paris: 1630). See Appendix A.

CHAPTER II

Public Welfare and the Bureau d'Adresse

FOR most Europeans of the early modern period, the grand issues of history had passed them by. Whether the mass consubstantiated or transubstantiated the body of Christ, whether the feudal bailiff should be replaced by an intendant responsible more directly to the central government of Paris, whether the planets revolved in circular or elliptical paths: these questions, made crucial to us through the luxury of historical hindsight, were often far removed from the concern of the majority of the population. The typical sixteenth and seventeenth century man had more pressing problems. He had to find enough food to stay alive.

Famine and disease were ordinary conditions of life; animal-like survival left little time for any other activity; food prices were the overwhelming expenses in one's budget.[1] To the French peasant, food meant black bread, soup, a few vegetables and, rarely, when a chicken would die or when he would be hungry or foolhardy enough to snare a rabbit, a bit of meat. Rural workers, according to a contemporary witness, "were compelled to labor from morning till evening, without having anything other than a morsel of dark bread and some water, considering themselves fortunate once or twice a year

[1] Perhaps the most successful attempt to portray this overwhelming cycle of poverty, disease, and malnutrition in terms understandable to twentieth century Americans is Robert Heilbroner's *The Great Ascent* (New York: 1963), pp. 23-28. The author describes conditions in the contemporary underdeveloped world, but the end result is to describe the conditions of poverty, disease, and malnutrition as graphically for the early modern period as for the twentieth century.

when they have some lard to put on their bread, and never have a taste of wine."[2] And even if he had enough to eat, this diet was of such miserable quality and variety that he had little resistance to disease. No wonder one-third to one-half of all children did not survive their first year; no wonder the average life span was only 20 to 25 years.[3]

Such problems were general. Against these, late sixteenth century France showed even more aggravating conditions. For two decades, the country was ripped by the Wars of Religion, and no war is as brutal as that in which God is a combatant. Even more than famine and plague—at least these were not human horrors—the Frenchman feared the soldiers: "their pay poor and often long overdue, they lived off the land, behaving everywhere as in a conquered country . . . relish for pillage and violence was their only motive."[4] Finally, a general rise in prices caused by the fall-off of new world gold and marketing changes, aggravated social and political instability. Some historians have referred to this as part of the "crisis of the seventeenth century," but its effects were just as brutal, in watered-down form, upon the late sixteenth century.[5]

Renaudot's France did not have to be reminded that the poor were everywhere. The principle was long established that each parish was responsible for its poor.[6] During the middle ages, autarkical theory reflected practical reality, but

[2] B.N. mss. f.fr. 21803, f. 234. Quoted also by R. Mandrou, *Introduction à la France moderne* (Paris: 1961), pp. 30-31.

[3] P. Goubert, *Beauvais et le Beauvaisis* (Paris: 1960) esp. pp. 30-82. Also see R. Mousnier, "Études sur la population de la France au 17e siècle," *Dix-septième siècle* (1953), pp. 527-42.

[4] P-G. Lorris, *La Fronde* (Paris: 1961), p. 28.

[5] An excellent summary of recent historiography on this crisis is F. Mauro, *Le XVIe siècle européen: aspects économiques* (Paris: 1966), pp. 209-34. Also see A. D. Lublinskaya, *French Absolutism: the Crucial Phase, 1620-1629* (New York: 1968), pp. 4-81.

[6] Article 73 of the Ordinance of Moulins officially put the burden on each parish. The injunction was designed to reduce pressure on Paris.

as society became increasingly mobile, the theory was tested beyond its breaking point. The local parish was barely a solvent concern in the best of times, and during famine and plague could not deal with its problems. Under the social and intellectual pressures of the sixteenth century, the local parish, hardly able to care for its own, now turned away the foreign poor. The poor flocked to the cities, where they could find more religious institutions, greater private households, and, when these failed, more streetcorners from which to beg. For thousands of poor Frenchmen, the city was Paris.

Marie de Medici's regency attempted to reform the institutions which dealt with the problems of beggars in Paris. Théophraste Renaudot was involved in these attempts. Why, however, were reforms needed? Why were already existing presuppositions and methods of poor relief ineffectual?

A number of factors coalesced to create a public welfare crisis in the late sixteenth century. On the one hand, there were popular attitudes which increasingly viewed the poor as pernicious threats to religion and society. And on the other, institutions devised to offer solutions had, in many cases, just aggravated the problem.

Christian Europe had venerated voluntary poverty long before St. Francis married Dame Poverty in the early thirteenth century. Involuntary poverty partook of some of this saintliness also. Even though St. Francis would say "I have worked with my hands, and I choose to work, and I firmly wish that all my brothers should work at some honorable trade, and if they do not know how, let them learn";[7] involuntary poverty was not seen as a crime. It was rather an unfortunate and inexplicable accident. Want was believed to be its own deterrent, and there was, therefore, no legal necessity to stamp it out. A *pauvre* was someone temporarily and inexplicably denied legal rights: because of the accident of poverty it was used

---

[7] B. Tierney, *Medieval Poor Law* (Berkeley: 1959), p. 11.

23

as the opposite of *potens*. Medieval poor law reflected this benevolence, protecting the pauper rather than pressuring him into work. With a relatively small amount of chronic unemployment, canon law and popular attitudes could afford such benevolence.[8]

The social and economic fluidity following the fourteenth century drastically increased the number of beggars and indigents, and the new threat made benevolence a luxury governments and the popular mentality could ill afford. Poverty took on pejorative connotations, and "miserable" and "indigent" became interchangeable with "truant" and "vagabond." Instead of being objects of Christian attachment, love, and respect, the poor were social threats—feared, hated, scorned. Certain towns would not bury the poor with other Christians.[9] Poverty as a religious and social value was attacked from humanistic quarters. The poor monks of Chaucer, Brandt, Erasmus, and Boccaccio were sorry souls indeed, far from any man's ideal. With so many deserving beggars about, Europe had no place for the voluntary poor.

Christian Europe's traditional poor relief methods—parish handouts, alms for holidays or funerals or weddings, the Hôtels Dieu—were not equal to the task. Nor did social institutions receive any particular help from Church canonists, whose late medieval attitudes to poor relief were unchanged from earlier doctrine.[10] The primary question facing town councils all over Europe was not the Eradication of Poverty or the Creation of a Christian Commonwealth, although such elements cannot be totally denied, but rather how to protect themselves against these armies of poor. The answer often took a simple, repressive form: close the gates to foreign poor, brand all healthy beggars, send them to the galleys,

[8] M. Mollat, "La notion de pauvreté au moyen âge: position des problèmes," *Revue d'histoire de l'Eglise de France,* LII (1966), 5-6; Tierney, p. 12.

[9] Mollat, pp. 5, 16-17.   [10] Tierney, pp. 109ff.

publicly whip them. But by the beginning of the sixteenth century, many secular officers were aware that highly skilled dependable city workers were often chronically unemployed, that the problem was one of the urban economy as much as public morality.

Juan Louis Vives' *De subventione pauperum*, written for the council and senate of Bruges in 1526, is one of the most revealing sources for this new outlook. Vives' tract influenced both Catholic and Protestant welfare innovators throughout Europe. Vives recognized the immensity of the problem: "In a state the poor members cannot be neglected without danger to the powerful ones. For the former, driven by their needs, in some cases turn thieves."[11] Bruges must plan an overall attack. First of all, the poor must be identified and counted. Foreign poor must be sent back to their own parishes. Children and the ill must be cared for. All able-bodied persons must be taught a trade, and even those otherwise too old or "too dull in intellect" should be set to sweeping streets, pushing wheelbarrows, or serving as ushers at court. Industry and commerce, as city fathers well understood, cried out for all kinds of workers, experienced and inexperienced alike. But since too many workers were so eager to avoid working, all poor must be made to labor, even those in the hospitals. "Since no one should die from starvation, those who have ruined themselves in disgraceful and base ways, such as gambling, immorality, luxury, greed, must indeed be fed . . . but the more disagreeable tasks are to be allotted to them and harder fare, so that they may be an example to others and may themselves repent of their former life: they will thus not easily fall back into the same vices, refrained therefrom by their scanty food and hard labor, not dying of hunger, but being made lean withal."[12] If great numbers of unemployed could be put to work, they could support themselves and even

[11] *De subventione pauperum*, ed., F. R. Salter (London: 1926), p. 6.
[12] Vives, pp. 12-13.

25

provide a surplus to support those too ill to work. Only as a last resort should poor boxes be set up around town.

The ideas expressed by men like Vives were becoming common currency in many enlightened quarters, and generated a veritable renaissance of urban-inspired public welfare reforms throughout Europe. Challenging Catholic and Protestant, Lutheran and Calvinist city alike, increased numbers of urban poor created a practical ecumenism cutting across confessional lines.[13]

By the end of the century, however, many of these reforms had failed. The hardening of public opinion and policy was not simply the result of crusading Calvinism or Counter-Reformation zeal, but rather the natural reaction of officials whose experiments had proven ineffectual. Such hardening of attitudes toward the poor was certainly evident in late sixteenth century Paris.

Henry IV's Paris had a population of at least 400,000, and estimates of the number of chronically unemployed poor ranged as high as 20 to 25 per cent.[14] Except on a quantitative

[13] "If sixteenth century poor laws did not spring from a new attitude toward property, their ambitious goal—to find practical means to eliminate all begging and death by starvation—did imply something new: now there are conditions of life that society should not and dare not tolerate *at all*, in Protestant Nuremberg and Norwich, in Catholic Ypres and Lyon. The suggestion is there, whether the urban welfare schemes succeeded or failed." Natalie Z. Davis, "Poor Relief, Humanism, and Heresy: the Case of Lyon," *Studies in Medieval and Renaissance History*, v (1968), 240. A recent study of interest is Robert N. Kingdon, "Social Welfare in Calvin's Geneva," *American Historical Review*, lxxvi (1971), 50-69.

[14] A. Feillet cited the same percentages during the Fronde 50 years later. *La misère au temps de la Fronde* (Paris: 1862). The population of Paris in the seventeenth century is difficult to establish: recent estimates have varied from a conservative 200,000 to as high as 500,000, depending upon one's statistical technique. See R. Mousnier, "Paris, capitale politique au moyen âge et dans les temps modernes," *Colloques, cahiers et civilizations* (Paris: 1962), pp. 39-80; R. Mols, *Introduction à la démographie historique* (Louvain: 1954-56), ii, 513.

level, Paris was no better equipped to deal with the poor than was the smallest provincial parish. It had various hospitals and asylums, such as the Hôtel Dieu, as well as the Bureau Général des Pauvres, created by Francis I on 6 November 1544. The records of the Bureau attest to its sad history during the reigns of Henry III and Henry IV: little public support, even from town fathers in the *échevinage* whom one would most identify with its success; irregular revenues; inability to ascertain who was worthy of aid; opposition from Church and corporate charity groups.[15]

These problems, however, were at base mechanical problems—finances, administration, statistics. Pressured beyond institutional limits, it is no wonder that the city fathers increasingly took a resolute stand against the poor. The emotions of distrust, fear, and hate confirmed the growing threat of extreme and pervasive poverty. More and more the welfare program in Paris reflected religious and emotional reaction. As severe as institutional limitations to reform, these psychological barriers were even more difficult to change.

First of all, and most glaring, is the fact that poverty and mendicity were seldom treated as problems in themselves. The preambles to these *arrêts* indicated why action was needed: beggars must be sent from the city because of fear of

[15] Records of the Bureau's activities during these years are found in the Bibliothèque Nationale, fonds français, mss. 8068, 8069, 8116 (Recueil de Dupré). For a full discussion of the Bureau's activities during the 1580's, see Howard M. Solomon, "The Innocent Inventions of Théophraste Renaudot" (Northwestern University: 1969), pp. 17-23. Also see A. Monnier, *Histoire de l'assistance publique* (Paris: 1866), pp. 313ff; M. Fosseyeux, "La taxe des pauvres au XVIe siècle," *Revue d'histoire de l'Église de France*, xx (1934), 407-34; Jean Imbart, "Les prescriptions hospitalières du Concile de Trent et leur diffusion en France," *Revue d'histoire de l'Église de France*, xlii (1956), 5-28; Michel Mollat, "La notion de pauvreté au moyen âge: position de problèmes," *Revue d'histoire de l'Église de France*, lii (1966), 6-24; R. Stauffenegger, "Réforme, richesse, et pauvreté," *Revue d'histoire de l'Église de France*, lii (1966), 47-58.

contagion;[16] they were disturbing church services and the peace and quiet of the city through "insolent nuisances and brigandage";[17] so many have entered Paris to beg that "there are hardly any workers to be found in the countryside to work in the vineyards and the fields."[18] The poor were manipulated in hopes of controlling other factors (contagion, the harvest) instead of other factors (unemployment) being manipulated first. There is no doubt that the appearance of poverty is related to larger and wider problems—this is a *quid pro quo* of modern poor relief—but in these official documents there was little awareness of the cause and effect of poverty. The age seldom saw poverty as an unfortunate situation within itself. Instead it saw only the obvious, ugly partners of poverty (no harvest, etc.) and branded them the problem. Bureau des Pauvres myopia translated itself into uncoordinated, ad-hoc attacks, aiming in all directions and accomplishing nothing.

There were other reasons why the age could not treat poverty as a distinct problem. For all of its Renaissance pretensions, Henry IV's France still took outworn and traditional concepts of order, station, and stability for granted. These concepts were reflected by law. "The status of each physical person is adapted to the place which he occupies in society, to the rank which he embodies and, to say it all in one word, to the function of general utility which he fulfils: the rights and privileges which are recognized and conceded to him have precisely as their end to facilitate the accomplishment of the social services he is expected to render and, additionally, to recompense him for them."[19] Every person was a public representative, a virtual personification of his social station. Life remained a constantly unfolding morality play.

---

[16] 14 July 1595, 24 October 1596. B.N. mss. f.fr. 8069, ff. 67, 143.
[17] 1 April 1605, 8 February 1607. B.N. mss. f.fr. 8069, ff. 321, 341.
[18] 22 April 1599. B.N. mss. f.fr. 8069, f. 195.
[19] E. Lousse, *La société d'ancien régime* (Louvain: 1943), p. 43.

The individual performed his social role for all to see—
working, speaking, sinning, and finally dying under the
gaze of his fellowman. The king, for example, was a public
figure who must act in a kingly manner. It mattered little
what his personality might be; in fact, as a private individual
he hardly existed. He wore the regalia, performed the ceremonies, embodied the traditions and powers which society
expected of the king and the king alone. In such a manner
lived all the members of the various estates and corporations
of the ancien régime. The *parlementaire*, for example, wore
the crimson robes of his office to make visible his public role;
the physician wore the red-bordered, gold-tufted cap so all
knew his station. The individual ceased to be a private person
when he was invested with his regalia of office or his corporate
robes. He became instead "monsieur le médecin," "monsieur
le parlementaire," the embodiment of the larger organism
which existed before and would exist long after the individual
médecin or *parlementaire*. His exterior robes were not trivial
decoration, but rather affirmation of his station. The lines of
precedence between a duke and a count, a bishop and an abbé,
a physician and a surgeon, a master and a journeyman must
never be reversed: to do so was to poison the air which man
breathed.[20] The more visible the distinctions between various
social groups, the greater the proof of society's viability.

So it was with the poor. Christ had said that "the poor
always ye have with you";[21] to sixteenth and seventeenth
century France, this was not only an observation, but an
injunction. To attempt reform was not only to change men,
but even more awesome, to change a universe responding to

[20] The hardening of prescribed patterns of behavior and dress reflected the social change then occurring. Such change did not make
these "externals" obsolete: instead it made the "theatrical exaggeration
of reality" of which they were a part all the more significant. See
Carl J. Friedrich, *The Age of the Baroque 1610-1660* (New York:
1952), pp. 45-47.
[21] John 12:8.

and reflecting God's will. "The desire to deal with [poverty] became almost a sacrilege, an arrogant revolt."[22] Instead of reform, one isolated and identified the poor, as one did the lawyer, the duke, the physician so that they could better perform their appointed social role. All those who had official permission to beg had to wear the red and yellow cross of the Bureau des Pauvres on their shoulder.[23] Those begging without permission would be shorn and shaved.[24] The poor must be isolated in hospitals and workshops.[25] These expedients did not change the face of poverty, but instead isolated it and made it more obvious.

The thin distinction between the temporary, legitimate poor and the professional vagabond who made a career out of bilking public institutions and private sympathies could quickly evaporate. The latter were "abominable and make in the Republic a sewer where all sorts of ordures flow, producing and nourishing an infinite number of perverse miseries, disgorging through the population, corrupting and destroying by their horrible license all religion and all civil decency."[26] Involuntary poor suffered irreparably from the excesses of these professionals. While one must publicly whip the latter, the former must be kept busy in unpleasant work, tasting in a lesser way the pain inflicted on those who took the easy road of vagabondage and public mischief.[27] *Ateliers* for these poor were less workshops than prisons, less reform institutions than way stations to keep them out of trouble.[28] The poor often worked on public projects, such as repairing

[22] Feillet, p. 53.

[23] 18 January 1606. B.N. mss. f.fr. 8069, f. 323.

[24] 24 October 1596. B.N. mss. f.fr. 8069, f. 143.

[25] 30 May 1595. B.N. mss. f.fr. 8085, f. 59.

[26] Louis Turquet, Sieur de Mayerne, *Apologie contre les détracteurs des livres de la monarchie aristodémocratique* (S.l. 1617), p. 226.

[27] 27 August 1612. B.N. mss. f.fr. 8082, f. 302.

[28] 15 March 1602. B.N. mss. f.fr. 8069, f. 261.

the city walls, and the wording of the *arrêts* suggests that keeping busy was much more important than urban improvement or security.[29]

Virtually every poor relief measure ordered non-Parisian beggars to leave the city. This was a standard part of the regime's approach to unemployment: in fact, it reflected the traditional responsibility of each parish to its own poor. As a practical device for large cities, however, it was patently unsuccessful. This tactic testifies to the attitude that one might reduce the number of poor, but dare not eradicate the group itself. The specific laws reflected the emotional and social assumption: decrease the number of individuals who may be poor, shift that group to another parish, but never do away with the poor.

According to Christian tradition, charity was best performed privately, between one man and another. Within a seventeenth century context, public corporations were private individuals writ large, "voluntarily performing a service of general interest and admitted in the State as a moral person," subject to the same sentiments and needs as a private person.[30] Moreover, as Bodin wrote, "all companies and colleges are instituted for religion or for administration [*police*]."[31] Corporations were therefore not only permitted to give charity (which was both a religious and a secular act), but were compelled to do so, just as any Christian individual was so compelled. This sentiment became more marked as the period went on. While the sixteenth century saw the foundation of innumerable public institutions (Hôtels-Dieu, etc.), the seven-

[29] B.N. mss. f.fr. 18605, f. 22.

[30] P. Avril, *Les origines de la distinction des établissements d'utilité publique* (Paris: 1900), p. 40. "*Corporation*" is primarily an eighteenth century term: the seventeenth century more often used the terms "*communauté*," "*confrérie*," "*corps de métier*." See E. Coornaert, *Les corporations en France avant 1789* (Paris: 1941), p. 23.

[31] *Six livres de la république* (Paris: 1583), III, Chapter 7, p. 478.

31

teenth century has been called "a golden age" of private charity.[32] The documents of any number of Parisian corporate bodies attest to this. For example, the fines imposed by the Community of *Patenôtriers et Bouchonniers* on its members guilty of shoddy workmanship went "half to the Hôtel Dieu, and the other half for the use of the Community."[33] The Cistercians included charity in their yearly expenses: "for the poor, the expenses of lanterns, and payment of rents owed by the College, and some expenses made on the days of St. Bernard and of St. Jean Chrysostom each year, about 120 *livres*."[34] All corporate entities—trade and craft guilds, religious houses, sociopolitical confederations—considered charity a religious and legal duty, faithfully performed and jealously guarded.

The Bureau des Pauvres was usurping the role of the Christian person, be it a private individual or a corporate body. By policing the poor, it removed from circulation the vessel through which the Christian became Christlike. Without beggars, no charity; without charity, no chance of being a good Christian. So many private persons ignored the bureau and gave alms to beggars that they were finally subject to fines.[35] Opposition to the Bureau was often even more direct: "it has also been thwarted by many persons without judgment or reason, such as pages, lackeys, grooms, kitchen boys, miserable workmen, and laborers, attacking and insulting the sergeants executing this police work, and saying that it

[32] L. Cahen, "Les idées charitables à Paris au XVIIe et au XVIIIe siècles," *Revue d'histoire moderne et contemporaine* (1900), 5.

[33] "Statuts et Règlements de la Communauté des Patenôtriers et Bouchonniers," 24 November 1614. B.N. mss. f.fr. 14462, f. 47. By encouraging such practices, government authorities escaped their own financial responsibilities as cheaply as possible.

[34] "Brief estat du gouvernement du college des S. Bernardins, Paris" (1634). B.N. mss. f.fr. 15770, f. 146. These expenses were for alms, and not for *boursiers*, which are listed elsewhere.

[35] 18 January 1606. B.N. mss. f.fr. 8069, f. 323.

was an offense to God to chase the poor, and that the Savior of the world had responded to Judas . . . that we shall always have the poor with us."[36] These, then, were some of the weaknesses of the Bureau des Pauvres, discharging social and civil responsibilities within religious and moral terms.

Repressive measures, such as public workshops, became increasingly prominent in Henry IV's reign, but there is no indication that they succeeded, even temporarily, to reduce the number of beggars in Paris.[37] In fact, there may have been an increase, since authorities were forced to intensify and regularize punishment. Previously punishment had consisted of flogging, expulsion from the city, or imprisonment.[38] During extreme conditions, as during the contagion of 1596, beggars were liable "to be hung and strangled without further ado."[39] During the first years of the seventeenth century, punishment was standardized: first offenders were caned, second offenders flogged, and third offenders sent to the galleys.[40] In spite of municipal rigor, the situation was becoming unmanageable. An anonymous writer has left a striking description: "This poverty was recognized as a veritable sewer of all sorts of filth, villanies, frauds and deceits. Some [beggars] pretended to be one-armed, lame, or ulcerated in

[36] Anon., *Mémoire concernant les pauvres qu'on appelle enfermez* (S.l.n.d.), p. 249. In a discussion of poverty in England, Christopher Hill believes that the major opposition to repressive treatment of beggars came from those members of the lower working classes and peasantry who themselves could not be "confident that eviction and vagrancy might not be their ultimate fate." "William Perkins and the Poor," *Puritanism and Revolution* (New York: 1964), p. 232.

[37] Often there was not enough money to keep them open. See the *arrêt* of 14 July 1595: B.N. mss. f.fr. 8069, f. 63. Moreover, not until 1 July 1603 is there any indication that these *ateliers* were at all permanent. In the document of that date, and after it, the Bureau referred to its *atelier* at the porte St. Antoine. B.N. mss. f.fr. 8069, f. 254.

[38] 14 July 1595: B.N. mss. f.fr. 8069, f. 167. 15 July 1587: B.N. mss. f.fr. 8068, f. 431. 9 February 1587: B.N. mss. f.fr. 8068, f. 401.

[39] 24 October 1596: B.N. mss. f.fr. 8069, f. 143.

[40] 8 February 1607: B.N. mss. f.fr. 8069, f. 339.

33

various parts of their bodies, disguising themselves with imitation skin and animal blood, bloated and jaundiced by the weight of suffering—horrible demonstrations, various sorts of shameful diversions, and infinite other inventions which abuse the word 'poverty' and the charity of good people and deceive the whole world. These tricks become obvious through the habits and behavior of those who, after making their daily rounds and returning to their homes (giving pleasure and enjoyment to these master beggars and counterfeit poor), are seen carrying their crutches on their shoulders, straightening their limbs which before had seemed broken and rotted, and enter as upright and gay as people without problems or cares: witness the place commonly known as the Cour des Miracles, behind the Filles Dieu near the ramparts between the gates of St. Denis and Montmartre, where you can see them every evening all summer long, dancing, playing, laughing, and having a great time. This place has that name because its beggars are lame and ulcerated only outside its walls."[41] Forty thousand within a population of 400,000, following their own social code, speaking their own language, occupying entire neighborhoods which no outsider dared enter: no wonder this rabble presented a pernicious, ugly threat to society.[42]

Even though there would be some temporary success in reducing the number of beggars in Paris during Marie de Medici's regency, the traditional poor relief methods of the

[41] *Mémoire concernant les pauvres*, pp. 250-51.

[42] Nineteenth century Parisian *classes dangereuses* bear at least a surface resemblance to this sixteenth and seventeenth century group: highly mobile residency patterns, a particular jargon and morality, and, above all, extreme social distance from the fearful society above them. Recent studies (A. Daumard, *La bourgeoisie parisienne de 1815 à 1848* [Paris: 1963]; L. Chevalier, *Classes laborieuses et classes dangereuses à Paris pendant la première moitié du XIX siècle* [Paris: 1958], for example) suggest some of the similarities: nineteenth century novels, especially Victor Hugo's *Notre Dame de Paris*—set in a world Renaudot would recognize—carry the comparison even further.

Bureau des Pauvres were ideationally as well as institutionally bankrupt.[43]

Théophraste Renaudot was vehemently opposed to social programs conceived on a local, and not a national, level. But this was not the only area of disagreement between Renaudot and traditional attitudes to poor relief. The specific conditions of urban economic life must also be reversed: "Among all the causes of poverty, the listing of which would be wearisome, we can assuredly say that one of the most manifest, and which reduces persons of the least condition to the miserable state of begging, or supporting themselves by illicit means and finally to the Hôtel Dieu (if worse does not first befall them), is that they flock to this city [of Paris] which seems to be the center and common country of everyone, in the usually vain and deceptive hope of finding some advancement here. Because after having spent the little they have on *bienvenues* and other useless expenses to which those who promise to find them jobs induce them, and on the debauchery to which they are susceptive and to which their idleness gives them easy access, they find themselves greeted by need before having found a master: from which they are led to begging, thievery, murder, and other enormous crimes; also because of the maladies which famine brings them, infecting the purity of our air and so overtaxing the Hôtel Dieu and other hospitals that, in spite of all the care which is expended on them, one can truly say that their great numbers renders them truly miserable. In place of this, henceforth, an hour after arriving in this city they can come to the Bureau [which shall be established] and inquire if there is employment or

[43] A series of asylums and workshops, created in 1612, helped reduce the number of beggars in Paris. But soon, "due to the misery of the recent wars, continued since 1614, shortcomings of the police, or, by God's punishment," the normal chaos returned, and in 1618 this program was abandoned (Anon., *Mémoire concernant les pauvres qu'on appelle enfermez* [S.l.n.d.], in *Archives curieuses de l'histoire de France*, xv, 241-70).

vacant positions, and thereby find positions more easily than they might have done after having sold, engaged, or even exhausted all their resources: and if there are no positions, they can appeal elsewhere. This would make it easier to identify the loafers and vagabonds and thereby their proper punishment."[44]

The poor, said Renaudot, were subject to debauchery not because they were naturally depraved, but because they had no work. These persons were not criminals, guilty in religious and political terms, but rather victims of social conditions. Authorities must prevent the disease rather than attempt to arrest it once it occurred.[45] Putting the unemployed to work would benefit the entire society. Obviously, and primarily, the individual could then control his basic needs as a free agent, resisting the seductions of those who falsely promise to find him employment.

Even more persuasive was Renaudot's hardheaded, bread-and-butter argument. Employment would reduce the pressure on overstrained institutions such as the Hôtel Dieu and the Bureau des Pauvres. Self-supporting, healthy workers would be less likely to infect the city with plague, and would be less likely to succumb to epidemics. No longer would the poor be reduced to "begging, thievery, murder and other enormous crimes": in one blow, police problems would virtually disappear.

This outlook was striking in its simplicity. To Renaudot the problems which until then the city of Paris had treated as primary—control of famine and plague, maintenance of the peace—in actuality were secondary to a more basic one, the large number of Frenchmen out of work. Chronic unemployment was nothing new, and it certainly was not limited to

[44] *Mercure françois*, Paris, 1641, 67-68. Virtually the same material appeared earlier in Renaudot's *Inventaire des adresses du Bureau de Recontre* (Paris: 1630), p. 12.
[45] *Inventaire des adresses*, p. 22.

rural workers; highly skilled artisans, shopkeepers, and nota-
ries often lived on the edge of poverty.[46] However, the civil
wars of the late sixteenth century and the agricultural and
commercial reverses of the early seventeenth century made the
problem all too obvious.

Renaudot was not the first, nor certainly the last, to recognize the magnitude of this problem.[47] To Antoine de Mont-
chretien, France was overflowing [*régorgeante*] with able but
unproductive workers. The Crown had a duty to harness these
tremendous resources, to create order from the chaos in which
the economy wallowed: "the greatest trait that can be practiced in a State is not to permit any part to remain idle."[48]
To many French mercantilists, lazy workers were particularly
characteristic of France. Barthelemy de Laffemas, for example,
preceded his 1602 treatise on *Le mérite du travail et labeur*
with the epigram:

> Dieu père du labeur donne la cognoissance;
> Faisant que le travail du commerce aye cours
> C'est le bien de l'Estat qui viendra tous les jours;
> Ostant l'oysiveté, malheur en c'este France.[49]

Mercantilist thinkers sensed relationships between unemployment, a stifled economy, and threats to public order from too
many beggars. Their diagnosis was sometimes wrong, often
believing that unemployment resulted from overpopulation

---

[46] Davis, "Poor Relief," pp. 221-26. Studying vagrancy in Norwich
in the 1570's, J. F. Pound discovered that while only a small percentage
of the population received public aid, "it would probably not be exag-
gerating to say that at least 50 percent of the English population in
the city were either poverty stricken or very near it and thus a potentially dangerous element in society." "Elizabethan Census of the Poor:
Treatment of Vagrancy in Norwich, 1570-1580," *University of Birmingham Historical Journal*, VIII (1962), 144.

[47] J.-P. Gutton, "À l'aube du XVIIe siècle: idées nouvelles sur les
pauvres," *Cahiers d'histoire*, x (1965), 87-197.

[48] *Traicté de l'oeconomie politique* (S.l.n.d.), p. 30.

[49] *Le mérite du travail et labeur* (Paris: 1602), Preface, p. 3.

and that forced emigration to the colonies was therefore the answer. This was a favorite suggestion of English projectors, and Renaudot even advocated this treatment for France's professional beggars.[50] But Renaudot and others before him recognized that chronic unemployment was a function of poor market mechanisms: the crown was the only agent able to improve existing economic mechanisms.

Barthelemy de Laffemas, Henry IV's Contrôleur Général du Commerce worked tirelessly to revitalize France's commerce. He suggested that the crown create a network of employment clearinghouses, "as necessary to the utility of the public and the convenience of private persons as anything ever invented for that end."[51] His son Isaac described these ideas: "I would mark this proposition among the finest that my father ever made to Your Majesty. In the first place, more useful and of great importance: it is also a tacit remedy for an infinity of abuses, and a preservative against the ruin of our commerce. Differing so much in diverse circumstances that it requires so many explanations for which, in any case, there is not sufficient time or paper, it suffices to say that here would be certain lines of communication [*correspondances*] which public agents would have through all the towns of your Kingdom, to make, manage, and negotiate all sorts of affairs which shall voluntarily and without constraint be referred to them in their bureaus, and by means of which Your Majesty himself can know, for his contentment and peace of mind, everything handled, deliberated, and executed in all the reaches and places of his dominion."[52] Laffemas acknowledged that these ideas occurred to him in reading Chapter 34 of Montaigne's *Essais*: "my father," wrote Mon-

[50] *Gazette*, 16 January 1632. For a discussion of this problem in England, see M. Campbell, " 'Of People Either Too Few or Too Many,' " *Conflicts in Stuart England* (London: 1960), pp. 169-202.

[51] Isaac de Laffemas, *l'Histoire du commerce de France* (Paris: 1606), pp. 102-04.

[52] *Ibid.*

taigne, "being aided only by experience and his naturally clear judgment, long ago told me that he had wished to set up in towns certain designated places to which those needing something could go and register their problems with an officer appointed for that purpose. I might seek to sell pearls, I could search pearls to sell; this one seeks company in traveling to Paris; another seeks a servant of a certain kind, still another, a master; someone else registers for a worker; this or that, each according to his needs. It would seem that this way of advertising among ourselves will bring more than minor convenience to our public commerce. Because at every turn there are positions which can be sought out, and which, when not filled, leave men in extreme want."[53] And Renaudot, too, acknowledged his debt to Montaigne.[54] From this common source, Laffemas and Renaudot arrived at different, yet complementary ends. To Laffemas, this institution would help revitalize France's moribund economy; to Renaudot it would be the cornerstone of his program as Commissaire Général des Pauvres.

Renaudot had been appointed a royal physician in 1612 and named Commissaire Général des Pauvres in 1618 in reward for offering his ideas on poor relief to the crown. His titles were repeatedly confirmed by royal council (30 October 1617; 3 February 1618; 28 February 1624; 22 March 1624; 31 March 1628; 8 June 1629; 13 February 1630). The Bureau d'Adresse was definitely in existence by 1630; it is quite possible, however, that the Bureau existed a year or two earlier.[55]

---

[53] Quoted in Renaudot's *Inventaire des Adresses*, p. 11. Montaigne, *Essais* (Paris: 1962), II, 53-54.

[54] *Inventaire des Adresses*, p. 11.

[55] Renaudot concluded his 1630 *Inventaire des Adresses* with "Lecteur, recoy par avance ces premières feuilles, que l'impatience de plusieurs a tiré des mains de l'Autheur, plustost qu'il ne pensoit." His 8 June 1629 request to Parlement indicated that others had already counterfeited or were soon to counterfeit his ideas (published in *Inventaire des adresses*, p. 14).

Renaudot's Bureau d'Adresse was a relatively uncomplicated institution. It was a clearinghouse, pure and simple, a public registry of goods and services for buyer and seller, employer and potential employee. The registry scheme, if successful, could perfect the existing labor market without enlarging it through massive infusions of new technology (such as draining swamps or new industry) or new capital (creation of joint-stock ventures). For three *sous* (the poor were not charged) all persons who had services or goods could register at the Bureau d'Adresse. All arrangements were made between the individuals, the bureau acting only as a noninvolved clearinghouse.

Renaudot was particularly attuned to the problems of the skilled and semiskilled worker. At the bureau, the individual worker met his prospective master on a face-to-face, one-to-one basis. As simple as this process seems, however, it was a radical innovation. If successful, the Bureau d'Adresse could destroy the unchallenged power of the *compagnonnages*, or journeyman organizations, in the existing French labor market. Without understanding these organizations, Renaudot's reforms remain meaningless.

Journeymen had first organized in the fourteenth and fifteenth centuries, seeking mutual protection against the domination of guild oligarchies. By the seventeenth century, journeymen of certain crafts had developed nationwide secret confederations, with local chapters throughout France.[56] A newly arrived "brother" knew in which local cabaret or hotel he could find the secret headquarters of his confederation.

[56] The basic works on these organizations are: Henri Hauser, "Les compagnonnages d'arts et métiers à Dijon aux XVIIe et XVIIIe siècles," *Revue bourguignonne*, XVII (1907), 1-220; Martin St. Leon, *Les compagnonnages* (Paris: 1901); Émile Coornaert, *Les compagnonnages en France du moyen âge à nos jours* (Paris: 1966). Hauser and Coornaert have appended a number of revealing documents (police reports, *compagnonnage* statutes, etc.) to their studies.

Here the owner, serving as *mère* or *père* of the local chapter, offered him bed and board, medical aid, and a loan until his "brothers" found him work. Protection, hospitality, brotherhood, employment—the journeyman organizations supplied thousands of peripatetic journeymen with all of their psychological and material necessities.[57] Even though municipal authorities attempted to destroy the organizations, dissension within the ranks of masters made such efforts ineffectual. By Renaudot's time, journeyman organizations monopolized hiring and firing and wage practices in many key crafts.

An unemployed journeyman, member of a confederation or not, was prohibited from appealing directly to a master needing employees. Instead, the unemployed worker would report early each morning to the *place d'embauche* of his occupation: in Paris, for example, the building trades traditionally assembled at the Place de Grève before the Hôtel de Ville (and hence the modern French word for "strike").[58] Some of the crafts gathered at hotels and cabarets, which doubled as headquarters of the secret groups. Here the unemployed met the *rôleur*, or foreman, of his craft. The foreman controlled hiring on a shop-to-shop basis, and masters who dared hire workers on their own risked a walk-out, a citywide strike, or even physical attack from journeymen.[59]

[57] The vocabulary and rituals of these groups reveal their "attempt to provide [their] members with a new family, a new inheritance." Natalie Z. Davis, "A Trade Union in Sixteenth Century France," *Economic History Review*, xix (1966), 55.

[58] Bronislaw Geremek, *Le salariat dans l'artisanat parisien aux XIIIe-XVe siècles: étude sur le marché de la main d'oeuvre au moyen âge* (Paris: 1968), p. 126; Henri Hauser, *Ouvriers du temps passé (XVe et XVIe siècles)* (Paris: 1898), pp. 61ff. Any member of the Jolis Compagnons Tourneurs of Bordeaux, for example, who dared find his own job had to pay a fine to the organization, and "il passera pour renégat et dernier des derniers." "Livre de règles des Jolis Compagnons Tourneurs (1731)," published in Coornaert, *Compagnonnages*, p. 363.

[59] Organizations could blacklist an entire town, as they did to the masters of Montpellier in 1677. Hauser, "Compagnonnages," 38.

41

Before the foreman would find him a job, however, the new man had to spend money on *bienvenues*, so-called "welcoming expenses" to wine and dine the foreman and other members of the organization. These payments were one of the most abused practices of early modern economic life. In cases where the journeyman did not have the cash, the organization would often seize his goods as payment of the *bienvenue*.[60] The unemployed worker had no assurance that his expenditures would result in the foreman finding him work, and as Renaudot had complained, he often "sold, engaged or even exhausted" resources which more realistically should have been saved for food and shelter.[61]

An employed journeyman could be "debauched," i.e. released from his job, if the foreman insisted that the master hire the new man instead. Masters lost hours of employment from journeymen who had hangovers from debauched activities the night before (if they showed up for work at all). And police authorities repeatedly had to squelch debauches which, fueled by too much wine, turned into violence between rival journeyman organizations. In fact, these debauches were considered a major obstruction to public order.[62]

---

[60] In 1626 the master carpenters of Dijon complained that "lesdits compagnons ont establi entre eux un ordre qu'ils observent, en telle sorte que de tous les compagnons qui arrivent en ceste ville et qui désirent de se mettre en bouticque, ils en dressent un ordre particulier, les imposent et cotisent en telle sorte qu'ils veulent pour leur bien venue. Et sy les compagnons qui arrivent en ceste ville n'ont argent pour payer à leur volonté, ils leur font mettre en gage leurs hardes, manteaux et habitz, les vendent et en ordonnent comme bon leur semble." "Supplique des maitre menuisiers," 28 April 1626, published in Hauser, "Compagnonnages," 79-81.

[61] *Mercure françois*, Paris, 1641, 67-68.

[62] "Ces compagnonnages sont suivis de plusieurs desordres. 1° Plusieurs de ces compagnons manquent souvent au serment qu'ils font de garder fidélité aux maistres, ne travaillans selon le besoin qu'ils en ont, et les ruinans souvent par leurs pratiques. 2° Ils injurient et persécutent les pauvres garçons du mestier qui ne sont pas de leur cabale. 3° Ils s'entretiennent en plusieurs débauches, impuretez, yvrogneries,

Journeymen who did not belong to the secret organizations were clearly at a disadvantage, and might never find work even though there were masters begging for skilled help. In a city as large as Paris, filled with refugees from war and famine, the number of disreputable foremen preying on their false hopes must have been large indeed. Renaudot's registries would eliminate the foreman and make the individual craftsman a free agent in the labor market.

Renaudot took the important functions of the journeyman organizations (providing jobs, supplying medical aid and cheap loans) and sought to generalize them for all of society. The Bureau d'Adresse—"ce lieu commun, ce moyen unissant, ce centre des desseins, cet avis innocent"[63]—would become the central *place d'embauche* for all skilled and unskilled Frenchmen alike. If it would end high wages for members of certain organizations, it would on the other hand enlarge the labor supply. In addition to non-*compagnonnage* journeymen seeking work, Renaudot won support from the masters of Paris who were unwilling or unable to pay the high wages extracted by the *rôleur*. And eventually, too, the civil authorities found cause to support Renaudot's Bureau d'Adresse.

Registry of unemployed workers remained voluntary until late 1639, when the pressures of war and public safety created

---

etc., etc., et se ruinent eux, leurs femmes et leurs enfans, par les dépenses excessives qu'ils font en ce compagnonage en diverses rencontres, parce qu'ils aiment mieux dépenser le peu qu'ils ont avec leurs compagnons que dans leur famille. 4° Ils profanent les jours consacrez au service de Dieu, parce que quelques-uns, comme les tailleurs d'habits, s'assemblent entr'eux tous les dimanches et ensuite vont au cabaret, ou ils passent une grande partie du jour en débauche." Introduction of the Sorbonne condemnation of the *compagnonnages* in 1655, published in Coornaert, *Compagnonnages*, p. 353.

[63] *Renouvellement des Bureaux d'Adresse* (Paris: 1647), p. 53. The medical faculty would complain that "d'establir des Bureaux d'Adresse, c'est à dire rendre toutes choses communes, et introduire l'heresie des Anabaptistes." *La defense de la Faculté de Médecine contre son calumniateur* (Paris: 1641), p. 53. See Chapter VI.

a perceptible shift in the Bureau's activities. Large numbers of military deserters had swelled the number of unemployed in Paris. Moreover, recruitment officers had nearly exhausted existing rural sources of troops, and the monarchy turned to the cities for recruits.[64] Isaac de Laffemas, one of Richelieu's most experienced and ruthless creatures, was appointed Lieutenant-Civil for Paris. His problems were considerable: to decrease the number of deserters in Paris, to enlist as many Parisians as possible without destroying the city's economy, to reestablish public order. To coordinate his activities, Laffemas quickly harnessed Renaudot's Bureau d'Adresse.

On 19 September 1639, "in order to make an exact and new investigation" of the number of vagabonds and military absentees in Paris, all tavern, cabaret, and hotelkeepers were ordered to register their clients with the civil authorities.[65] Except for the threat of "exemplary punishment" this was nothing but old legislation restated. Moreover, it was still the old approach, with lists maintained from *quartier* to *quartier*.

On 9 December 1639 these registrations were centralized finally at the Bureau d'Adresse. The problem was not only the soldiers returning from the wars, but their deleterious effect on local life: "Remonstrances [have been] made by many artisans and craftsmen, that they are unable to have in their shops journeymen uncorrupted by those returning from the armies:" these former soldiers encourage them "to follow their debauchery and to live by their wits like themselves, no longer able to reduce themselves to work, having once tasted that freedom." All previous edicts must be executed and all "hotel and cabaret-keepers, and others" must register their tenants with the police, under threat of fines of 500 *livres*. "All those who are seeking a master will be expected to register at the Bureau within 24 hours of their arrival in this city,

[64] V. L. Tapié, *La France de Louis XIII et de Richelieu* (Paris: 1967), p. 369.
[65] B.N. mss. f.fr. 8083, ff. 25-27.

and to take the positions indicated to them at the said Bureau, under penalty of the galleys as vagabonds and vagrants."[66] Those who could not afford the ordinary registration fee were inscribed gratuitously. On 27 February 1640 free registration was extended to those masters themselves too poor to pay.[67] On 22 June 1640 the regulation was broadened. Hotel and cabaret-owners were prohibited from lodging for more than one night any strangers who had not first registered at the Bureau d'Adresse.[68] Although the *arrêts* say nothing directly on the problem, these measures would make it much easier to monitor hotels and boardinghouses reputed to be secret meeting places of journeyman groups.

This action perceptively changed the function of the registries. Military needs, police problems, and economic pressure had forced civil authorities to seek Renaudot's aid. Public safety had triumphed over free-market mechanisms. The unemployed now registered under threat of the galleys. In its own way, this was as prohibitive a regulation as the older *bienvenue* system which Renaudot was so eager to contain.

Due to usual problems of police enforcement, these regulations had no more success than others. They suggest, nevertheless, the double-edged thrust of Renaudot's conception of public welfare. Poor relief was at heart an economic problem, finding the unemployed and putting them to work. The Bureau would establish a single registry for the entire city, cutting away the entangling confusion of statistical methods varying from one parish or neighborhood to the next. Centralized information could make a general attack upon unemployment and poverty possible.[69] Moreover, these registries

[66] "Ordonnance pour ceux qui arrivent dans Paris pour y chercher Maistre, et autres faits de Police," *Gazette*, 9 December 1639.

[67] "Ordonnance pour la defence faite à tous hostes de loger plus d'une nuit les estrangers et forains qui cherchent employ," *Gazette*, 13 March 1640.

[68] B.N. mss. f.fr. 21801, f. 32.

[69] A helpful discussion of the emergence of statistical methods and

would make policing more clear cut; registration, and not the easily counterfeited criterion of appearance, would determine who in fact was liable to arrest and who was permitted to beg. In this instance, Renaudot's Bureau was clearly serving a governmental function. It had become the focus of attempts at civil order, while dealing with the equally acute problem of putting skilled artisans to work.

Finding jobs was only part of the Bureau's activities, and Renaudot anticipated the other needs of those under his surveillance. Here they could find legal aid. Knowing that illness was a step-sister to poverty, the poor "will find here the address of physicians, surgeons, and apothecaries who, without doubt will not wish to yield to others the honor of consulting, bloodletting, and preparing gratuitously some remedies for these poor people who are referred to them. . . . All the experiments which one has or wishes to give to the public showing the admirable effects of simples and other remedies, will be faithfully registered here."[70] Response for this information must have been overwhelming, and much of it from Parisians too poor to afford medical advice and not sick or destitute enough to be admitted to the Hôtel Dieu. Perhaps as early as 1632, Renaudot was providing free medical consultations at his Bureau.[71]

Each Tuesday afternoon, all persons could consult Renaudot's staff for medical advice. The patient would appear before a board of three physicians, who would examine him, publicly diagnose his ailment, prescribe necessary chemical treatments, and then refer the patient to a physician willing to

---

attitudes is R. Mousnier, "Études sur la population de la France au XVIIe siècle," *Dix-septième siècle* (1952), pp. 527-42.

[70] *Inventaire des adresses*, p. 24.

[71] In his *Response . . . au libelle fait contre les consultations charitables* (Paris: 1641), Renaudot said that he had been offering consultations at the Bureau for over 10 years.

treat him gratuitously. Soon treatment and remedies were being offered at the Bureau, in conjunction with the original diagnosis. These charitable consultations were among the most popular and controversial activities of the Bureau d'Adresse.[72]

Faithful to his 1612 charge to use "all other means and inventions discovered by him for the employment of the healthy poor and treatment of invalids and the ill, and in general everything useful and suitable for the regulation of the poor,"[73] Renaudot realized that the hordes of poor flocking to his Bureau often lacked the most basic elements of food, shelter, and clothing. He was also aware of the lack of readily available capital in the French economy. As a result, he instituted the first pawnshops, or *vents-à-grâce*, in France. In so doing, Renaudot encountered vehement criticism from specific business interests in Paris and irritated some of the most deeply rooted sensitivities of his age.

Few issues in European history offer more striking contrast between theory and practice as does the role of usury. Both classical and religious authorities were adamant: broadly interpreted, usury was undue or excessive profit. As St. Thomas Aquinas defined it, "profit proceeding from a loan without intermediary and by agreement" was considered usurious.[74] Long before Renaudot's time, religious and philosophical arguments were conveniently sidestepped by those lacking ready cash, be they bourgeois, prince, or pope. That these injunctions were often ignored does not mean that they had disappeared, however.

Sixteenth century businessmen cleverly disguised their profits behind highly involved business transactions, such as bills of exchange and *rentes* on the Hôtel de Ville at Paris. Traffic

---

[72] See Chapter VI. [73] *Inventaire des adresses*, p. 12.
[74] Quoted by Renaudot in his "Si l'établissement des monts-de-piété est nécessaire en France," *Gazette*, 13 March 1636.

47

in *rentes* reached a peak in the period 1560-1580, as authorities refused to permit straight interest profits.[75] Certain secular authorities, however, responded to such trafficking by permitting government-supervised interest and profit charges. Charles V, for example, licensed interest "to good merchants according to the profits that they might be able to gain reasonably."[76] Whether the Church admitted it or not, interest was a reality of sixteenth century life.

With calls for liberalization of usury bans coming from Protestant, Catholic, and secular sources, Catholic orthodox opinion was forced into an untenable scholastic rigidity by Renaudot's time. Indeed, it would maintain its theoretical opposition to uncontrolled interest until the 1745 bull *Vix pervenit.*

No matter how vehement its objection to uncontrolled interest, however, the Catholic Church did recognize the necessity of low-cost loans for the poor. Even before the meeting of the Lateran Council on 4 May 1515 which approved church pawnshops, or *monts-de-piété*, there were already such institutions in several Italian cities. Here they had been set up to protect the poor against the machinations of Jews and usurers.[77] The Catholic Church, then, did not categorically deny interest, but instead railed against high and uncontrolled interest rates. Its motives were often humanitarian and social, well founded and sincere.

[75] M. Venard, "Catholicisme et usure au XVIe siècle," *Revue d'histoire de l'Église de France,* LII (1966), 63. For early modern methods of disguising profits in transactions, see H. Lapeyre, *Une famille de marchands: les Ruiz* (Paris: 1955), esp. Chapter 5 and 7. A good study of the intellectual development of usury is B. N. Nelson, *The Idea of Usury* (New York: 1969).

[76] Venard, "Catholicisme et usure," p. 61.

[77] As a preacher said when a *mont-de-piété* was established in Amelia in 1470, ". . . orribile et grave peccatum esse in toto populo Amerino, tam usure quam etiam ratione excommunicationis, vigore capitulorum iam factorum cum Ebrais." Quoted by A. Ghinato, *Monte de pietà e monte frumentari di Amelia* (Rome: 1956), p. 19.

Opposition to low-interest loans for the poor seemed particularly persistent in France. The Parisian business community was certainly not against loans per se: the buying and selling of *rentes* permitted them all of the profits they wanted. But new forms of credit appear to have been particularly suspect. In 1548 and 1566, for example, the *Échevinage* of Paris refused to approve new credit-granting institutions.[78] The Estates General of 1614 considered a proposal to legalize low-interest loans. The proposal originated in the Second Estate. With inheritances jeopardized by years of civil and natural disasters, many impoverished nobles were unable to perform their traditional military function. Second Estate petitions advocated government *monts-de-piété* where they could borrow money to rearm themselves for royal service without being forced to go to usurious Jews and Lombards. The Second Estate pointed out the religious and moral benefits to be gained—these institutions would aid the poor, the Jews would be destroyed, etc. But the Third Estate, represented by municipal officials and businessmen, refused to consent to their recommendation.[79] They considered it a covert

[78] P. Harsin, *Crédit public et banque d'état en France du XVIIe et XVIIIe siècle* (Paris: 1933), pp. 8-9.

[79] F. Rapine, *Recueil très-exact et curieux de tout ce qui s'est fait et passé de singulier et mémorable en l'assemblée générale des estats tenues à Paris en l'année 1614* (Paris: 1651), pp. 347-55. For an analysis of the composition of the 1614 meeting, see R. Mousnier, *État et société en France au XVIIe et XVIIIe siècles* (Paris: 1969), pp. 30-34; George A. Rothrock, "The French Crown and the Estates General of 1614," *French Historical Studies*, i (1958), 295-318, and "Officials and King's Men: A Note on the Possibilities of Royal Control in the Estates General," *French Historical Studies*, ii (1962), 504-10; J. Michael Hayden, "Deputies and *Qualités*: the Estates General of 1614," *French Historical Studies*, iii (1964), 507-24. On the related problem of *dérogeance*, see G. Zeller, "Une notion de caractère historico-sociale: la dérogeance," *Cahiers internationaux de sociologie* (1957), 40-74; G. Richard, "Un aspect particulier de la politique économique et sociale de la monarchie au XVIIe siècle: Richelieu, Colbert, la noblesse et le commerce," *Dix-septième siècle* (1960), pp. 11-14.

attempt to legalize usury in France. In fact, however, were Third Estate representatives not motivated by more realistic economic considerations?

There were a number of attempts to establish government-directed *monts-de-piété* in France. Louis Turquet, Sieur de Mayerne had been a leading spokesman for this sentiment. True, he argued, there were religious and moral factors to consider: the state should "loan to common artisans and laborers small amounts and at reasonable interest, in order to protect them from the pillage of usurers, of whom the good towns of France are too well supplied." But Turquet de Mayerne recognized, as did Renaudot after him, that loans were only part of a larger, total attack upon chronic poverty to be centered in a nationwide, state-run bureau.[80] Turquet de Mayerne and Renaudot knew that without low-interest loans, the worker was forever enslaved to the usurer. Under such conditions, he had no recourse but to work for starvation wages.

It is this recognition which brought the greatest opposition to government sponsored low-interest loans in France. It was believed that cheap loans "would foment laziness."[81] As long as interest rates remained high, salaries could remain low: lower interest rates, and the poor will borrow cheaply rather than work cheaply.[82]

[80] *Epistre au Roy* (Tours: 1592), pp. 24-25. Turquet de Mayerne developed these ideas in his *Monarchie aristodémocratique* (Paris: 1611) and *Apologie contre les détracteurs . . . de la monarchie aristodémocratique* (S.l. 1617).

[81] Renaudot argued against this sentiment in "Replique aux nouvelles objections contre les monts-de-piété," *Extraordinaire*, 25 March 1637.

[82] These loans had to be carefully regulated. As Richelieu observed, "tous les politiques sont d'accord que si les peuples étaient trop à leur aise il serait impossible de les contenir dans lès regles de leur devoir." Quoted by H. Hauser, *Pensée et action économiques du Cardinal de Richelieu* (Paris: 1944), p. 145.

Although Richelieu considered instituting government-sponsored low-interest loans in 1626, the project never succeeded.[83] Except for *monts-de-piété* under the control of the Duke of Lorraine at Sedan and Nancy, and the papacy in Avignon, none were legal in France. None whatsoever existed in Paris, the capital and center of the realm.

On 13 March 1636 Commissaire Général des Pauvres Renaudot appealed to the King and his ministers in the name of an impoverished nobility eager, yet financially unable, to equip itself for royal service. "The principal impulse for the establishment of *monts-de-piété* has been the abolition of usury, an abominable sin by all divine and human laws." He cited religious authority (Aquinas, Cajetan, Valerius Reginaldus, the Lateran Council *arrêt* of 4 May 1515) and historical precedent (Charles V established a *mont-de-piété* at Naples in 1539, later protected by Cardinal Aquaviva). To say that these institutions will stop commerce was to reason, argued Renaudot, "that the rain will dry up the earth."[84] Renaudot directed his remarks to counteract the intransigent influence of the six *corps des marchands* at Châtelet and at Parlement, where these *arrêts* had to be registered.

Renaudot continued the campaign two weeks later.[85] His only aim was to serve "the public utility and embellishment of this Kingdom," and not to serve his own profits. He scoffed at those businessmen who feared that he would "be master of all the wealth of the city." One can appreciate their fears: as director of the Bureau d'Adresse and as Richelieu's

[83] Richelieu's scheme provided for *monts-de-piété* and letters of credit, but an ordinance of 16 June 1627 killed the entire plan. J. Caillet, *De l'administration en France sous le ministre du Cardinal de Richelieu* (Paris: 1857), p. 242.

[84] "Si l'établissement des monts-de-piété. . . ," *Gazette*, 13 March 1637.

[85] "Replique aux nouvelles objections contre les monts-de-piété," *Gazette*, 25 March 1637.

51

newspaper voice, Renaudot had already inextricably insinu-
ated himself in the city's life, and there seemed no limit to
his ambition and power.

On 27 March 1637, the Crown entrusted Renaudot with
establishing low-interest loans. Permission was granted because "every day many gentlemen and other subjects of His
Majesty present themselves at his Bureaus, having a great
desire to serve in his armies if they could, in their great need,
be promptly assisted and aided with money, in order to outfit
and equip themselves."[86] Renaudot had used arguments which
the Second Estate had used in 1614. The war-weary monarchy
could well understand them: the *Gazettes* of 1636 and 1637
were packed with calls to arms and threats to nobles who
were not at war.[87] By borrowing from Renaudot with goods
left as collateral, such service would be possible. Noble bor-
rowers would avoid the loss of property and estate which
illegal borrowing risked. Moreover, Renaudot would protect
their anonymity. He was empowered to establish a *mont-
de-piété* in Paris, lending money for six *deniers* per *livre* of the
price of the item sold or exchanged.[88] In the patent signed by
the king on 1 April, these *monts-de-piété* were joined to the
Bureau d'Adresse, giving Renaudot authority to establish them
not only in Paris, as the earlier *arrêt* stated, but throughout the
realm.[89] Renaudot had audaciously appealed to the Crown
in the name of an impoverished nobility. But even more than
the nobility, these pawnshops would serve the chronically unemployed urban poor.

Every Thursday, unredeemed items were sold at public auc-

[86] B.N. mss. f.fr. 21741, f. 228.

[87] These occur throughout the *extraordinaires* of 1636 and 1637;
stories of officers away from their units without permission, the problems of the *ban* and *arrière-ban*, etc.

[88] "Arrest du conseil, commission et brevet de Sa Majesté pour
l'achat, troque et vente au Bureau d'Adresse et toutes choses licites,"
Gazette, 9 April 1637.

[89] *Ibid.*

tion. The profits from the sale were held for a certain length of time, and if the owner paid back his loan promptly, he received the proceeds of the sale less a fee for holding and damages. These fees, plus the initial three *sous* fee of the Bureau d'Adresse, less operating costs, provided the funds from which persons could borrow at the six *deniers* per *livre* rate.[90] In spite of numerous other attempts to establish *monts-de-piété*, Renaudot ran the only authorized low-interest loan institution in Paris.

If the Bureau aided the poor, "the most agreeable end," said Renaudot, "that I could ever consider,"[91] it seems that upper and middle-class citizens were the financial mainstays of the Bureau. *Les Tables des choses dont on peut donner et recevoir advis au Bureau d'adresse* is a veritable index to their world.[92] One could find carriages, manorial lands, jewelry, tapestries, and rugs listed for sale. Persons on the make could find "the names and residences of all persons of importance, such as Princes and Officers of the Crown, of the sovereign and inferior courts, the royal household," and lists of vacancies, secular and religious. Officers could locate "soldiers to enroll for the service of the King." The Bureau registered the names of colleges and academies, teachers of "Arms, Navigation, Artillery, Penmanship, Mathematics; French, Latin, Greek, Spanish and other foreign languages; lute-playing, dance, and other disciplines." And if that did not satisfy, Renaudot would gladly provide the address of persons teaching "brief methods" for learning other sciences. One could find the addresses of genealogists, of "banks, bankers and agents at Rome," "benefices to exchange or put into escrow," "attorney and notary practices to sell or buy," "gazettes of foreign news, and the price of merchandise," "marriages," etc.

In addition to regular *Prix Courants des Marchandises*,

[90] *Mercure français*, Paris, 1641, 57-60.
[91] *Inventaire des adresses*, p. 12.   [92] See the Appendix.

Renaudot published monthly excerpts of the Bureau's listings. Several examples taken from the *Quinzieme Feuille du Bureau d'Adresse, du premier Septembre 1633* suggest Renaudot's wide clientele:

Seigneurial lands for sale. A seigneurial estate, with all rights of justice, four leagues outside of Orleans, in the forest, consisting of a lovely comfortable chateau, arable lands, vineyards, pastures, lordship of a village, hunting and fishing rights, many small farms [*métairies*], *rentes*, privileges, patronage and other seigneurial rights. It has a yearly revenue of 2000 *livres*. Its price: 60,000 *livres*. V.3f. 252 à 3.v. . . . *Parisian house for sale.* A house near the old rue du Temple, consisting of a *porte-cochère*, carriage garage, courtyard, stable for five horses, three drawingrooms, two bedrooms, one of which has a *cabinet* adjacent, all well-embellished with very lovely pictures; two other bedrooms, a large attic; another two-room house behind the kitchen. Its price: 30,000 *livres*. For ten years it has been leased for 1200 *livres*. V.3. f. 248 à 8v. . . . *Goods for sale.* A new coat which is still not finished, scarlet with silver braid, lined with satin of the same color. The price: 18 *écus*. V.8f.253 à 3.r . . . *Miscellaneous.* Someone is looking for a craftsman who works in coral. V.3.f.251 à 1.v. Another offers to disclose how to feed large numbers of fowl cheaply. V.3.f.254, art. 10v. For sale. An atlas of Henricus Hondius. The price: 48 *livres*. V.3.f.251 à 1.r. Someone is looking for a traveling companion to go to Italy in two weeks. V.3.f.249 à 3.v. For sale. A young dromedary camel, at reasonable price. V.3.f.253 à 11.v.[93]

After coming to the Bureau and paying the registration fee, the client received the address. This was all: identities were

---

[93] Republished in *Variétés historiques et littéraires* (Paris: 1859), IX, 51-61. The last listing is particularly intriguing: what is a "reasonable price" for a dromedary?

disclosed after the Bureau had ceased to be involved, and then at the participants' own risk. Each type of listing was done in a separate room, so that, for example, a cook seeking a new position would not pass the major domo of his household, registering for a new butler; a hard-pressed advocate selling his office would not have to worry about bumping into his next door neighbor, hoping to find a well-placed fiancé for his daughter.[94]

By the late 1630's, Renaudot the projector-entrepreneur was at the height of his success. His Bureau d'Adresse was located in his Maison du Grand Coq, on the Ile de la Cité's Rue Calandre. This was one of the busiest areas in Paris. Renaudot was a few steps from the Marché Neuf and the Pont Neuf, the Cathedral of Notre Dame and Hôtel Dieu, and the Palais, with its offices and chambers housing the sovereign courts. Crowds flocked to the Maison du Grand Coq—newly arrived provincial artisans, speaking a babel of dialects; Parisian lawyers, artisans, masters; victims of plague, war, and chronic illness seeking free medical aid; Richelieu's officers bringing articles for the *Gazette*; colporters buying copies of the *Gazette* to sell throughout Paris; teamsters unloading barrels of ink and reams of paper to supply his presses; university professors, lawyers, and gentlemen virtuosi come to discuss questions of science and philosophy at his weekly Conferences, all joined by people wishing to borrow money.

During these years, the Maison du Grand Coq was one of the most teeming households in Paris. A single bourgeois dwelling could hardly serve all of Renaudot's needs.[95] It is very likely that the Maison du Grand Coq consisted of a central house with rooms or small buildings attached to it, built in any available space (such as a courtyard or over existing

[94] *Le renouvellement des Bureaux d'Adresse* (Paris: 1647), pp. 7, 40.
[95] For a description of Renaudot's neighborhood and a discussion of housing in seventeenth century Paris, see O. Ranum, *Paris*, pp. 11, 83-95.

structures) or leased from neighbors. We know that the *grande salle* of the Maison accommodated the public medical consultations, periodic auctions of goods left on collateral, and had to be large enough to seat up to one hundred participants at the weekly conferences. At least two rooms housed the registries of the Bureau d'Adresse, and another room stored goods left on collateral. It is unlikely that Renaudot would keep his furnaces and chemical equipment in a public place, so another separate room would be needed for his apothecaries.[96] By 1644, Renaudot had a printshop of 4 presses on the premises, probably housed in a ground level shop in an adjoining building. Renaudot's private living quarters were on the second and third floors of his home, and probably served his son's families until they were able to form their own households. The upper stories, as well as rooms leased or owned in adjoining buildings, were occupied by the servants, clerks, printers, and apprentices who worked for Renaudot.

Renaudot had several clerks to keep his inventories and accounts, and they may also have helped to translate and edit the *Gazette*. His printing presses employed four printers each, and by 1644 he had 4 presses in operation. Add to this another 12 to 15 compositors, proofreaders, and errand boys, and Renaudot must have had at least 30 employees. In addition to these, a large staff of consulting apothecaries, surgeons, and physicians were constantly on the premises.

The Bureau d'Adresse enjoyed a remarkable success. At times, bragged Renaudot, the street in front of the bureau was blocked with people.[97] In 14 years of operation, over 80,-000 persons used its job-referral services, to say nothing of its

[96] Renaudot was granted permission to establish chemical furnaces in 1640. See pp. 173ff.

[97] *Requeste présentée à la Reyne par Théophraste Renaudot* (S.l.n.d.), p. 2. Guy Patin scoffed that it would not require a very large crowd to block such a narrow street! *Examen de la requeste présentée à la Reyne par le Gazetier* (Paris: 1643).

other registries.[98] This is an impressive record—if we can believe Renaudot's own statistics, an average of 5,700 employment transactions per year from 1630 to 1644 at his single bureau in Paris. By 1638, Renaudot had established similar bureaus "in some other towns."[99] The Bureau d'Adresse was also the subject of several ballets performed for the court.[100]

Not only was Renaudot an intermediary for commercial activities, but he had become actively engaged in commerce himself. His critics' fears were certainly understandable. They attacked Renaudot's desire to maintain anonymity, seeing it as a guise to protect thieves selling stolen goods.[101] Others

[98] He wrote this in 1647 (*Renouvellement des Bureaux d'Adresse,* p. 8) after 3 years of inactivity. The statistics therefore refer to the period 1630-1644.

[99] *Gazette,* 14 October 1638. It is impossible to determine to which "other towns" Renaudot was referring. There is evidence that he attempted to establish a bureau at Lyon: an anonymous editor discovered a request to the Consulat of Lyon, dated 21 June 1639 (Archives Lyonnais, BB193), but could find no further mention of Renaudot's activities. "Théophraste Renaudot et les petites affiches et avis divers à Lyon," *Bulletin historique et archeologique du diocèse de Lyon,* 1 (1930), 92-94. Perhaps these other bureaus were associated with the men who were licensed to publish provincial editions of the *Gazette,* but information here is just as sketchy.

In 1638 Charles I granted a patent to Captain Robert Innes to establish an "Office of Intelligence" in London, supposedly inspired by Renaudot's Parisian bureau. There is no evidence that it took root. See H. Brown, *Scientific Organizations in Seventeenth Century France.* (Baltimore: 1934), pp. 30ff; see also pp. 94ff.

[100] There were at least two editions of ballets performed in Paris: *Ballet du Bureau de Rencontre dansé au Louvre devant Sa Majesté* (Paris: 1631); *Ballet du Bureau de Rencontre ensemble le remerciment du maitre du Bureau d'Adresse, à ceux qui dansent son ballet* (Paris: 1632). A similar ballet was performed before Monsieur, and was published as *Ballet du Bureau des Adresses* (Dijon: 1640).

[101] He included the following notice in the *Extraordinaire* of 20 May 1637: "Ceux ausquels on aura derobé quelque chose sont avertis qu'en envoyant le mémoire en ce Bureau, lesdites choses y seront arrestées si on les y apporte, en n'y seront pas vendues: non pas mesmes à grace et faculté de rachat comme toutes les autres qui y sont tous les jours exposées à un chacun."

claimed that by controlling the only legal low-interest loans in Paris, he hoped eventually to control all of the city's economy. Still others said that his activity was not a *mont-de-piété* (i.e., a church-sponsored institution) but instead "a downright veritable junkshop" more at home in the Jewish quarter.[102] At first these attacks seemed to have had little effect, other than to pique Renaudot. But as his fortunes changed after the death of his protectors, such criticism became associated with and strengthened by the antagonisms of groups Renaudot had managed to challenge elsewhere.

In these two concerns, the directory of addresses and low-interest lending, Renaudot exhibited a certain sophistication in recognizing the importance of basic economic matters to the general problem of poor relief. In his desire to find jobs for the poor, and in his establishment of the *mont-de-piété*, religious and moral arguments were secondary. Indeed, they were mentioned (granting good advice, in the words of St. Bernard, was a high form of charity; establishing the *monts-de-piété* would banish usury and the Jews with it), but they appear more decorative than substantive. Renaudot never denied the validity of traditional religious and moral arguments; he chose instead to treat them as subsidiary. Such Christian approaches to poverty and usury were explicable after the fact. In attempting to prevent the problem first instead of curing it later, Renaudot had no need for such apologetic arguments.

We may accuse Renaudot of a certain amount of naivete in assuming newly arrived unemployed in Paris would voluntarily take a job. In a constricted economy, with low, often starvation-level wages, high prices and few consumer goods, idleness is an understandable recourse. Moreover, there is little reason to believe that the transition to an urban environment was any easier for sixteenth and seventeenth century

---

[102] *Requeste présentée au prévôt de Paris par . . . la faculté de médecine contre Théophraste Renaudot* (S.d.: 1643).

man to make than it was for his nineteenth or twentieth century counterpart.

Given all this, there still is no denying Renaudot's attempts to aid the chronically unemployed skilled and semiskilled worker. In a milieu convinced that sloth and idleness were the absolute forms of pride, that forced confinement in endless labors "without utility or profit" was the only way to punish these social deviates, Renaudot's approach remains unique.[103]

[103] See E. Chill, "Religion and Mendicity in Seventeenth Century France," *International Review of Social History,* VII (1962), 400-25; and M. Foucault, *Madness and Civilization* (New York: 1965), pp. 38-64, which discuss the reasons and methods of the "Great Confinement," culminating in the establishment of the Hôpital Général in 1656.

CHAPTER III

The Conferences at the Bureau d'Adresse

THÉOPHRASTE RENAUDOT enjoyed a significant role in the popularization and diffusion of letters and science in seventeenth century France. He was by no means an original thinker, certainly not when compared to the genius of many contemporaries. But as was true of his medical, public welfare, and publishing activities, he responded to his century with a fresh and enthusiastic dedication, spreading ideas far beyond the intellectual and social elites in which they were developed and first tested.

By the early seventeenth century, the University of Paris cast only a shadow of its former glory. The intramural disputes of the fourteenth and fifteenth centuries, the religious disputes and economic reverses of the sixteenth century had irreparably weakened the university. Pierre Ramus' *Advertissements sur la réformation de l'Université de Paris* tells it all: teachers who would not teach, students who would not study, too many banquets, not enough scholarships, disputes and rivalries among the various faculties, *et cetera ad nauseam*.[1] The university continued to license various guilds, crafts, and corporations, but it had earned this privilege in an earlier, more intellectually vibrant age. One attempt after another was made to revitalize higher education at Paris, from the establishment of the Collège de France outside the University in 1530 to the internal reforms instituted by Henry IV in 1595. But like most legislation, these efforts reflected old weaknesses more

[1] Ramus, *Advertissements sur la réformation de l'Université de Paris* (Paris: 1562), passim.

than they reflected a new vitality. The University was more destitute than ever before or since, with no money for the most basic expenses. Curricula remained virtually unchanged. The university was "the citadel of Routine" and "the temple of Immobility."[2] Renaudot would fault university medical instruction, but this was merely one facet of a general degeneration.

The curious Frenchman could hardly expect to find the latest ideas at the university, when in fact innovations were born outside its walls, directly challenging its religious, moral, medical, or scientific orthodoxy. There was another reason, much less lofty but just as important: formal courses of study were not always fun. The intellectual man-in-the-street wanted his knowledge direct, clear, concise, and, if possible, painlessly administered. The university was justifiably unwilling and unequipped to do this, since popularization directly conflicted with its traditional purposes. Disdaining the faculties on the one hand, being shut out from them on the other, French intellectuals had reacted by forming academies and scientific organizations.

French intellectual academies trace their lineage back to the Florentine Academy of Ficino and Pico. Neoplatonism had seeped into France by the period of the early Pléiade in the mid-sixteenth century. And to Catherine de Medici, it seemed natural to encourage the academic tradition founded by her ancestors Cosimo and Lorenzo il Magnifico.[3]

In the original letters-patent for the Académie Royale de Poesie et de Musique, of November 1570, the major concern was to affect morality through the harmonious powers of music: "for the minds of most men are formed and their behavior influenced by its character [music], so that where

---

[2] René Pintard, *Libertinage érudit dans la première moitié de dix-septième siècle* (Paris: 1943), p. 88.

[3] F. Yates, *The French Academy of the Sixteenth Century* (London: 1947), p. 20.

music is disordered, there morals are also depraved, and where it is well ordered, there men are well disciplined morally."[4] The harmony of music reflected the harmony of all morality and of all knowledge (*encyclopedia*). Under Henry III, ethical and moral discussions took precedence over the music and poetry earlier favored by his brother Charles IX. With its encyclopedic outlook, its attention to ethics and morality, this royal academy remained loyal to its Italian Renaissance roots.[5] More important to our discussion, it provided some of the characteristics of the next academy with royal backing, the academy of Renaudot.

From the disappearance of the royal academy in the late 1580's, until the founding of the Académie Française in 1635, "there is a tract of time in which the history of [French] academism has hardly been studied."[6] Except for an abortive attempt to revive such an academy in 1612, no other officially supported academy existed before the Académie Française in 1635. But the Académie Française was hardly a popular, public venture. In its own way, it was as elitist as any of the Renaissance academies in Italy, or the academies supported by Henry III and Catherine de Medici.

Slightly before the founding of the Académie Française, several scientific and literary circles appeared in Paris. Most notable and influential was the Cabinet of Pierre and Jacques Dupuy. Here "the taste, or even better, the frenzy for books" was supreme.[7] *Parlementaires* and priests, Catholics and Protestants, lawyers, historians, astronomers, mathematicians, and poets met together regularly to discuss topics as varied as the membership. The Cabinet followed the elitist academic tradition by remaining private, and jealously fighting against any

[4] Quoted by Yates, *French Academy*, p. 23.

[5] *Ibid.*, pp. 23ff.

[6] *Ibid.*, p. 275. Although patents were granted in 1635, Parlement did not register them until 1637.

[7] Pintard, *Libertinage érudit*, p. 190.

who would bring the glare of public attention upon it. Even more important, its members were similar to those of earlier French academies, men of high birth or of comfortable status. The practicing barrister or physician was unable to penetrate their circle. Under the best of circumstances, pure scholarship and mass audiences do not mix; under the stultifying pressure of seventeenth century Parisian social and intellectual pretensions, the gap remained nearly unbridgeable. Except for Renaudot.

His numerous patents and privileges gave Renaudot a wide range of freedom to do whatever he felt necessary under the auspices of the Bureau d'Adresse. Renaudot had participated regularly in Scévole de Sainte Marthe's circle at Loudun, and Sainte Marthe himself had likewise been a pillar of Henry III's academy. Sainte Marthe had written a history of this academy, and it was likely that Renaudot knew this work and even discussed it with his beloved Sainte Marthe.[8] Although Renaudot's academy would maintain an encyclopedic outlook, he would depart from the model in having a truly popular, open academy.

There were other reasons why Renaudot wished to form an academy. Throughout his life, he was greatly interested in renovating pedagogical theory and practice. He conceived of his academy much as he conceived of the press, as a public trust. Information, be it applied propaganda or pure science, was a necessity to seventeenth century life. A man without the news was liable to believe "various rumors which often ignite intestine disturbances and sedition." A man without a solid intellectual foundation was like a starving man confronted by "artificial meat or wax fruits" mixed "among real and verifiable meats and fruits."[9] What better way to prove the

---

[8] See Sainte Marthe's *Éloges des hommes illustres* (Paris: 1644), pp. 47-48.

[9] "Preface au Lecteur," *Recueil des Gazettes de 1631*, p. 5; Conference of 4 March 1641.

efficacy of one's theories than to put them into practice? What better way to demonstrate the effect of a popular academy than in fact to institute one?

The "Inventaire des Adresses" of the Bureau d'Adresse already provided the addresses of a variety of educational services: "Summary of sciences and brief methods of learning them, Arts, sciences, and exercises to learn. . . . Experiments, courses, lessons, debates, lectures, and other acts in Theology, Medicine, Law, philosophy, and the humanities. . . . Experiments in Medicine, agriculture, and others. . . . News which one may wish to learn. . . . Questions to resolve."[10] Soon these "experiments, courses, lessons, debates, and lectures" were being held on the premises.

The conferences were held regularly from 22 August 1633 through 1 September 1642, each Monday afternoon. In all likelihood several conferences preceded this first public meeting.[11] From the outset, the doors were open to all; "and if all persons of the necessary quality have not been able to find a place, the most diligent can testify to the others that this is attributable to the location which, as spacious as it is, still cannot accommodate all the late arrivals."[12] Only French was to be spoken.[13] There was no limit to the number of speakers, nor was there a moderator to summarize the positions of the participants. Obviously, this open-endedness upset some members of the conference. "It seemed necessary that with so many differing opinions, they be gathered together so that the Reader could follow them, it seeming improper to leave him wandering in incertitude. But having been considered many times,

[10] See *Table des choses dont on peut donner & recevoir advis au Bureau d'adresse*, Appendix A.

[11] The first published conference, dated 22 August 1633, referred to "la dernière conference," indicating that at least one and probably several sessions preceded the 22 August meeting.

[12] "Avis au Lecteur," *Première Centurie*.

[13] "Preface," *ibid*.

more inconveniences have been found in summarizing each point than in letting each Reader [or Auditor] do so himself. ... The Conference thereby shows how it defers judgment to its Reader, having a better opinion of him than of itself." The members of the circle themselves chose the weekly topics, "there being no better way to have us agree on a proposal than by making us its authors. ... I having found nothing more expedient in contending with so many different tempers than to let them choose themselves the subject they wish to discuss."[14] All subjects were admitted, with two very important exceptions: "the innocence of this exercise is most remarkable. Not only is slander banished, but for fear of irritating minds easily upset by problems of Religion, all such concerns are referred to the Sorbonne. The mystery of affairs of State, partaking of the nature of divine things, of which those who have the most to say, say the least, we refer them to the Conseil [du Roi] from where they proceed. All the rest are here, to give free play to your imagination."[15] Renaudot was very much aware of the limits of free inquiry; in fact, however, his academy was no less free than any other academy was, or could be, at that time. Religious discussion was the exclusive bailiwick of the Sorbonne, and other faculties within the University knew not to step on its prerogatives. And even though he had been baptized in the Catholic Church, Renaudot remained a reprobate Protestant to most of his critics. One could never be too careful in avoiding religious controversy. As for problems of practical political significance, these were the concerns of the court, and not the marketplace.

Reports of the conferences were published each week. From 1634 to 1641, Renaudot published four collections of these conferences, and in 1655 his son Eusèbe published the fifth. These went through several editions during the following years, often without acknowledgment of their origin. Several individual

---

[14] "Avis au lecteur," *ibid.*   [15] "Preface," *ibid.*

topics were translated into English *ca.* 1640 (i.e., "Whether there be nothing new;" "Which is to be most esteemed, an inventive wit, judgment, or courage;" "Whether truth begets hatred, and why;" "Of the cock, and whether his crowing do affright the lion;" "Why dead bodies bleed in the presence of their murtherers."[16] In 1644 and 1665 two folio editions of the conferences were published in London, as the *General Collection of the Discourses of The Virtuosi of France*, possibly as a result of public interest in the newly formed Royal Society.[17]

Four-hundred sixty different subjects were discussed in the 345 meetings of the conference. Through the 115th session (2 June 1636), two topics were considered each week; from then on, only one subject was treated weekly. During the early days of the conference, there was also an hour devoted to inventions. This third section of the conference lasted regularly until 5 December 1633, when it was dropped due to a lack of time. The conference continued to consider inventions, at least on an irregular basis. At least one summer (1634), and possibly others, was devoted exclusively to inventions submitted to it.

Renaudot's academy broke all the rules that were followed by the Académie Française, the circles of Dupuy or Rambouillet. It was public, and not private; it sought publicity, rather than fleeing from it; it was directed to rhetorical ends, as much as to informational and scientific ends. In addition to all of this, we must imagine the activity at the Maison du

[16] Republished in *The Harleian Miscellany* (1808), I, 439-41; (1809), II, 35-37.

[17] The translator's dedication states: "I shall not undertake to determine whether the restitution of Philosophical Liberty began first by the French, or by some great Personage of our own, particularly the renowned Lord Bacon (from whom, 'tis said, not improbably, their Des-Cartes took the grounds of his new Theory) but 'tis certain that his way of Experiment, as now prosecuted by sundry English Gentlemen, affords more probabilities of glorious and profitable Fruits, than the attempts of any other Age or Nation whatsoever."

Grand Coq, where the meetings took place. Renaudot's house on the Rue Calandre hardly breathed the sweet air of Parnassus. Charles Sorel, who wrote a contemporary account of the early years of the Académie Française, captured the atmosphere: "no end is attained in treating of them [the *conferences*] with contempt because of the variety of affairs which were carried on there, such as the sale and distribution of the *Gazette*, and the consultation there permitted of the registers of investments and houses for sale, and because of the valets found for hire there, the money loaned on security, the unredeemed goods for sale by auction, which sometimes made this house a real secondhand shop. That did not prevent its appearing at other hours a school of philosophers; and one may say that its various uses were created to make it a model of our civilization, and a mirror of human life. As for its disputes or doctrinal discourses, although they were not performed with as much formality and order as they might have received in the houses of the nobility, yet they represented what a private person could achieve; and in comparison with many others this assembly had had its excellence."[18] Other contemporaries were much less generous. In his *Roman bourgeois*, Furetière described a no-account lawyer who "for twenty years never missed a morning at the Palais [de Justice]: even though he has never had consultation, written documents, or pleaded for a client. In place of this, he was busily involved in discoursing on a variety of false news, which he broadcast at his accustomed pillar [in the gallery of the Palais de Justice]; and he offered much advice on public affairs, and on the government: he associated with a horrible bunch of useless people, who every morning came to the Palais and talked about all sorts of news, as if they were *controlleurs d'État*, offices very popular and very much in vogue. . . . In the afternoon he used to go to the Conferences of the Bureau d'Adresse, to the lec-

[18] *Discours sur l'Académie Française* (Paris: 1654), pp. 176-77.

67

tures given by the teachers in the colleges, to the sermons, to the concerts of church music, to see the seller of Orviétan, and to all the other public games and amusements which cost nothing, for he was a man entirely governed by his avarice."[19] And Tallement des Réaux, never one for gilding the lily, prefaced his derogatory description of the novelist-dramatist La Calprenède, "He came to Paris very young, and although he played the man of rank, he was long one of the buttresses of the Bureau d'Adresse, and never missed one of the conferences."[20] Much of Renaudot's reputation came from the fact that his bureau was a meeting place of "libertine physicians, vagabonds, heretics and Huguenots"—in a word, all of the people associated with his medical clinic.[21] It would likewise win a reputation as a "luago troppo Vituperoso," no doubt because of the mystical and hermetic topics treated there.[22]

Renaudot's academy drew from a wide public. There were professional scholars, recognized throughout Europe, such as Jean-Baptiste Morin, Tommaso Campanella, and Étienne de Claves. But the rest remain nameless. What kind of men were they?

Many of the regular participants were dilettantes, or, as the English translator of Renaudot's conferences referred to them, "virtuosi." These terms did not yet have pejorative connotations. For all of his delight in learning, the seventeenth century virtuoso pursued scholarship in deadly seriousness, and this is the spirit in which the conferences at the Bureau d'Adresse were held. It was assumed that the virtuoso was a man of rank, leisure, and wealth who devoted full time to his

---

[19] Le roman bourgeois (Amsterdam: 1714), pp. 112-13.

[20] Historiettes (Paris: 1960), II, 584.

[21] Faculté de Médecine, Examen de la Requeste présentée à la Reyne par le Gazettier (Paris: 1643), pp. 18-19.

[22] "Questi avvisi," B.N. mss. f.fr. 18600, f. 491.

study.[23] This social connotation colored Sorel's and Furetière's view of Renaudot's audience. But in addition to such virtuosi, the conferences drew the bulk of its audience from other sources.

We can infer much about the audience since it chose the discussion topics. The large number of medical and legal subjects indicates the presence of these professional groups. The discussions of status, education, and social behavior indicate that members of the nobility were attracted to the conferences. Renaudot considered service to this group among his major responsibilities.[24] There are a number of topics dealing with the role and goal of femininity, and some have argued that women were regular participants at Renaudot's academy.[25] This is impossible to prove. What is important is that this popular academy is full-square in the *précieuse* movement. In addition to sessions devoted specifically to the topics of *préciosité*, all of the sessions were directed to a nobility sorely in need of social grace and intellectual sophistication.[26] For Renaudot, vulgarization was serious business.

In its 9 years, the academy discussed all manner of subjects. At first, it appears that a conscious attempt was made to balance the content of the weekly sessions, pairing a naturalistic-scientific topic with one of a literary-moral-philosophical content. Such pairing may have been more fortuitous than in fact conscious. Analyzing these conferences quantitatively, on a subject basis, is complicated by a much more subtle problem.

During Renaudot's lifetime, knowledge was not compart-

[23] W. E. Houghton, Jr., "The English Virtuoso in the Seventeenth Century," *Journal of the History of Ideas* (1942), 51-73, 190-219.

[24] See pp. 84ff.

[25] G. Reynier, *La femme au dix-septième siècle* (Paris: 1929), pp. 142-49.

[26] R. Lathuillère, *La préciosité* (Geneva: 1966), pp. 627-29. See J. H. Hexter's article, "The Education of the Aristocracy in the Renaissance," in *Reappraisals in History* (Evanston: 1961), pp. 45-70.

mentalized as it is today. The Faustian dream of total knowledge was, if no less quixotic, at least theoretically possible. Thinking, reasoning, and discussion on most subjects was still couched in traditional Aristotelian terms. The Aristotelian world view provided single vantage points, single sets of keys by which one could interpret all phenomena, natural and moral alike. It was intellectually reassuring and as theoretically simple as could be. The principle of the Aristotelian outlook expressed itself in quadratic terms. The world was composed of four elements, which paralleled the four seasons, the four cardinal directions, the four bodily humours, the four sensations, etc. Even when weakened by a variety of specific discoveries, the outlook still maintained a seductive and secure hold on the minds of most thinkers.[27] Astronomy provides a perfect example. In spite of hundreds of discrete discoveries and modifications which exposed the potential weakness of the Aristotelian-Ptolemaic cosmology, the cosmology itself remained intact. The system absorbed these potshots by adding epicycle after epicycle, and if the cosmic maps of the sixteenth century were far more complex than those of the fifth century, the basic cosmology was nonetheless still as strong and consistent as ever.[28]

The quadratic scheme could be applied as successfully to morality, physiology, personality, and the nature of different political systems as it could to the nature of physical matter, the revolution of the planets, the character of disease and diet.

[27] In spite of the significance of many of these individual discoveries (those of Tartaglia, Cardan, Scaliger, Benedetti, and other sixteenth century critics of Aristotle's physics), these men still remain "en deça de la ligne de partage qui separe la science de la Renaissance de la science moderne." A. Koyré, "La Renaissance: les sciences exactes," *Histoire générale des sciences* (Paris: 1958), ii, 91-107.

[28] Perhaps the clearest scholarly treatment of the vitality of the Aristotelian-Ptolemaic world-view is T. Kuhn, *The Copernican Revolution* (New York: 1959), esp. pp. 83-84. For a general discussion of the methods and forms of early modern thought, see M. Foucault, *The Order of Things* (New York: 1970), esp. Chapter II and III.

Such syncretism lasted as long as it did, impervious to the piddling threats of unrelated and diverse intellectual break-throughs, because it was so overwhelmingly consistent with the world as it was actually perceived.[29] The outlook lasted, quite simply, because it worked.

If the four elements of the earth had relationships which extended horizontally to each other, they likewise extended these relationships vertically, to plants, gems, animals, body types, etc. All things, no matter how insignificant in them-selves, were potentially significant. A discussion of plants was likewise concerned with the *correspondances* of the plant in the animal and mineral world, the humours it would activate when used as food, its relationships to others on the basis of its shape and color.[30] Analysis by particularization and reduction—the hallmark of a modern scientific attitude—is not only anathema to the operation of these minds, but more important, psycho-logically impossible. And as slowly as scientific viewpoints changed after the mid-sixteenth century, literary and religious metaphors grounded in this premodern outlook were even more impervious to change. In addition, this psychological set endured longest among the dilettantes, precisely the persons who attended Renaudot's academy. The list of subjects of the academy reflected this syncretism; our categorization is, at best, artificial. If Renaudot had attempted to divide his 460 con-ferences by subject, he certainly would have arrived at con-clusions far different from ours. If nothing else, our inability to apply neat, discrete twentieth century labels to Renaudot's

[29] "Aristotle was able to express in an abstract and consistent manner many spontaneous perceptions of the universe that had existed for centuries before he gave them a logical verbal rationale. In many cases these are just the perceptions that, since the seventeenth century, elementary scientific education has increasingly banished from the adult Western mind . . . much of the appeal of the Aristotelian doctrine must lie in the naturalness of the perception that underlies the doctrine." T. Kuhn, pp. 96-97.

[30] This element of ratiocination paralleled the pedagogical-rhetorical use of "common places," or *lieux communs*. See pp. 82ff.

71

seventeenth century conferences indicates the mental distance between our age and his.

The conferences covered the obvious scientific questions, problems as basic to physical science today as they were in the seventeenth century, or 2,000 years earlier. Sessions were devoted to the elements ("Basic matter," "Fire," "Air," "Water," "The fifth essence," "Earth"),[31] motion ("Perpetual motion," "Movement," "Why motion produces heat"),[32] and other physical phenomena ("The vacuum," "Weight and causes of weight," "If the heavier of two bodies of different weight descends more quickly than the other, and why," "The cause of vapors").[33] A large number were concerned with weather ("Thunder," "The origins of winds," "Dew," "Evening dew," "Why it is colder at midnight than at any other hour of day or night")[34] and the related problems of navigation ("Various movements of the sea and rivers," "Navigation and longitude," "Why there are more winds on sea than on land," "The ebb and flow of the sea").[35]

These topics gave Renaudot's participants a chance to expose new ideas and even engage in scientific demonstrations and experiments. For example, Jean-Baptiste Morin, professor of mathematics at the Collège de France, first publicized his controversial methods of determining longitude to the conference in the Spring of 1633. He repeated the demonstrations at the Arsenal before a number of Richelieu's councilors, who had sponsored a competition to find better methods of navigation.[36] On 23 April 1635 the conference considered "Navigation and longitude," and Morin's method was cited as one of

[31] 12 September 1633; 26 September 1633; 3 October 1633; 8 January 1635; 17 October 1633.

[32] 12 September 1633; 29 January 1635; 27 March 1635.

[33] 3 July 1634; 14 January 1636; 5 November 1640; 2 June 1636.

[34] 2 April 1635; 19 December 1633; 17 March 1636; 22 June 1637; 7 December 1637.

[35] 6 July 1637; 23 April 1635; 26 January 1638; 28 December 1633.

[36] *Gazette*, 1, 22, 29 April 1634.

the most effective. Morin's ideas embroiled him in a lengthy battle with Gassendi, Bernier, and other defenders of the new astronomy, but for all of his controversiality, Morin remained one of the most famous mathematicians of his age.[37]

Ismaël Boulliau was another probable member of the assembly. Boulliau, as was Renaudot, was born at Loudun and later renounced his Calvinism for Catholicism; unlike Renaudot, however, Boulliau entered the priesthood and became a well-respected astronomer. He was a regular correspondent of Gassendi and Galileo, and Gassendi took for granted that Boulliau and Renaudot were friends.[38]

Jacques Dupuy also knew Renaudot and seemed to follow the conferences regularly. It is doubtful if he participated actively in the weekly sessions, Renaudot's popular, open academy so different from his own circle. Even though Dupuy said that he had "little communication with M. Renaudot," his correspondent Peiresc seemed to assume that the two of them were associates.[39]

Marin Mersenne followed Renaudot's conferences and publicized them to his far-flung correspondents.[40] It is impossible to identify him in specific conferences, but he and Renaudot collaborated in publicizing one of the most controversial scientific events of the century. On 24 October 1633 the assembly considered "The movement or immobility of the earth," a session in which Mersenne may have participated. Renaudot was aware of the controversial nature of this topic, but did not yet know that the Vatican had condemned Galileo's writings on 22 June. He learned of the Vatican decision at the beginning

[37] R. Lenoble, *Mersenne, ou la naissance du mécanisme* (Paris: 1943), pp. 409-13.

[38] Gassendi to Boulliau, 24 January 1634 in M. Mersenne, *Correspondance* (Paris: 1943), IV, 11.

[39] Jacques Dupuy to Peiresc, 17 February 1634; *ibid.*, p. 46.

[40] J.-J. Denonain, "Les problèmes de l'honnête homme vers 1635: Religio Medici et les Conférences du Bureau d'Adresse," *Études anglaises* (1965), p. 254.

of December, and printed the entire condemnation in the *Relation* of December 1633 "so that this question should no longer be disputed."[41] Renaudot may have first learned of the decision from his normal news sources in Rome. Peiresc however took for granted that Renaudot learned it from Mersenne, "who has let it out of his hands a bit too easily."[42]

In addition to discussing scientific issues, the assembly often participated in scientific demonstrations. The first months of the assembly saw demonstrations of Hero's Aeolipyle, as well as a perpetual motion device, a submarine, a more effective windmill, a one-man cart capable of carrying extremely heavy loads, and techniques for producing high-quality charcoal.[43] This latter invention was demonstrated by a Sieur de Lamberville, probably an Englishman, who later repeated the demonstration before Louis XIII.[44] Although regular sessions devoted entirely to inventions stopped by the beginning of 1634, the assembly continued to consider them occasionally. During the summer of 1634, the commissioners examined 44 different inventions, devices, and schemes: the list indicates the range of the assembly's interests.[45] In 1640 Renaudot received permission to erect a chemical laboratory at his Bureau, and this would be used for demonstrations during the weekly conferences.

Francis Bacon was widely read in Paris, and Renaudot and his colleagues took Bacon's attitudes toward the responsibility of science very seriously.[46] Even though they were as intrigued by card tricks and perpetual motion machines as by practical

[41] *Gazette*, 5 January 1634.
[42] Peiresc to Pierre Dupuy, 6 February 1634; Mersenne, *Correspondance*, IV, 31.
[43] 12 September, 3, 10 October 1633; 24 April 1634.
[44] *Gazette*, 6 May 1634.
[45] This list is reproduced in the Appendix.
[46] H-J. Martin's research has indicated the popularity of Bacon's writings in Parisian libraries of the 1630's. *Livre, pouvoirs, et société à Paris au XVIIe siècle* (Geneva: 1969), p. 509.

74

inventions, throughout the published records of the academy runs the assumption that science and technology could be used for social amelioration. Indeed, the government exploited Renaudot's academy as a sort of research laboratory and brain-trust. Not only did the government examine Lamberville's charcoal schemes and Morin's navigational methods, but like-wise petitioned Renaudot's confederates for ideas on economic reform.[47] Bacon might have objected to the rhetoric, but he would have appreciated this part of Renaudot's activities.

The most popular realm of science treated in the weekly sessions was that of medicine and its allied fields. Part of this interest may be attributed to Renaudot: he was a physician, the conferences were held under his auspices and, as time went on, the Bureau increasingly took on the characteristics of a medical faculty.[48] Nor can one deny the abundance of maladies, the chronic morbidity of the entire population during this period.[49] But the interest is broader than that.

Medicine remained loyal to its ancient past much longer than did its sister sciences. Long after astronomers had ac-cepted the Keplerian cosmology and physicists the Newtonian system, physicians were still using much of the vocabulary, manner, and methods of Hippocrates and Galen. Modern medicine cannot date its birth before the new empiricism of the end of the eighteenth century, and the resulting changes in methods of diagnosis and description.[50] Medicine remained an unspecialized, unwieldy hybrid, neither science nor art, but a combination of the two. " 'Medicine' in one word perfectly says 'Encyclopedia' because it so well contains all the other sciences and arts in it, that whosoever would dare to separate one from another would completely destroy the composition, in that respect resembling the statues of the great sculptor Phydias (of

[47] See p. 89.   [48] See p. 175.
[49] Mandrou, *Introduction à la France moderne*, p. 46.
[50] M. Foucault, *Naissance de la clinique* (Paris: 1963), p. viii.

75

whom Antiquity has reserved the memory until the present), which were so cleverly constructed that a single collapsing stone meant the indubitable ruin of the entire statue."[51] Medical lore was the most unaffected by change of all during Renaudot's lifetime. Men who knew the classics "knew" medicine. It maintained its theoretical simplicity longer than its allied disciplines and consequently was understood by a wider range of the public than other, increasingly specialized sciences.[52]

Because medical theory changed less radically than other fields, this did not mean that medicine was therefore less fascinating to the layman. Just the reverse is true. It was the science most directly related to his daily life, be he peasant, bourgeois, or nobleman.[53] Diet, the weather, the changing of the seasons, bodily effects of witchcraft, the use of cosmetics—all were as legitimately medical as the problems of disease, treatment, physiology, and prescription. A grasp of the humoural theory did not give the layman professional competence—after all, it took four years of study to get a medical license at the University of Paris—but it did permit him to

[51] D. de Planis Campy, *Bouquet composé de plus belles fleurs chymiques* (Paris: 1629), p. 3.

[52] See pp. 170ff. The history of medicine has continued to suffer from this identity problem. Historians of science often avoid medicine, either discussing it separately or relegating it to the less glamorous realm of agriculture, technology, metallurgy, etc. This tradition is still so strong that René Taton felt compelled to apologize in the Preface of volume II of *Histoire générale des sciences*: "l'Inclusion de l'histoire de la médecine dans notre programme ne constitue pas une exception à cette règle car, si par son objet, la médecine est une technique de l'amélioration humaine, son developpement est lie trop intimement à celui de la biologie pour qu'il soit possible de l'en dissocier." (Paris: 1958), II, vii.

[53] A major content of the popular press of the seventeenth and eighteenth centuries continued to be medical handbooks, diet guides, etc., intended for the literate, but uneducated rural classes. See R. Mandrou, *De la culture populaire aux XVIIᵉ et XVIIIᵉ siècles: la Bibliothèque bleue de Troyes* (Paris: Stock, 1964).

hold opinions about the most efficacious way to bleed a patient, the proper mixture of such and such a remedy, what weather was the best for melancholics, etc. Everyone was medically aware, potentially an expert on medical theory and practice. Those who marvel at Shakespeare's and Molière's mastery of medical lore are missing the point. It suggests less an extraordinary medical sophistication on their part than it does the high level of medical understanding of their audiences.[54]

"Medicine is useful not only to the body but also to the soul, from which it may contemplate nature, the mental faculties, and [human] actions;"[55] in a word, all things of interest to man were ultimately of a medical import. The humanistic philosophy of the sixteenth century saw man as the measure of all things, the microcosm of the forces, powers, and mysteries of the universe. Push these humanistic attitudes one step further, and they become medical attitudes.

Since the medical vocabulary was common currency, medical metaphor described phenomena of society and philosophy which had nothing to do with physical medicine. Society was an organism, with a prince at its head, a nobility at its heart, the judiciary as eyes, ears, and tongue, the peasantry at its feet; nonbelievers were "cancers on the body politic" who were to be cut out and destroyed for the general well being of society; exile "was like a beneficial purging which cures the Kingdom of the evils which menace it," etc.[56] The popularity of these shopworn metaphors into the seventeenth century indicates that social and political theory was still basically of an organic nature. Medical theory, unchanged in principle in the seven-

[54] The large number of popular medical handbooks likewise helped spread the vocabulary of medicine to the nonprofessional audience. See R. Mandrou, *Culture populaire* and B. Quemada, *Introduction à l'étude du vocabulaire médical 1600-1710* (Besançon: 1955), p. 34.

[55] Conference, 24 November 1636.

[56] Richelieu speaking of Marie de Medici and the Duc d'Orleans leaving France after the Day of Dupes. Quoted by Hanotaux, III, 345.

teenth century from that of the twelfth, could be used by Richelieu to describe social and political phenomena with the same effectiveness as it was used by John of Salisbury in the *Policraticus*.[57] Political metaphors had changed little, medicine had changed little during this period.

Medical discussion, therefore, was by no means a monopoly of the medical profession. It was the diversion and the responsibility of all men to be interested in medical problems. Without minimizing Renaudot's influence as a physician in the choice of medical topics at the conferences, the popularity of these subjects well reflects one of the age's major fixations.

Medical and medically related discussions provided the greatest variety of subjects treated at the Bureau d'Adresse. There were those that concerned specific maladies and diseases ("Leprosy," "Gout," "Sea-sickness," "Smallpox," "Scurvy").[58] Added to these were such topics as "Dreams," "Sexual frenzy," "Epilepsy," "Drunkenness," "Sterility," "Ecstasy," "If the touch of a seventh son can cure warts, and why."[59] All of these problems were medical at core, but took the discussions far afield. The whole range of dietary subjects was at base medical: "Which is better, meat or fish"; "Is dinner better than supper"; "If it is true that eating hare will help one acquire beauty, and why"; "If it is unhealthy to sleep after dining"; "If wine aids or hinders digestion, and why."[60] Weather and climate were

---

[57] Examples are numerous. The following Mazarinades suggest the popularity of medical analogy: *Le médecin politique, ou consultation pour la maladie de l'État* (Paris: 1649); *Deuxiesme visite du médecin politique* (Paris: 1649); *Consultation et ordonnance des médecins de l'État pour la purgation de la France malade, par le Sieur de-Teil* (Paris: 1649); *l'Antidote pour guerir la France* (S.l.: 1649).

[58] 30 April 1635; 18 February 1636; 1 December 1636; 26 January 1637; 27 January 1642.

[59] 9 January 1634; 14 May 1635; 12 June 1635; 19 February 1635; 22 June 1638; 23 April 1640; 21 April 1642.

[60] 6 March 1634; 9 March 1637; 28 April 1642; 16 July 1640; 1 December 1637.

directly related to personal health: "What is the most bearable, heat or cold"; "What is more healthy, damp or dry weather"; "What is more healthy, the summer or winter"; "What climate is most conducive to a long life."[61]

Discussion of physiology reflected Renaissance humanistic attitudes toward medicine: "What is the most noble part of our body"; "Are persons with large heads more intelligent"; "If physical beauty is indicative of spiritual goodness and beauty."[62] Such qualitative standards as nobility and beauty are anathema to twentieth century medical science, but to Renaudot and his post-Renaissance, post-Paracelsian contemporaries, the body could be described in extranaturalistic terms because it was more than a simple amalgam of physical matter. It was the seat of the soul, the microcosm of the greater world, the reflection of religious grace or moral perfection.

Some 101 discussions were held directly on medical topics, in addition to 19 on zoology and biology, 35 on physics, 5 on diet. These conferences were taking place in the same building, at the same time, as were Renaudot's public medical consultations and his chemical experiments.[63] No wonder Renaudot's enemies feared that he was creating a rival medical school at his Bureau d'Adresse, in direct confrontation with the University of Paris.

If the sheer number of discussions did not terrify the medical establishment, their content did. There were the old but still controversial questions, such as "Bloodletting," "Antidotes," "Bezoard," and "Purgation."[64] Others were more contemporary, more embarrassing: "If there are remedies specific to each malady"; "If it is useful to use chemical remedies"; "The principles of chemistry"; "If maladies are cured by similars or

---

[61] 3 December 1635; 10 December 1635; 6 May 1641; 17 November 1636.

[62] 23 January 1640; 27 May 1641.   [63] See pp. 170ff.

[64] 10 March 1636; 28 April 1636; 6 August 1640; 24 February 1642.

opposites"; "If more benefit than not has come from the division of Medicine into the three parts of Physicians, Surgeons, and Apothecaries."[65] While faculty members might have discussed these things privately, Renaudot was making them public issues by exposing them in the Bureau d'Adresse.

Only three conferences dealt directly with monsters or curiosities of nature, and all three were prompted by specific local interest: "The two monstrous brothers"; "The hairy young girl seen in this city"; "The water-drinker of the St. Germain market" (famous for drinking extraordinary quantities of water, talking with his mouth full—in Italian—for 15 minutes, and then spitting out "a red liquid which seemed like wine but which only had its color").[66] These topics were a mainstay of the popular press before and after the 1631 appearance of the *Gazette*, but within Renaudot's circle they were losing much of their fascination as topics of serious discussion.[67] *Jeux de nature* would continue to appear in seventeenth and eighteenth century *cabinets des curiosités*, but the society from which Renaudot drew his academy seemed to view them more skeptically than the so-called cultivated classes in general.

A number of topics concerned occultism, sorcery, and astrology. These topics were the most hybrid of all. The discussion of "Incubi and succubi, and if demons can reproduce" and "The appearance of spirits or phantasms," for example, combined the medical and judicial with the legendary.[68] It is possible that the sensational trial and execution of Urbain Grandier on 18 August 1634 prompted the 14 May 1635 discussion on "Witches." There was no mention of the specific

[65] 24 July 1634; 1 April 1636; 3 September 1640; 17 September 1640; 22 November 1638.

[66] 24, 31 October 1633; 5 March 1640.

[67] The academy also discussed "Eunuchs," "Hermaphrodites," and "Satyrs," but these were more in the realm of classical topics than of naturalistic topics.

[68] 9 February 1637; 4 June 1635. See R. Mandrou's discussion in *Magistrats et sorciers en France au XVIIᵉ siècle* (Paris: 1968), pp. 301-303; see also p. 190.

trial, however. The participants here, as elsewhere, maintained the general nature of the academy's discussions.

All of the conferences, but especially these on demonology, astrology, and the occult, indicate a general and persistent skepticism. The weekly sessions did not aim at a conclusion, permitting as a result an extravagant free-for-all of opinions, from the slavishly orthodox to the most rational, secular, or radical. Throughout there remained an invigorating flavor of skeptical questioning of these subjects. Much has been made of the pre-Cartesian skepticism of Louis XIII's reign, particularly in groups such as the Tétrade and the Cabinet, but a perusal of the conference indicates that it was not a monopoly of these groups alone.[69] In its discussion of witchcraft and related problems (problems as contemporary and significant as any discussed at the bureau) one is struck by the diversity of opinions, by the absence of blind, uncritical belief in any single explanation. Partially it reflected the general method used throughout the meetings, but likewise it reflected the attitudes of the participants themselves. Modern scientists may reject most of their conclusions and observations, but can at the same time admire the skepticism which permeated their thought.

Many topics concerned Cardan, Postel, Paracelsus, Lull, Campanella, and their interest in numerology and the occult. These include "The Cabala," "Artificial memory," "The philosopher's stone," "The virtue of numbers," "Hieroglyphs," "Ways to write occultly," "Talismans," "The Brothers of the Rosicrucian Order," "What did Paracelsus mean by the Book

[69] "Cartesian philosophical ideas are not merely discussed in the salons of the *précieux* and the *bas-bleu*; its principles are here brought before a bourgeoisie interested in culture, and the Cartesian methods of reasoning and criticism are here used by the speakers." L. M. Richardson, "The Conferences of Théophraste Renaudot," *Modern Language Notes* (May 1933), 316. The classic study of the *Tétrade* and the *Cabinet* is R. Pintard's *Libertinage érudit*. And as R. Mandrou has indicated, these attitudes likewise remained strong in the more popular *Bibliothèque bleue*.

'M'," and "The art of Raymond Lull."[70] Discussion of these dangerous and controversial authorities is striking, and suggests that the entire academy itself may have attempted to serve Campanellian and Postellian ends.[71]

When participants discussed morality and daily conduct, they continued the Renaissance academic tradition of "problem" topics: "If it is easier to resist voluptuousness than pain"; "Why men are more inclined to vice than to virtue"; "If pardon is worth more than vengeance"; "Which is better, the active or contemplative life"; "Which is better, company or solitude"; "If one must do well to everyone"; "Who loves his children more, the father or mother."[72] Obviously these questions were unsolvable, but in terms of the academy's purposes, this was their greatest virtue. These questions served to display the rhetorical arts at their grandest. They were generally discussed through the use of "common places." The speaker attacked the subject from all sides and with all of his rhetorical skills—simile, metaphor, quotations, amplification—the variety of his attack was as important as its content.[73] As rhetoricians, the *conférenciers* sought to persuade, rather than convince, their listeners. If most obvious in the treatment of morality and daily conduct, such ends were also obvious elsewhere, including medicine, science, and literature. If a subject appears silly to us, "Which came first, the chicken or the egg," for example,[74] it is because we do not appreciate the rhetorical ends the academy sought to achieve.

Such rhetorical ends were in fact the major ends of Renau-

[70] 2 May 1634; 23 January 1634; 10 July 1634; 7 January 1636; 21 January 1636; 7 April 1636; 16 May 1639; 20 June 1639; 27 June 1639.

[71] See pp. 91ff.

[72] 31 October 1633; 9 January 1634; 29 May 1634; 10 December 1635; 22 March 1638; 29 October 1640; 15 May 1642.

[73] An excellent discussion of the aims and methods of Renaissance rhetoric, which remained unchanged in principle in Renaudot's era, is Hannah H. Gray's "Renaissance Humanism: the Pursuit of Eloquence," *Renaissance Essays* (New York: 1968), pp. 199-217.

[74] 3 February 1642.

dot's academy. While governmental and social business was increasingly being written down, it is highly dangerous to exaggerate the impact of the so-called "paper revolution." Men thought less in written than in oral terms, and "the great purveyor of their imaginations was the sense of hearing."[75] Life was oriented to the sermons, the court pleas, the verbal exegeses on medical problems. It was still possible for Richelieu to speak for an hour and have the entire audience follow and remember his oration.[76] The government adviser was defined, quite literally, as he who had access to the royal ear.[77] Well-cultivated Frenchmen were expected *sur le champ* to be able to cast an epigram in polished verse, or to recite such and such an author.[78]

[75] Mandrou, *Introduction à la France moderne*, p. 69. The classic treatment of this fascinating problem is L. Febvre, *Le problème de l'incroyance au XVIe siècle* (Paris: 1942), esp. pp. 464ff.

[76] *Gazette*, 21 January 1634.

[77] Richelieu's *Testament politique* provides a striking example of this taken-for-granted definition: "Ce n'est pas assez aux grands Princes de n'ouvrir jamais la bouche pour mal parler de qui que ce puisse être: mais la raison requiert qu'ils ferment les oreilles aux médisances et faux rapports: qu'ils chassent et banissent ceux qui en sont auteurs comme pestes très dangereuses, qui empoisonnent souvent le coeur des Princes et l'esprit de tous ceux qui les approchent. Si ceux qui ont libre accès aux oreilles des Rois, san le mèriter, sont dangereux, ceux qui en possedent le coeur par pure faveur le sont bien davantage, pour conserver un tel trésor, il faut, par necessité, que l'art et la malice suppleent au défaut de la vertu, qui ne se trouve pas en eux." (Paris: 1947), p. 274. He attributed his own control of power to his "ouie monstreuse." M. Deloche, *Autour de la plume de Richelieu* (Paris: 1920), p. 72.

[78] Renaudot himself gave an example. In the midst of the Fronde, the young Louis XIV paid a surprise visit to Renaudot's printshop at S. Germain en Laye. "Selon l'inclination qu'il a à toutes les belles inventions, ayant voulu faire imprimer quelque chose, ne se trouvant rien lors qui eust un sens complet pour luy donner ce divertissement, sans l'ennuyer par trop de longeur," Renaudot quickly recited a verse "sur le sujet de cette heureuse et inopinée venue," which the king quickly had printed. The verse: "J'accepte cet augure en faveur de l'Histoire/ Qu'à l'instant que Paris se met à la raison,/Mon Prince visitant sa Royale maison,/Va fournir de sujet aux outils de sa gloire./ Embrassez-vous François: Espagnols à genoux/Pour recevoir la loy: car la Paix est

Renaudot believed that participation in the conferences could help develop this aspect of man's social equipment. There was no better apprenticeship for the student entering the world of affairs and unable to receive this training at the schools and colleges. There, unfortunately, the teacher's opinions were presented ex cathedra. "One of the greatest defaults of teachers, which we increasingly abhor as we advance in age, is pedantry, too often accompanied by indomitable obstinacy; instead of persuading us, this entirely alienates our sympathies."[79] Seventeenth century education, both in theory and practice, strove to maintain a sharp distinction between the life within the college and the everyday world outside.[80] Renaudot called for a greater correspondence between the two, an education that would prepare youth for society. The popularity of the weekly conferences suggests that many others were equally disillusioned and dissatisfied.[81]

---

chez nous." *Le Siege mis devant le Ponteau de Mer* (S. Germain: 10 March 1649), pp. 4-5.

[79] Conference, 4 April 1641.

[80] See G. Snyders, *Pedagogie en France aux XVIIe et XVIIIe siècles* (Paris: 1965), Book I, "Éducation traditionelle." The development of the postscholastic academy, "semi-scholastic and semi-military in character," was an attempt to modify these distinctions. P. Ariès, *Centuries of Childhood* (New York: 1965), pp. 203-08.

[81] This rhetorical-educational function was evident when Jean de Soudier de Richesource established his *Conferences de l'Académie des Orateurs* in 1653. Richesource, a Loudun-born teacher of rhetoric, had been an habitué of the weekly sessions at the Bureau d'Adresse: "Après tout, amy Lecteur, je vous diray que pour me delivrer utilement, de la louable persecution de plusieurs personnes de mérite et d'érudition, qui me demandent les recueils et les résolutions des belles choses qui se debitent dans nos Conferences académiques et oratoires, sur toutes sortes de sujets libres et honnestes, que nous continuons depuis sept années, et que quelques-uns appellent la suite de celles qui se tenoient au Bureau d'Adresse, nous avons commencé par l'impression de ce première Volume." (*le Première Partie des Conferences* [Paris: 1661]).

The topics were similar to those discussed at the Bureau d'Adresse, except that scientific and medical topics were quite rare. The development of an effective orator was more important than the diffusion of

The participants at the conferences never denigrated the study of Latin; they were too much men of the seventeenth century to do that. But they vociferously attacked the exclusive use of Latin in the schools. Everyone affected Latin, and even "the majority of beggars ask for alms in Latin."[82] Latin was associated with scholastic obscurantism, with syllogistic argumentation. As Renaudot said: "those [who have] recently left the schools find themselves incapable of attending the Court and the other places which they should frequent. This incapacity comes from the coarseness of sessions at school and from the humour which schoolboys usually learn from debate, where they learn never to yield: one of the most uncivil qualities and one of the most inept that a young man can have in society."[83] Social grace, on the other hand, was synonymous with effective use of French, and Renaudot's academy was one of the few places in Paris which treated the use of French seriously. Many of the general problems of education (as opposed to the problems of *enseignement*) had been batted about for centuries, but they had new relevance in the first half of the seventeenth century. Sessions ranged from "Must one join arts to letters," "How to acquire nobility," and "Is travel necessary to a cultivated man," to "Jokes, and if they are permitted to a cultivated man" and "Can man have too much knowl-

---

information or opinion. In order to prepare his remarks, each speaker received the subject six weeks in advance (at Renaudot's academy, the subjects were chosen a week in advance). The sessions were tightly organized, with the chairman (Richesource) opening the session with a general statement. After all had spoken, he would then "decide la Question et donne le Resolution de toutes les difficultez; ou, enfin, il prend le party de celui dont l'opinion a esté suivie d'un plus grand nombre de partisans." ("Advis de l'Académie au Lecteur," *Première Partie des Conferences*). Richesource interrupted and criticized his young speakers; clearly this was more of a formal school than was Renaudot's academy. See M. Revillout, *Un maître des conferences au milieu du XVIIᵉ siècle: Jean de Soudier de Richesource* (Montpellier: 1881).

[82] 19 September 1633.   [83] 4 March 1641.

edge?"[84] Even though the topics often appear to be hackneyed and warmed-over, they were nonetheless being discussed out of school and in French. In this regard, Renaudot's conferences served as a way-station between the cloistered academy and the world of affairs, between the Latin school and the French-speaking salon.

There were discussions of general principles of teaching and learning: "If reading books is a better way of learning than by word of mouth"; "If one profits more from rules than example"; "Which is the more conducive to study, the evening or morning"; "The Conference, and if it is the most instructive way to teach."[85]

In addition to these topics treated during regular sessions, the assembly considered a series of inventions of specific methods of applied education, including "How to teach a root language [*une langue matrice*] of which all the other languages are dialects and which can be learned from it: the projector will demonstrate all of the grammar in only six hours, it being so simple, but six months is necessary to learn the meaning of the vocabulary"; and "How to debate successfully in all sorts of methods and styles with all kinds of persons, to be learned in only a quarter of an hour."[86] In the first conference of which there is a transcript, commissioners were appointed to investigate the theories of a man who claimed to be able to teach "a perfect logic" in only eight hours, and of another who offered a method of learning through play everything from the ABC's to the most advanced study.[87] Perhaps some of these inventions were no more than get-rich-

[84] 19 September 1633; 10 April 1634; 6 August 1635; 4 February 1641; 16 September 1641.

[85] 19 May 1636; 3 February 1637; 14 March 1639; 4 March 1641.

[86] "l'Ouverture des Conferences de Bureau d'Adresse. Pour le premier Lundi du present mois de Novembre 1634," *Seconde Centurie*, pp. 1-8.

[87] 22 August 1633. Unfortunately Renaudot did not publish the commissioner's report.

quick schemes. But it is more likely that they instead represent the academy at its most purposeful. Throughout his career Renaudot had great respect for the problems of education. He is in the same tradition as Ramus and Bacon. In his career, as in theirs, the interests of scientific method and pedagogical reform intersect.

In 1543, when he made his famous frontal attack upon Aristotelianism, Pierre Ramus was less concerned with Aristotle as a scientist than with his stranglehold upon the study of rhetoric and logic. Ramus felt that medieval writers had too long embellished and enshrined Aristotelian precepts instead of reforming them. Since rhetoric was the basis of university education, to reform one was to reform both. Ramus believed that Aristotelian rhetorical and logical traditions taught schoolboys to argue about arguments instead of arguing about things.[88] Students should instead seek the clearest, most useful arguments, rather than the most complex. Clarity of arrangement was synonymous with the clarity of the idea, and "to command the true laws of logic, it is not enough to know how to babble the rules of school, but instead one must exercise and practice them as poets, orators, philosophers; that is, in all kinds of activities."[89] Ramus was not a particularly original thinker, but without his call for rhetorical clarity, subsequent developments of scientific method would have been impossible.[90]

Ramus would have felt at home at Renaudot's weekly academy. In form, participants used Ramist commonplaces to impress their ideas upon the audience; rhetoric was used to persuade the assembly; there was no formal conclusion, leaving

[88] W. J. Ong, *Ramus, Method and the Decay of Dialogue* (Cambridge, Mass.: 1958), pp. 140ff. In addition to Ong's excellent study, also see N. W. Gilbert, *Renaissance Concepts of Method* (New York: 1960), esp. Chapter V, "The Single Method of Pierre Ramus."

[89] Ramus, *Dialectique . . .* (Paris: 1555), p. 137.

[90] For Ramus' influence upon Bacon, see P. Rossi, *Francis Bacon* (Chicago: 1968), esp. pp. 152ff.

that to the auditor. In content, child education and pedagogical method were treated with the same seriousness as were topics of science and morality. All of these were legitimate intellectual concerns. Renaudot had developed "a method for the instruction of children even briefer than current methods." While still at Loudun, "I gave the rules to one of my brothers, who in company with some others so effectively applied them that they quickly received results surpassing all belief: there still is proof of this, which I can demonstrate to the curious. As a result, some of my friends begged that their children, when they became old enough to learn, might study under the same precepts as my own children, and would do so under the best masters that I could choose for them."[91] Renaudot did not explain this "even briefer" method, but it may have figured among the *inventions* presented to the assembly, thus giving rise to allegations that Renaudot was no more than a provincial schoolmaster.[92]

Political discussion was taboo, politics "partaking of the nature of divine things."[93] But general discussions of social conduct, even when of a traditional rhetorical nature, impinged on politics: "If it is better for a state to have slaves"; "Commonwealths"; "If it is better to guard one's frontier than to carry the war to the enemy," etc.[94]

[91] *Response au Libelles* (Paris: 1641), p. 42.

[92] In 1641, the Faculté de Médecine charged that "depuis trente-six ans qu'il dit estre Docteur, il a fait tout autre estude que celle de la Medecine. A Loudun d'ou ce Demon es venu nous obseder, son employ estoit d'enseigner des enfans qu'il tenoit en pension, & qu'il promettoit de rendre scavans dans deux ou trois mois." *La Defense de la Faculté de Médecine de Paris contre son Calumniateur* (Paris: 1641), p. 21. It was likely that Renaudot had medical students (the title of his *Oraison funebre pour Monsieur de Sainte-Marthe* [Samur: 1623] indicated that the eulogy was pronounced "Par Jean Cesuet estudiant chez Théophraste Renaudot"), as did many physicians, particularly in the smaller towns, but not necessarily *pensionnaires* as the faculty charged.

[93] "Preface," *Première Centurie*, p. 1.

[94] 3 October 1633; 7 May 1635; 11 January 1638.

The small percentage of economic and social discussions probably reflected as much a naive and underdeveloped appreciation of these problems as a desire to avoid controversy. But several of these topics were specific and topical, reflecting Renaudot's direct influence; these included "The regulation of the poor," and "Monts-de-piété."[95] The conference likewise considered very significant problems of economy and trade. They include "Is barter better than buying and selling" and "Does commerce derogate nobility."[96] More remarkable, the entire summer of 1638 was devoted to a discussion of the French economy. The pressures of a war economy were overwhelming for the monarchy, and Richelieu seemed eager to act decisively and broadly at this time; his *Règlement des Finances*, for example, was promulgated in July 1638. Renaudot's academy met informally throughout the summer of 1638, and prepared a report for the crown on ways of reestablishing commerce in France. The summarized recommendations ran the gamut of mercantilist ideas: currency stabilization, encouraging nobles to enter commerce, supporting retail as well as wholesale trade, regulating prices, improving canals and roads.[97] It was likely that the conferences discussed problems referred to it during other summers, not published in the collected *Centuries*.[98]

No sessions were devoted exclusively to history or geography.[99] It was for the *Gazette*, and not the conferences, that

[95] 19 April 1634; 12 June 1634.

[96] 15 May 1634; 1 February 1638.

[97] "Resultat des Assemblées tenues dans le Bureau d'Adresse durant les vacations de la present année 1638: touchant les moyens de restablir le Commerce," 15 November 1638.

[98] H. Hauser, *La pensée et l'action économiques du Cardinal de Richelieu* (Paris: 1944), sees Richelieu's patronage of the Bureau d'Adresse as a very conscious attempt to implement ideas for the revitalization of the French economy. They definitely accepted questions for discussion in the summer of 1634, 1635 and 1638: why not some, if not all, of the other summer periods?

[99] R. Mandrou recognized the academy's interest in geography, if

Renaudot saved his descriptions of foreign lands. But interest in exotica, be it medical, zoological, or meteorological, provided conference participants ample opportunity to engage in the imaginary voyages so important to the psychological expansion of the age.

Only once was a specific work of *belles-lettres* discussed directly, and then not in a regular session, but as an *invention.* A Latin epic entitled "Fulmen in Aquilam," concerning the life and death of the king of Sweden, was presented to the company, the poet "believing that he could have no better way to write long-lasting things than to have many persons pass judgment."[100] Commissioners were appointed and, the following week, gave an hour-long report to the company. The *Centuries* tell us nothing of their evaluation, other than congratulating the author for writing such a long work (twelve books, of 1,000 verses each)![101] This was the only mention of a specific literary work treated as such, and here it was part of the section on *inventions* rather than a regular discussion topic. It is likely that the conference did evaluate other works, on a regular basis, during its first years.[102]

Topics related to literature were discussed fairly regularly, including sessions on "If one must write as one pronounces, or follow the traditional and accepted orthography"; "Is it better to speak well than to write well"; and "Is poetry useful."[103] These topics, however, were primarily vehicles with which to display one's rhetorical skills.

Topics on the occult parallel another large group of topics, those dealing, *grosso modo,* with the unity of knowledge and

---

somewhat overstating the evidence: "une fois par semaine, une séance est consacrée à l'histoire et à la géographie, et attire forces beaux esprits" (*Introduction à la France moderne,* p. 317). Also see F. de Dainville, *La géographie des humanistes* (Paris: 1940), p. 365.

[100] 29 August 1633.   [101] 5 September 1633.

[102] See pp. 95ff.

[103] 24 January 1639; 31 July 1634; 4 December 1634.

the possible reduction of all science to a central, single source. Such topics by themselves may just appear to be more seventeenth century curiosities. In fact, however, these subjects reflect the extraordinary role Renaudot's conferences played in the history of French academism.

From Henry III's academy until the establishment of the Académie Française, there was no royally supported academy in France. During this interim, well-positioned persons promoted the reestablishment of academies after the sixteenth century model. In the dedication of his *Quaestiones in Genesim* (1623), Marin Mersenne asserted that unifying all knowledge through the formation of Europeanwide academies in the Renaissance encyclopedic mode could lead to the political and social unity of the world itself.[104] In 1635 Tommaso Campanella established himself, under the protection of the court, at Paris. More than any other man of his half-century, Campanella devoted himself to promoting world unity through the unity of knowledge. His astrological-political-religious ideas and political activism earned him a prison cell for 27 of his 71 years. Campanella enthusiastically promoted the ideas Mersenne, and, before him, Guillaume Postel, had articulated: "Prior to its material creation, Postel maintained, the universe was a structure of ideas. The Fall, however, shattered the divine system of correspondences and symbols, scattering them to all parts of the earth. The task of the humanist movement, he felt, was to gather together and restore the original body of learning in preparation for a Golden Age, when the union of peoples would become part of a culminating concord of all Creation under God's law, made manifest by the reestablished harmony of natural and revealed knowledge. This great enterprise was to be made possible by philology on one hand and world empire under French leadership on the

---

[104] Yates, *French Academies*, pp. 285-88, see also the unpublished M.A. thesis of Richard Merbaum, "The Role and Goal of Science in the Life and Works of Marin Mersenne," New York University, 1968.

other. . . . Postel merely associated reason with political authority; Campanella fused the two and developed a theory of a perfect society conforming in every respect to the laws of nature."[105] In a dedication to a 1637 edition of his *De Sensu Rerum*, Campanella called on Richelieu to establish the society "which I have delineated" in the *Civitas Solis* "and which you must erect."[106] Richelieu himself was well acquainted with the Renaissance tradition of academism.[107]

These clues suggest that Renaudot's encyclopedic academy, protected by Richelieu, was dedicated to Campanella's mission of uniting the world through academic means. Campanella was one of a handful of contemporaries mentioned in the published records of the conferences. He could never pass up a public platform, and enthusiastically used Renaudot's conferences and even the pages of the *Gazette* to express his ideas. An *Extraordinaire* of the weekly *Gazette*, for example, recounted Campanella's observations on the birth of the future Louis XIV, the Sun King.[108] He was one of a handful of contemporaries specifically mentioned in the 9 years of the conference, and Renaudot hailed the "great reputation of his learning" in his obituary in the 28 May 1639 *Gazette*. The conference had a long interest in topics directly or indirectly related to hermeticism and magic—memory systems, the philosopher's stone, egyptology, cabala, hieroglyphs—but in the weeks immediately preceding and following Campanella's death the assembly paid special attention to these topics. It was as if the ailing Campanella, spurred on by the long-awaited birth of the Sun King, was working at a feverish pace to convince the world of his hermetic prophesies. The con-

[105] L. Rothkrug, *Opposition to Louis XIV: The Political and Social Origins of the French Enlightenment* (Princeton: 1965), pp. 75-76.

[106] Quoted by P. Treves, "The Title of Campanella's 'City of the Sun,'" *Journal of the Warbourg and Courtauld Institutes* (1939-1940), III, 250.

[107] Yates, *French Academies*, p. 279.

[108] 31 March 1639.

ference discussed "The Method of Raymond Lull," "What did Paracelsus mean by the Book 'M'," and most striking, "The Brothers of the Rosicrucian Order."[109] The last topic was certainly unique; of the 460 topics discussed at the Bureau d'Adresse, it is only one of 3 summarized in 8 pages instead of the normal 4.

Rosicrucianism is one of the greatest enigmas of European intellectual history. Except for scattered traces very little is known of its history in the first half of the seventeenth century: Christian Rosenkreutz, a German influenced by Giordano Bruno and Campanella, supposedly founded a secret sect dedicated to their hermetic ideas; the mysterious appearance in 1614 of *Fama Fraternitatis Roseae Crucis*, the handbook of the order; reports in 1623-1625 of the brotherhood's existence in Paris.[110] As the 16 May 1639 discussion at the Bureau d'Adresse indicated, interest in the organization and its ideas never failed. Indeed, much of the popularity of Renaudot's academy derived from discussions on hermetic subjects.

Until his association with Campanella, Renaudot's conferences were not particularly controversial. But the renewed attention to hermeticism and occultism in 1638-1639, precisely when Renaudot's privileges and power were on the ascendant, could only frighten the Parisian intellectual and religious establishment. The faculty's attack upon Renaudot reeked of fear and suspicion, and they made much of his association with paracelsianism, protestantism, witchcraft, and the occult. Among Renaudot's circle of "libertine physicians, vagabonds, heretics and Huguenots" there must have been many who were as strongly attracted to Rosicrucianism as Campanella himself had been. The faculty had good reason to fear that

[109] 27 June, 20 June, 16 May 1639.
[110] On this fascinating subject, the research of Frances Yates is essential: *Giordano Bruno and the Hermetic Tradition* (Chicago: 1964), esp. pp. 190ff, 400ff; *The Art of Memory* (Chicago: 1966), pp. 304, 368-73. On the background to the 1623-1625 rumors, see Lenoble, *Mersenne*, pp. 27-31.

Renaudot was knowingly protecting them and that, perhaps, the entire conference was a Rosicrucian front.

Renaudot's encyclopedic hopes may have influenced Comenius' English friend, Samuel Hartlib. Corresponding with continental religious and scientific figures, Hartlib was familiar with Renaudot's academy.[111] In 1647 he asked for Parliamentary support to establish an Office of Address. This would consist of two parts, an Office for Communication and an Office of Accommodations. "The Office of Addresse for Communications is as far beyond that of Accommodations in Usefulnesse, as the Matters of the Mind are above those of the Body. It is then to be erected for Addresses and Informations in Matters of Religion, of Learning, and of all Ingenuities, which are Objects of Contemplation and delight unto the Mind, for their strangenesse and usefulnesse unto the life of Man." This Office of Communication would be a clearing-house "of Advices, of Proposalls, of Treatises and of all Manner of Intellectual Rareties freely to be given and received, to and from, by and for give notice of the best Helpes and Overtures, and of the most Profitable Undertakings, Discoveries, and Occurences; whereby Godlinesse, Truth, and Peace, and all the Ways and Means tending to the harmlesse Advancement of Divine and Humane Wisdome and Perfections may be set forward in Church and Common-wealth."[112] Hartlib asked Parliament to appoint him "Superintendant Generall of all Offices of Addresse instituted in the Kingdom of England and Dominions of Wales,"[113] a word-for-word equivalent of Renaudot's title. Hartlib never realized his projected Office of Address, although Henry Robinson would establish a similar institution briefly in 1650.[114] Both Robinson and Hart-

[111] G. H. Turnbull, *Hartlib, Dury, and Comenius* (London: 1947), pp. 80, 81-87.
[112] Quoted by M. Purver, *The Royal Society* (Cambridge, Mass.: 1967), pp. 203-05.
[113] *Ibid.*, p. 205.
[114] W. K. Jordan, *Men of Substance* (Chicago: 1942), pp. 250-53.

lib hoped to accomplish many of the social welfare ends which Renaudot's Bureau d'Adresse sought, but Hartlib was particularly attracted to Renaudot's academy as a model for furthering the unity of knowledge.

Given all of this, the limited and circumscribed activities of Richelieu's Académie Française disappointed those of the epoch nurtured on these older, idealized aims. Many contemporaries must have welcomed Renaudot's academy, even with its disregard for academic decorum, as a final attempt to revive the lofty dreams of Renaissance pansophism in France.[115]

The letters-patent for the Académie Française were granted on 10 February 1635, but were not registered in Parlement until 10 July 1637. The Bureau d'Adresse was solidly established by this time, and like the Académie Française was responsible to Richelieu for its existence. Many contemporaries saw an identity between the two groups. Some of the topics discussed at the bureau would form the basis of the Académie Française's program, such as the problems of grammar, criticism of specific literary works, the reform and direction of the French language. But this identity was more than simply the similarity of their topics. On one hand, both institutions were lumped together by those condemning Richelieu as patron of letters; on the other, the genuine interests of the two groups overlapped directly.

Mathieu de Morgues, at first in Richelieu's service and then, after the Day of Dupes, the most able of those pamphleteers opposing him, damned the servility of Richelieu's writers. "I have never seen a man more unfortunately eulogized than His Eminence, who has never been assessed by a single decent man or praised by a clever or intelligent writer. He has recognized his shortcoming and endeavoring to escape from it, has erected a school or, perhaps better, an aviary of Psaphon, the academy which meets at the home of the Gazeteer, the father of lies. A large number of poor zealots meet there, learning to

[115] Yates, *French Academies*, p. 297.

mix cosmetics to plaster over the ugly deeds and make un-
guents to dress the sores of the public and of the cardinal. He
promises some promotion and gives token assistance to his
canaille, who combat the truth for a crust of bread."[116] Elsewhere, he ridiculed Jean Sirmond, one of Richelieu's most
ardent pamphleteers: "Messire Jean Sirmond will take on the
titles of the Duke Sabin and of the Marquis de Cleonville: he
will wear a sword at his side, and will have in his train five
or six zealots of the *Académie Gazetique*, whose courage to
lie about everything they are told in the praise of Monseigneur
the Cardinal Duke we have restored; and to that end they
will learn all the Poems, Epigrams, Elegies, Acrostics, Ana-
grams, Sonnets and other compositions of Latin and French
poets to spread their pretty merchandise everywhere."[117] The
two groups were well separated in fact, if not in substance,
and Pelleson-Fontanier's classic treatment of *l'Histoire de
l'Académie Française* (1652) did not even mention the Renaudot circle.[118] Another contemporary distinguished the two
groups: "l'Abbé de Saint Germain [Mathieu de Morgues] de-
ceives himself in the gross libelles which he writes in Flanders,
when he mistakes their Academy [*Académie Française*] for
an assembly of a few poor pedants who meet at the home of
the Gazeteer."[119] Morgues had to fight Richelieu's propaganda
machine, the *Gazette*, and the pamphlets written by Sirmond,
Chatelet, and other polemicists. By focusing on Renaudot's
academy, he hoped to attack both at the same time. Separated
by distance and by hate from the French capital, Morgues had
understandably confused the two groups.

The activities of the two groups added to the confusion. In

---

[116] "Jugement sur la preface," in *Diverses pièces pour la defense de la
Royne Mere* (S.l.:1643), p. 4. Also quoted by L. Delavaud, *Quelques
collaborateurs de Richelieu* (Paris: 1915), pp. 35-36.

[117] *l'Ambassadeur chimerique* (S.l.:1643), p. 3.

[118] *l'Histoire de l'Académie Française, depuis son établissement
jusqu'à 1652* (Paris: 1729), pp. 5-14.

[119] Charles Sorel, *Discours sur l'Académie François*, pp. 15-16.

its early days, Renaudot's academy enjoyed a semi-official position as an arbiter of literary practice among foreign writers.[120] In the "Ouverture" of the 1634-1635 session, Renaudot appealed "to those who might earnestly set their hands to constructing this Republic of letters [*Republique lettrée*], founded to honor the French language and nation, to support our designs if they find them useful to the public just as the public, which cannot lie, approves of them by their attendance."[121] Renaudot at this time seemed to anticipate that Richelieu's projected Académie Française might take over his functions. Charles Sorel, who delighted in writing parodies of Renaudot's *Gazettes*, assumed the same. Sorel published an anonymous parody of the first meeting of the new Académie Française, dated 13 March 1634. It recounted a visit from Renaudot, "petitioning that he be compensated for the losses he has been forced to suffer since the establishment of the *Grand Jours de l'Éloquence*, evidence being that the Germans and other nations no longer refer to his Bureau for the addresses of masters of French language."[122] With one exception,[123] references to specific literary works did not appear in the published collections of Renaudot's conferences. The Académie Française seems to have assumed the role of arbiter of literary and grammatical practice from Renaudot's academy.

The topics treated at the Bureau d'Adresse became more and more ephemeral as the sessions wore on, and in several instances the same topic, or nearly the same topic, was repeated.[124] Perhaps the conference was simply running out of material. By the summer of 1642, moreover, Renaudot was

---

[120] 29 August 1633. See p. 90.   [121] 3 November 1634.

[122] *Role des presentations faicte au Grand Jour de l'éloquence François* (S.l.n.d.), p. 138.

[123] 29 August 1633, discussion of "Fulmen in Aquilam."

[124] "Du flux et reflux de la mer" (28 December 1633) and "Des divers mouvements de la mer et des fleuves" (6 July 1637); "Si les sciences sont utiles à un Estat" (28 January 1641) and "Quelle science est la plus necessaire à un Estat" (11 March 1641), for example.

embroiled in his lengthy and exhausting litigation with the medical faculty. The last published conference was dated 1 September 1642, and unlike those preceding, it did not list the titles of following sessions. There is no solid evidence that the conferences continued.[125]

When one considers the milieu in which Renaudot's academy existed—a Paris of renewed Catholic zeal, scientific orthodoxy, professional and faculty rivalry—it is remarkable that it survived for so long.[126] Renaudot's success reflected the protection a creature of Richelieu could enjoy. But there was more to it than that. Richelieu exploited Renaudot's academy just as he exploited Renaudot's *Gazette* and Bureau d'Adresse. The weekly conferences provided Richelieu with opinion, information, and technical expertise, all critical to an expanding government.

The crown had always received private *mémoires* and public petitions, but beyond the royal bureaucracy itself there was no existing institution to channel expertise and opinion to the court. The Estates General and Assemblies of Notables had fulfilled some of these functions, but these institutions were not convened beyond 1614 and 1626, respectively. Renaudot's conferences provided the crown with some of the benefits of the suspended institutions without any of their political dangers. The conferences were a place to solicit opinion without having to listen to political grievances, a laboratory to ex-

---

[125] The subtitle of Guy Patin's 1644 attack on Renaudot suggests that the conferences may have resumed immediately after the 1 March 1644 session of Parlement (*Le nez pourry de Théophraste Renaudot . . . et la ruine de tous ses fourneaux et alambics excepte celle de sa Conference, retablie depuis quinze jours . . .*). There is no solid proof elsewhere that the conferences existed beyond September 1642. Moreover, the circle of Pierre Michon, l'Abbé Bourdelot (1610-1685) began meeting at the Hôtel du Condé in 1642. This group would serve some of the same ends as Renaudot's circle, and perhaps began in order to fill the void it left. R. Taton, *Les origins de l'Académie Royale des Sciences* (Paris: 1965), p. 16.

[126] See Ranum, *Paris*, esp. Chapter XII, VIII, and IX.

plore new technology without investing government funds or royal confidence. This function is most apparent in the 1638 discussions devoted to the French economy, but it is likewise true throughout its 9-year history.

Richelieu's efforts as government reformer were directed to improving the collection and dissemination of information; witness the intendency system, the *Gazette*, the Académie Française. Renaudot's academy was part of this effort. As a government resource, it anticipated the royal societies and economic commissions of Louis XIV, as well as the "think-tanks" of the twentieth century. As did so many of Renaudot's experiments, the conference began without any apparent encouragement from Richelieu. As happened with all of Renaudot's innocent inventions, Richelieu was quick to recognize and exploit its potential.

CHAPTER IV

The Founding of the Gazette

PUBLISHING in France underwent profound and radical change during the first decades of the seventeenth century. The publishing world had to react to new realities of lower profits and poorly trained craftsmen, to say nothing of changes in reading interest and the reading public. And above all of this stood the monarchy, increasingly uncompromising in its demands upon the printed word. It was in this fast-changing scene that the political press was born: it is for this reason that the publishing career of Théophraste Renaudot takes on significance.

Printing first appeared in Paris in 1470, within a generation of the discovery and application of moveable type in Germany. Ulrich Gering, of Constance, and Michel Friberger, of Colmar, published humanist texts needed by members of the University of Paris. The University realized the importance of the new invention, and soon supported its printers openly and actively.[1] Printers were as essential to the University as were the booksellers and paperdealers, who could trace their association with the University back to 1275.[2] From its appearance in Paris, therefore, printing was ancillary to education, and only secondarily a part of the world of commerce and the mechanical arts.

But just as important in distinguishing printing from the mechanical trades were the conditions unique to the craft. From the 1470's, and certainly through the mid-sixteenth century, the printer was a highly trained and specialized artist. The bulk of material published during this period was in the

[1] L. Febvre and H-J. Martin, *l'Apparition du livre* (Paris: 1958), pp. 266-68.

[2] H. Falk, *Les privilèges de librairie sous l'ancien régime* (Paris: 1906), p. 8.

classical languages and/or humanistic topics.[3] Consequently, the printer knew his Greek and Latin, both as printer and as author or editor of the text itself. Many early printers designed their own typefaces and were involved with the decoration and illustration of their books. Clearly, these printers were not simple mechanics, but highly trained, sophisticated intellectuals. Even though the printer-scholar would become a rarity by the seventeenth century, the Paris printing establishment never forgot its artistic and intellectual past.

From 1500 to 1600, the number of printshops in Paris increased from 75 to 112; by 1625, the number had exploded to 270.[4] Those Latin Quarter printers publishing religious and humanistic texts for the scholarly community were increasingly threatened by a growing number of printers publishing scientific, legal, and popular materials. For the most part, the latter grouped near the Palais on the Île de la Cité, where the hurly-burly of town life brought them the customers they needed. They often published cheaper, portable, smaller format

---

[3] A good introduction to the problems of analyzing reading interests is H-J. Martin, "Ce qu'on lisait à Paris au XVIe siècle," *Bibliothèque d'Humanisme et Renaissance*, XII (1959), 222-30. For the seventeenth century, Martin's *thèse d'état* is an inexhaustible source of information: *Livre, pouvoirs et société à Paris au XVIIe siècle* (Geneva: Droz), 1969.

[4] An inventory done during the Revolution offered the following profile of the number of printshops in Paris: 1473-1500, 75; 1500-1525, 80; 1525-1550, 90; 1550-1575, 102; 1575-1600, 112; 1600-1625, 270; 1625-1650, 240; 1650-1675, 120; 1675-1794, 60. (B.N. mss. f.fr. 22106, f. 19.)

These statistics vary from one contemporary source to another. A 1645 *mémoire* spoke of 76 shops with 183 presses in Paris (B.N. mss. 18600, ff. 693-696: reprinted by F. Funck-Bretano, "l'Imprimerie à Paris en 1645," *Revue des études historiques* [1902], 483-86); an *enquête* the year before visited 75 shops, with a total of 181 presses (B.N. mss. f.fr. 18600, f. 671-686; reprinted by G. Lepreux, "Une enquête sur l'imprimerie de Paris en 1644," *La bibliothèque moderne*, XIV, 5-36). The 1644 and 1645 *mémoires* seem to be concerned only with the recognized corporation printers, and their total of 75 seems conservative. Perhaps the source of confusion is the seventeenth century interchange of *"l'imprimerie"* with *"presse"*: the term can either mean "printshop" (with multiple presses) or a single "printing press."

books for their nonstationary, nonscholarly audience. They also tended to publish fewer copies per edition than did their university oriented counterparts. Many of these printers, particularly journeymen and apprentices, were poorly trained and little interested in maintaining standards which many Left Bank printers still took for granted.

If publishing a deluxe edition was a costly and time consuming job, printing broadsheets, bottle labels, or sensational pamphlets was very easy. In spite of a few refinements, the press used by Gutenberg remained virtually unchanged through the eighteenth century. Indeed, it was so simple that any carpenter could build one.[5] An enterprising journeyman could open a print shop in an abandoned loft or under a bridge for as long as business would last, and then move on. These men printed anything and everything, and their shoddy standards and anonymity threatened the hard-earned reputation of the craft. With the demands for cheaper popular editions, with a shift away from deluxe editions of religious and secular classics, many old publishing families could not make the change and found themselves in financial difficulties. Moreover, printing was, at best, a financially precarious business, and the cost of paper and ink increased in the first half of the seventeenth century.[6] All of these economic threats— from costs of material, to the competition of hack printers, to a reading public becoming accustomed to and satisfied with cheaper paper, sloppier editing and cast-off typesets—demanded regulation if the venerable craft would survive.

Since 1492 printers, along with booksellers, illuminators, and copyists, had formed themselves into the *Confrérie de St. Jean de la Porte Latine* or of *St. Jean d'Evangile.* The confraternity was a religious and social association, only second-

---

[5] Febvre, *l'Apparition du livre*, p. 86. See also n. 52.

[6] H-J. Martin, "l'Édition parisienne au XVIIe siècle," *Annales* (1952), VII, 310-12.

arily concerned with economic matters.[7] Under the protection of the University, as an ancillary to education, there was little reason for the printers to organize further.

The religious and social turmoil of the sixteenth century forced the trade to police itself. As we have seen, publishing in its youth was concerned primarily with religious and humanistic treatises. All books, no matter what their subject, had to be submitted to the theology faculty for approval. The University, and not the state, served as censor. In 1547, however, the University's authority was limited to approving religious publications.[8] According to an *arrêt* of 10 September 1563, all books, regardless of subject, required royal permission. Theological consideration had given way to political necessity: the theology faculty had been reduced from official censor to critic.[9] In 1571 enforcement of the law was put into the hands of printers and booksellers sworn to the Crown.[10] These two events signaled the growing power of the press— no longer a cloistered adjunct to the University, but a social and political force subject to strict government surveillance.

Subject to economic and manpower problems, subject likewise to political and civil pressures, the leaders of the publishing community repeatedly appealed for tighter organization. On 16 June 1618, the Crown approved the 38 statutes of the Corporation of Printers and Booksellers, and they were registered in Parlement on 9 July.[11] Until this date, publishing remained a quasi-educational activity, without a clearly defined status in the Parisian commercial and financial community.

[7] Falk, *Privilèges de librairie*, p. 9.

[8] P. Mellottée, *Histoire économique de l'imprimerie* (Paris: 1905), pp. 47, 50.

[9] Falk, *Privilèges de librairie*, p. 26.

[10] D. Pottinger, *The French Book Trade in the Ancien Régime 1500-1791* (Cambridge, Mass.: 1958), p. 59.

[11] B.N. mss. f.fr. 8110, ff. 75-88. The *règlement* was extended throughout France on 29 January 1626.

It had now definitively emerged as an active participant in the political, social, and economic life of the nation.

The 38 statutes restated existing but diffused legislation. They made a conscious effort to curtail the plethora of fly-by-night printshops. No one was permitted to publish in a private home; only members of the corporation were permitted to publish in Paris; no one could be certified until he had two fully equipped presses belonging to him alone. Two copies of all publications were to be sent to the royal library, and all publishers of defamatory books or libels would be considered "disturbers of public tranquility," and lose their rights and privileges.[12]

Parisian printers were now subject not only to government imposed controls, but also to those imposed by the mutual agreement of corporation members. Printers could wield social and political power, just as older corporations in Paris had long done. As a group they could influence the police powers of the city, and in addition maintain their own corporate standards. The full weight of the corporation fell upon those within the organization: corporation privileges and honors came only after accepting the responsibilities of membership.

But as was true of all corporate groups, its requirements were binding upon its members, but not those outside. The latter, of course, provided the most embarrassment for the government. Many of them, without ability, capital, or training, produced the anonymous broadsheets and political pamphlets which the government was most eager to silence.

Renaudot was outside the corporation. Its requirements re-

---

[12] B.N. mss. f.fr. 8110, ff. 75-88. The original motive for demanding two copies of each publication was to increase the size of the royal library (first imposed in 1537: B.N. mss. f.fr. 22076, f.2). But quickly enough the police function became more important. The 1618 *arrêt* sent one copy to the royal library and the other to the corporation. In 1638 the Chancellor was authorized a copy, and by 1658, a fourth copy went to the Cabinet du Roi at the Louvre. See R. Estivals, *Le dépôt légal sous l'ancien régime* (Paris: 1961).

mained, for him and other *nonjurés*, simply recommendations, and little more. But in civil matters, the *nonjuré* was definitely at a disadvantage. When involved in a civil suit, he had to press his claims alone, as an individual against the political and social power of one of the city's most prestigious and influential groups. During the 1630's, Renaudot was the only publisher in Paris openly existing—and thriving—outside the corporation.

The printing press and its methods, first developed and applied in the 1440's, were substantially unchanged in 1631, when the periodical press made its appearance in France. The two-century delay in the development of the political press was not due to a lack of technical or mechanical sophistication, but rather to social changes which demanded a new genre of news diffusion.[13]

There were four major forms of published news in France before the appearance of the *Gazette* in 1631: royal proclamations and edicts, the *canard*, the *relation*, and the *annuel*. All of them, and none of them, are forerunners of the regularly appearing newspaper. They continued to exist after 1631, and this shows that they had ends to serve different from those of the political press.

During the 1560's, the monarchy and the parlements became particularly eager to distribute their published decisions throughout the realm. Since it was essential that the printing be faultless, a royal printer, known and trusted for his skill, was appointed. In addition to government decisions, it became

[13] See M. Varin-d'Ainvelle, *La presse en France: genèse et évolution de ses fonctions psycho-sociales* (Paris: 1965), p. 60. Although offering enough random information, the study hardly lives up to its subtitle. Elizabeth L. Eisenstein has published excellent introductions to the problem of literacy and printing: "The Advent of Printing and the Problem of the Renaissance," *Past and Present*, No. 45 (1969), pp. 19-90; "The Advent of Printing in Current Historical Literature: Notes and Comments on an Elusive Transformation," *American Historical Review*, LXXV (1970), 727-43.

customary for private individuals and corporations to publish summaries of litigation in which they were involved. But while these legal publications could inform and influence, they lacked the personality and regularity of a conventional journal. J-P. Seguin studied over 500 *canards* published in France before 1631.[14] These pamphlets appeared irregularly and reported a variety of current events, the most popular including crimes, natural calamities, astronomical and celestial phenomena, and a whole variety of marvels, sorcerers, and strange births. This literature was primarily sensational, not at all concerned with the political and social events which concern the modern press. The anonymous, irregularly appearing press would thrive through the eighteenth century, offering its readers a potpourri of popular myths and medical and astrological information.[15] The *Gazette* itself, aimed at a smaller middle and upper-class audience, was remarkably devoid of these subjects.

The political and diplomatic *relation* also appeared irregularly, when events warranted it. It was usually four to eight pages long, anonymous, and always *engagé*—varying in style from sheer and outrageous propaganda to straightforward news reporting. The *relation* shared the weaknesses of the *canard*. Appearing irregularly and unsigned, it could not develop a regular and dependent readership. Anonymity may have been an asset when attacking an enemy, but it obviously raised doubts of the reliability and authority of the news.

There was also the *annuel*, the most noteworthy of which was the *Mercure français*. Founded in 1605 by Jean Richer, the *Mercure* was the official compilation of news of the court and crown. It was directed by Père Joseph from 1624 until his death

---

[14] *l'Information en France avant la périodique: 517 canards imprimés entre 1529 et 1631* (Paris: 1964). His earlier study is also helpful: *l'Information en France, de Louis XII à Henri II* (Geneva: 1961).

[15] See R. Mandrou, *De la culture populaire aux XVIIᵉ et XVIIIᵉ siècles: la bibliothèque bleue de Troyes* (Paris: 1964).

in 1638, when Renaudot assumed the editorship. Its limitation in influencing public opinion is obvious from its publication dates. The *Mercure* of 1637-1638, for instance, was published in 1646; the *Mercure* of 1643 appeared in 1648. No wonder this was its last edition. It provided a stylistic model for the *Gazette*, and was at least a regular, government supported publication, no matter how great the intervals between editions might have been.

Periodic publications existed in Europe long before the *Mercure françois*. As early as 1587, *Relations semestrielles* appeared in Latin and in German, in Frankfort. In 1604 a *Mercurius gallo-belgicus* appeared, also at Frankfort. And Abraham Verhoeven's Antwerp-based *Wekelyke tyndike* (or *Nieuwe tidjingen*) is cited as having possessed the oldest privilege in Europe to publish news for its government. There was also the *Frankfurter oberpostamtszeitung*, a semi-official bulletin of the Imperial office of posts, directed by Jacques de Birghden. After 1617 a large number of *courantos* were published in Holland, and then distributed in England. In 1618 Nathaniel Butter began publishing his *Weekly News* in London.[16]

Renaudot therefore can hardly be credited with founding the first newspaper. Nor can he be credited with having founded the first French newspaper, as there were French *courantos* published in Amsterdam for distribution in France as early as 1618.[17] Renaudot even acknowledged in his dedication to the *Recueil des Gazettes . . . de 1631* that he had followed "the example of other States and even of all of [France's] neighbors."[18] In the preface to the same collection, he said that the

---

[16] R. Livois, *Histoire de la presse française* (Lausanne: 1965), p. 18. On antecedents to the modern press, see G. Weill, *Le journal, origines, évolution et la rôle de la presse périodique* (Paris: 1934). Similar foreign papers were on sale at Renaudot's Bureau d'Adresse. See the Appendix.

[17] F. Dahl et al., "Les débuts de la presse française," *Acta Bibliothecae Gotoburgensis* (1951), pp. 7, 21.

[18] *Recueil de 1631*, p. 3.

107

publication of the *Gazette* was indeed a novelty, but only in France.[19] The other informational devices—published edicts, *canard*, *relation*, and *annuel*—existed long before 1631. The question, then, still remains: why did the periodical political press appear in France in 1631?

Étienne Thuau thoroughly analyzed the theoretical and practical use of government propaganda during the first half of the seventeenth century.[20] His study indicated that few men more keenly appreciated the power of the engaged pen than did Richelieu. By ignoring the ancient tradition of royal direction of thought, however, Thuau implied that this control appeared only with Richelieu. Nothing could be more misleading.

In traditional political theory, the metaphor of the organic state attributed to the Crown the direction and supervision of its subjects' thought. The prince served the function of the good father, a preceptor educating his subjects. One had a good government if one in fact had a good, a just, a wise ruler, not because he would be a more effective statesman, but because he would serve as an example to his people.[21] Royal direction resulted from simple and direct emulation: subjects followed the king on the strength of his moral and spiritual superiority. Even more than other individuals, the prince was a public figure, larger than life. His career was spent in public acts—on horseback, under a tree at Vincennes dispensing justice, so that the populace could follow his behavior. And royal administration was predicated on a single postulate: to communicate throughout the realm the justice and charity of the ruler.

[19] "Preface," *ibid.*

[20] *Raison d'État et pensée politique à l'époque de Richelieu* (Paris: 1966).

[21] In his *Testament politique*, Richelieu spoke constantly of princely attributes, more important than any technical or administrative abilities of the ruler: "La pureté d'un Prince chaste bannira plus d'impuretés de son Royaume que toutes les diligences qu'il sauroit faire à cette fin." *Testament politique*, L. André, ed., p. 322.

Government remained tied to the person of the king, and it was his personal commands which were communicated. If the crown, in all of its panoply, was the head of an organic society, the administration was its mouth.

In practice, premodern French administration corresponded very closely to this theoretical construct. The royal official was charged with broadcasting the works of the crown. All royal documents concluded with an obligatory "the present judgment shall be read, published, and posted everywhere necessary so that no one may claim ignorance of it." The official was the mouth through which the king, far away in Paris, spoke. The poverty of early seventeenth century French political theory accounts for the continuation of these traditional metaphors into the reign of Louis XIII and Richelieu,[22] but not only the metaphors remained. Royal administration, no matter how sophisticated and efficient it might become, was still an extension of the royal person, serving essentially an informational function.

To these medieval constructs were added the maxims garnered from Machiavelli, the great source for political writers of the seventeenth century. No matter the morality or justice or goodness of informing one's subjects, to the Florentine's disciples the essence of governing was controlling public opinion. Subjects served for nothing if they could not be directed and channeled. If theological tenets held that man was too weak to be left to his own religious devices, the same held true for man as political and social animal: "the character of the

---

[22] "Les idées qu'exposent couramment les publicistes royalistes du XVIe et du XVIIe siècles paraissent souvent banales à quiconque a feuillété la littérature des périodes précédentes. Elles n'étonnent qui si l'on ne sent pas en elles le long héritage mediéval; pas plus en histoire des doctrines politiques qu'en toutes autres sortes d'histoires, il ne convient de prendre trop au serieux la coupure traditionelle que, à la suite des humanistes, nous pratiquons d'ordinaire dans le passe de l'Europe aux alentours de l'an 1500." M. Bloch, *Les rois thaumaturges* (Paris: 1961), p. 347.

people is not to be blamed any more than that of princes, for both alike are liable to err when they are without any control."[23] Direction of one's proper thought on royalty, power, and authority, to the extent that they could be separated from purely theological matters, had to come from secular authorities. The prince who did not harness the power of the pen left his state open to disorder and rebellion, a religious sin as well as a political blunder. "Those desiring to trouble a State try by all kinds of means to imprint a bad opinion of the Prince in the subjects' minds. Writings are the first preparation which fashion the design. They are the doors through which respect exits and rebellion enters: all the other resources are weak when he who commands them has a bad reputation. Everything said and everything done is evilly interpreted, his most just actions are censured and if he works miracles, they would pass them off as illusions."[24] From here to a purely secular, Machiavellian use of propaganda was but a short and obvious step. The power of opinion in domestic affairs was as potent as the sword in military affairs. They both led to the same end, namely, the application of power. If war was the extension of diplomacy, the control of public opinion was a legitimate extension of politics.

To modern men, propaganda is a loaded word, connoting specious argument to justify actions that men in power undertake regardless of any considerations beyond simple self-interest. Expediency and self-justification were both liberally present in Richelieu's propaganda, yet total dedication to state and king lifted his propaganda beyond mere self-justification. His propaganda rings with the missionary's self-assurance, the conviction that he was justifying policies in accord with the highest purposes of the French state.

[23] Machiavelli, *Discourses*, Modern Library edn., Book I, LVIII, p. 262.
[24] "Discours au Roi touchant les libelles faits contre le gouvernement de son État," quoted in Thuau, p. 170.

More than any of his contemporaries, Richelieu sensed the importance and latent power of the pen. He was a voracious writer, and his letters are models of organization and clarity. It was through correspondence, rather than through direct speech or the intervention of lesser officials, that he "sought to conquer the assent of others."[25] During his early career he had written theological tracts, and continued to dabble in drama and poetry. Richelieu understood the role of creative, persuasive writing, and recognized and rewarded its potential in others.

As early as 1614, he had collected the pamphlets inspired by the meeting of the Estates General, well aware even then of the politically tuned press.[26] When he came to power, he would develop it with authority and dispatch. Richelieu's involvement in the production of royalist pamphlets was personal and direct, ranging from suggesting a title to rewriting a finished draft. He supervised his political writers as he supervised his military and diplomatic underlings. These writers often acted as a team, the Cardinal demanding a series of pamphlets written from different points of view of a single problem, knowing "that a varied number of small pamphlets broadcast at different times is more effective than one large volume."[27]

In the year following the Day of Dupes, the French royal family was divided and, with it, so was much of France. Monsieur, the Duke of Orleans had fled with his armies to Lorraine, while the Queen Mother continued to intrigue against Louis XIII and the Cardinal-minister at home. Richelieu's polemicists, Sirmond, Balzac, Hay du Chastelet, Mézeray, were never busier than in the first half of 1631.[28] Richelieu

---

[25] L. Delavaud, p. 7. Also see O. Ranum, *Richelieu and the Councillors of Louis XIII* (Oxford: 1963), p. 14.

[26] Richelieu, *Lettres* (Paris: 1853-1877), edited by M. Avenel, I, 144; cited by Thuau, p. 173.

[27] Charpentier, quoted by Thuau, p. 175.

[28] R. Kerviler, *La presse politique sous Richelieu et l'Académicien Jean de Sirmond 1589-1649* (Paris: 1876), pp. 28-29.

himself authored several *relations*, including the important
"Relation de ce qui s'est passé pendant le sejour du Roy à
Dijon, et depuis qu'il en est party, jusqu'au 8 Avril 1631." The
relation published Louis XIII's declaration of 30 March, brand-
ing his brother's followers traitors to the state. Although his
political press was working as it never had before, by mid-1631
it was obvious to Richelieu that these propaganda methods
had limited effect. Renaudot's *Gazette* dates from this era. It
is as a result of political exigencies that the modern press was
born.

Ever since January 1631, Jean Martin, Louis Vendosme, and
François Pommerai, members of the Corporation of Printers
and Booksellers, had been publishing a weekly *couranto* entitled *Nouvelles ordinaires des divers endroits* in Paris.[29] Their
format was exactly that which Renaudot would use: short news
dispatches printed without comment, the more recent dis-

[29] According to H-J. Martin, Vendosme and Martin were suspect for
being Protestant. "Une projet de réforme de l'imprimerie parisienne en
1645," *Humanisme actif* (Paris: 1968), II, 261.

The only copies of the *couranto* are found at the Bibliothèque de
l'Arsenal, in a volume entitled *Gazette 1631. Table alphabetique des
Gazettes de l'année 1631* (Rés. 4° H. 8918). The following is written on
the inside cover: "Ce tome II contient, outre la table, quelques feuilles
et cahiers de la Gazette de Renaudot de 1631 avec les Nouvelles des
divers endroits qui en font partie, les nos. 27 à 49 d'une gazette portant
ce meme titre de 'Nouvelles ordinaires de diverses endroits' mais
avancé de Jean Martin et Louys Vendosme. Le no. 27 est daté du 17
juillet 1631, le première numéro de l'année a donc du paraître en
fevrier: cette gazette est par consequent antérieure d'au moins quatre
mois à celle de Th. Renaudot. C'est vraisemblement le premier journal
paru en France. Le première tome de ce recueil renferme les doubles,
des nos. 36 et 37 du 19 et 26 Septembre. Le premier exemplaire de
cette gazette a été découvert à la Bque. Royale de Stockholm, il porte le
no. 42, du 31 oct. 1631. On ne connait pas actuellement d'autres nu-
méros que ceux ici contenus. 13 Octobre 1949. Mlle. Pettibon—Bibliot.
à la B.N."

Contrary to Mlle. Pettibon's calculations, the first number of the
Nouvelles ordinaires would have appeared on 16 January, counting
back week by week from the date of the twenty-seventh number, 17 July.

patches appearing last. Louis Epstin, a German, edited their newspaper. Epstin enjoyed a wide correspondence with Dutch and German businessmen, perhaps analogous to the Fuggers' printing and information agency. It was through Epstin that news from Amsterdam, Danzig, Leipzig, Frankfort, and other cities appeared.[30] The *Nouvelles ordinaires* must have been a successful venture, so well-received and lucrative, in fact, that others would try their hand. On 30 May 1631, four months after the first issue of the *Nouvelles ordinaires*, with exactly the same format, appeared Renaudot's *Gazette*.[31] Renaudot had been publishing since 1629, but was not a member of the corporation. Neither of the rival publications carried a royal privilege, since publishers of *courantos* never bothered to get one.

By the summer of 1631, Martin, Vendosme, and Pommerai were feeling the pressure of their new competitor. With corporation support, they appealed to civil authorities at Châtelet, indicating that Renaudot had not paid the necessary fees to register his *couranto*. All publications had to be approved by the nearest civil court, in this instance, the civil authorities at Châtelet.[32] Ordinary legal procedure was on the side of the three members of the corporation. Renaudot, however, claimed exemption from payment on the basis of permission he supposedly received from royal council, dated 31 May 1631. Nowhere does this *arrêt* exist, either in original or in manuscript copy,[33] although Renaudot referred to it in his February

---

[30] F. Dahl et al., p. 52. B.N. mss. f.fr. 22084, f. 222v.

[31] The date and place of publication ("Du Bureau d'Adresse au Grand Coq, rue de la Calandre sortant au Marché neuf près le Palais à Paris") does not appear until the sixth weekly issue, on 4 July 1631. The 30 May date is therefore by deduction.

[32] F. Dahl et al., pp. 57ff.

[33] The 30 May letter does not appear in "Lettres du Roy en forme de Chartre" (S.l.n.d.) B.N. mss. f.fr. 21832, ff. 164ff., which Renaudot had drawn up. The letter is cited in Louis XIII's often-republished letter of 11 and 18 October 1631, and elsewhere, but an original text does not exist.

1635 *Gazette*. Moreover, there was no meeting of the council on that date. Within the normal bounds of precedence and practice, Martin, Vendosme, and Pommerai were publishing according to the law, Renaudot was not.

The *procureur-général* authorized the seizure of Renaudot's illegally published *Gazettes*. Corporation members went to the shop of Michael Blaegaert, Renaudot's neighbor who would continue to print the *Gazettes* for him, and impounded the copies and typeface.[34]

Without recourse within the procedures of normal civil law, Renaudot appealed to Richelieu and Louis XIII. His royal protectors were certainly aware of Renaudot's difficulties, and also knew that the earlier they incorporated one of the two Parisian newspapers into their public opinion machine, the better. The *Nouvelles ordinaires-Gazette* litigation gave them an ideal pretext. On 11 and 18 November, the crown stated that Renaudot "alone, exclusive of all others, shall enjoy our privilege and permission to make, print, sell and distribute the aforementioned *Gazettes, Relations* and *Nouvelles* of this kingdom as well as of foreign countries: either in his Bureaus or in whatever other places he might wish to choose; with prohibition to all other persons to do so, under whatever penalties pertain."[35]

Not only were Martin, Vendosme, and Pommerai ordered to cease publishing their newspaper, but Renaudot was so sure of himself that he stole the *Nouvelles ordinaires* title as his own, long before 5 December 1631, when his own *Nouvelles ordinaires* appeared as part of the *Gazette*. More important, he evidently stole Louis Epstin away from them also. With their chief correspondent went the source of their news. Increasingly

---

[34] This was the standard procedure in such cases. See B.N. mss. f.fr. 8069, f. 525.

[35] B.N. mss. f.fr. 21832, f. 164. This is reprinted by E. Hatin, *Histoire politique de la presse* (Paris: 1859-1861), 1, 92; F. Dahl et al., pp. 49-50.

Renaudot had the news quicker and in greater depth than they.[36] The three corporation members soon stopped publishing, probably by the beginning of 1632.[37]

An idea, an editor, a title stolen from others; flagrant disrespect for normal civil procedures; undisguised royal favoritism in granting a monopoly—thus the modern political newspaper was born. Renaudot may indeed remain as its father, but its birth was a bit more sordid than his nineteenth century biographers would admit.

In protecting Renaudot's *Gazette*, Richelieu does not appear to have followed any premeditated schemes to cripple the Corporation of Printers and Booksellers, no grand blueprint to destroy corporatism. Always the pragmatist, he seized the opportunity to protect a favored creature. In so doing, Richelieu was assured of receiving Renaudot's full service, as well as serving notice to the printers that they could not take their traditional corporate autonomy for granted. This is an example, one of several in the Richelieu-Renaudot collaboration, where a specific situation had the effect of diluting the power of a specific corporation.

Renaudot soon learned that holding a monopoly de jure was not synonymous with enjoying it de facto. The corporation

[36] They complained to the king that Renaudot, "non plus l'autheur, n'estant que une Traduction de celle d'Amsterdam, Anvers, Bruxelles, Francfort, Ambourg, Zurich, Venise, Rome et autres lieux, qu'en recoit chaque semaine à Paris, ensemble de quelques Lettres des Banquiers. Que c'est un nommé Epstin qui les recoit et les luy traduit moyennanant une Pistole chaque semaine, lequel, devant qu'audit Renaudot, les bailloi audit Vendosme. . . . Qu'il n'est pas vray qu'il face un denier de depense pour avoir des intelligences étrangeres, le tout ne vanant que par le moyen desdites Traductions, et de quelques lettres desdits Banquiers. Qu'à l'egard des Nouvelles de Paris, et d'alentour, il n'y a aucune difficulté ny peine de s'en acquitter." "Réquête au Roy des Syndic et Adjoints de la Communauté des Imprimeurs, Libraires et Relieur . . . contre Renaudot," B.N. mss. f.fr. 22084, ff. 222-223.

[37] The last *Nouvelle ordinaire* in the Arsenal volume is dated 19 December 1631 (no. 49).

continued to hound Renaudot in defense of its three members. They were ordered to return the *Gazettes* and typefaces they had seized at Blaegaert's shop, but refused to do so.[38] Constantly Renaudot appealed through the court to get his copies and equipment back, and constantly they ignored the court requests. For impeding the *arrêts* of 31 March 1628 and 13 February 1630, which had given Renaudot undefined powers under the aegis of the Bureau d'Adresse, Martin et al. were fined 6,000 *livres*, plus costs and damages.[39] On 11 March 1633, Renaudot's prior *arrêts* were all confirmed, and wider privileges were added to them. "THE KING IN HIS COUNCIL . . . prohibits the Syndic and Adjuncts of the Printers and Booksellers of Paris, together with the aforesaid Martin, Vendosme, Pommerai and all others, be they of the city of Paris or of any other place of this Kingdom, from printing or having printed, selling or supplying, troubling or obstructing the aforesaid Renaudot and his associates in the impression at his Bureau d'Adresse of the *Gazettes, Nouvelles, Relations, Prix courant des marchandises, Mémoires, Affiches*, and other dependences of his Bureau, nor to meddle therein having now been so informed, under penalty of confiscation of their books and proofs, type and presses: of a fine of 6,000 *livres*, plus expenses, damages, and interest: nor under the same penalty to intimidate or obstruct the Master or Journeymen printers which Renaudot might choose to work at the presses in his Bureaus."[40]

This *arrêt* joined the activities of Renaudot the publisher to those of Renaudot the director of the Bureau d'Adresse. He could publish whatever he considered necessary to the operation of the bureau. He soon had his own presses in his home on the Rue Calandre. In fact, he had received virtual carte blanche powers. Now that he controlled his own presses and his own

---

[38] B.N. mss. f.fr. 21832, f. 168.
[39] 11 March 1633. B.N. mss. f.fr. 21832, f. 168-69.
[40] B.N. mss. f.fr. 21832, f. 164ff. Reprinted by F. Dahl et al., pp. 72ff.

printers, relations with the corporation grew even more strained.

Renaudot saw his *Gazettes* counterfeited. As soon as the weekly journal would appear, "many Printers, Colporters, and others, through contempt and infringement of the law, daily print and publish *Relations* and *Nouvelles* of diverse titles, without Renaudot's permission."[41] Renaudot again had such counterfeit *Gazettes* seized and their publishers and distributors prosecuted. As was general with such clandestine publications, colporters were more easily apprehended than were the publishers. Renaudot acted in contravention of the privilege granted to the 50 colporters distributing such publications within Paris. The Royal Council acted to "sustain the Suppliant in the possession and exercise of his power to make, sell, and distribute the said *Gazettes, Nouvelles* and other things printed at his Bureau, by whomsoever he wishes."[42] Renaudot, unlike other Parisian printers, could sell his publication however, through whomever, he wished.

Finally, in a charter of February 1635, the crown confirmed all of Renaudot's privileges. To these was added the keystone of his power, a monopoly to publish the *Gazette* granted to "his heirs, successors, or assigns: fully, peaceably and perpetually, without suffering or permitting any trouble or obstacle to the contrary to be made or inflicted upon them."[43] Renaudot had entered the Parisian publishing world by openly flaunting tradition and civil law; he prospered in it through the sustained encouragement of Richelieu and Louis XIII. In sheer volume Renaudot was the most important publisher in Paris during the period 1631-1644. His *Gazettes, Nouvelles ordinaires,* and *Relations* appeared each Saturday and *Extraordinaires* at various times during the week; the *Conferences* each Monday; his *Feuille du Bureau d'Adresse* each month;

---

[41] Conseil du Roi, 7 November 1634. B.N. mss. f.fr. 21816, f. 93r; B.N. mss. f.fr. 21832, f. 164.

[42] B.N. mss. f.fr. 21832, f. 164.   [43] B.N. mss. f.fr. 21832, f. 172.

editions of royal edicts and laws whenever he saw fit or was ordered to do so;[44] yearly *Recueils* of the *Gazette* and fairly regular collections of the *Centuries des Conferences*; the *Mercure françois* (after 1637); as well as his own medical writings. The monopoly which he had sought de jure in 1630-1631 was, by 1635, a fact. Counterfeiting would continue, and Renaudot would continue to prosecute the printers and colporters contrevening his monopoly. Nevertheless, his monopoly was as complete as the loose administration of the period could permit.

Renaudot's *Gazette* appeared each Saturday. On 5 December 1631 the 4-page *Gazette* was joined by the 4-page *Nouvelles ordinaires*. According to his *Relation* of 2 September 1632

[44] Renaudot's privilege to publish government documents as part of his weekly *Gazette* brought him into direct conflict with the royal printers. Ever since 1474 certain printers in Paris had had the right to publish all government laws and declarations. These printers included, among others, François Pommerai and Louis Vendosme (publishers of the abortive *Nouvelles ordinaires*) and Sebastien Cramoisy, the most powerful publisher of the seventeenth century. Repeatedly the corporation of printers and the royal printers themselves cited Renaudot for publishing material which they considered theirs alone: "les Edicts et Declarations, Lettres Patentes, Ordonnances, Mandemans, Arrêts, Reglemens, Baux Generaux et particuliers, et autres expeditions concernant les Finances, Aydes, Tailles et Gabelles, et généralement ce qui intervient en conséquence des Traitez faits avec sadite Majesté en son Conseil, Ensemble tous Contracts, Commissions et autres Expeditions des Greffiers des Commissions extraordinaires, soit par traité ou autrement" (*arrêt* of 18 March 1639, *signification* to Renaudot on 7 January 1640: B.N. mss. f.fr. 16744, ff. 34-36).

There was no clear distinction between the extent of their privilege and the extraordinary power which had been granted to Renaudot. The establishment of the Imprimerie Royale in 1640 under Cramoisy's direction simply intensified their rivalry. This is another example of Renaudot's special ability to antagonize and offend the most powerful interests and individuals.

There are several lists of these royal printers. Perhaps the most complete is "Liste et origine des Imprimeurs ordinaires du Roi," B.N. mss. f.fr. 21819, f. 24ff. On Cramoisy's career, see H-J. Martin, "Un grand éditeur parisien au XVIIᵉ siècle: Sebastien Cramoisy," *Gutenberg-Jahrbuch* (1957), 179-188.

Renaudot intended the *Gazette* for foreign and domestic news originating to the east and south of Paris, and news from the west and north for the *Nouvelles ordinaires,* but such a plan was hardly followed.[45] The *Gazette* and the *Nouvelles ordinaires* were epistolary in format; dispatches were printed in chronological order, preceded only by the place and date of origin. Maps, pictures, and diagrams never appeared. The number of dispatches varied, but most weekly editions of the *Gazette-Nouvelles* carried between 20 and 24 different articles. In 1639, many *Gazettes* were 8-pages long; by 1642, the practice was general, making the total weekly publication 12-pages long.

The first *Relations des nouvelles du monde* appeared on 4 February 1632. At first this was a recapitulation of news of the prior month, along with items not treated elsewhere—extended transcripts or excerpts of decrees, laws, speeches, and treaties, "to clarify what is too brief in my *Gazettes* and *Nouvelles*."[46] On 3 March 1634 the monthly *Relations* were replaced by the *Relations extraordinaires,* which appeared more often than once a month, often each week, pushing the weekly publication up to 20 or 24 pages. These *extraordinaires* are particularly fascinating, for it was here that Renaudot consciously cast off the mantle of anonymity to offer his opinions on the role of the press and the Bureau d'Adresse and, increasingly, to confront his many critics.

Scholars have tried to convert the price of Renaudot's *Gazette* into comparative terms. It sold for four *sous* per 12-page issue,[47] the cost of 900 grams of high quality white bread, or of 1,800 grams of the ordinary *pain des pauvres.*[48] By today's standards,

---

[45] "Les nouvelles comprenans ordinairement les pays qui nous sont Septentrionnaux et Occidentaux, et la Gazette ceux de l'Orient et du Midy: si la conjoncture des affaires de la France (ausquelles cette-cy est dediée) n'en interrompt l'ordre." *Relation,* 2 September 1632.

[46] 1 July 1632.   [47] *Extraordinaire,* 22 September 1650.

[48] M-N. Grand-Mesnil, *Mazarin, la Fronde et la presse 1647-1649* (Paris: 1967), p. 36.

the same amount of bread costs about one *franc*. "If Renaudot would return to offer his *Gazette* to us at that price, would we buy it from him? Probably not: we consent to paying from one to two *francs* for a magazine of a hundred pages, a large political weekly. But the *Gazette* offers only 12 small pages, the printed text on each page covering an area from 18 to 20 cm. high by 10 to 12 cm. wide: thus the printed surface of an entire edition of the *Gazette* is only equal to that of the first 2 pages of a daily like *Le Monde*. Who would pay a franc for a one page, *recto-verso* printed weekly?"[49] The *Gazette* was not directed to the majority of Frenchmen by content or design, and certainly not by price. If he wished, a reader could pay a monthly fee and read it in a shop or at a stand on the Pont Neuf.[50] By any standard, however, the *Gazette* was expensive.

In 1632, after the corporation finally returned what it had seized, Renaudot found himself with hundreds of unsold back copies of his weekly publications. Always the astute business-man, Renaudot bound these weekly issues into a deluxe *Recueil des Gazettes de l'année 1631*, with an introduction, dedication, preface, and table of contents, and offered them for sale. The *Recueil* was so well received that he produced and sold such a collection each year. He numbered each page of the weekly editions consecutively for future binding into the collection.

Renaudot wrote that he published 1,200 copies of the *Gazette* each week.[51] For certain *extraordinaires*, such as celebrations of the birth of the Dauphin or the treaties of Münster and Osnabrück, he probably increased the number of copies; these *extraordinaires* are much more numerous in existing archival and library holdings than normal weekly issues are. At first, Renaudot was a publisher-merchant, "putting out" his copy to Michael Blaegaert's print shop.[52] But eventually, Renaudot

[49] Grand-Mesnil, pp. 36-37.
[50] Anon., *Commerce des nouvelles restably* (Paris: 1649), p. 9.
[51] *Gazette*, 1 May 1638.
[52] Throughout the sixteenth century, and even in Renaudot's time,

established his own presses at the Maison du Grand Coq. By 1644, he had at least 4 presses in operation. With 3 working at capacity, he could produce 1,200-1,500 copies of his 12-page *Gazette-Nouvelles* in one day.[53]

In addition to Epstin, Renaudot probably employed a few clerks to translate extracts from foreign journals for inclusion in the *Gazette*. His sons Isaac and Eusèbe worked actively with him, and during the 1640's would assume much of the editorial responsibility. Renaudot received information from a variety of friends and associates, but the day-to-day editorial and commercial concerns remained a Renaudot family affair.[54]

Renaudot by no means had a limited view of the power of the press: instead he had to contend with the limited goals imposed upon him, and all printers of the era, by the mechanical exigencies of the craft. The 1635 patent gave Renaudot privilege "to compose and have composed, print and have

---

it was relatively rare for an important publisher-merchant to have his own printing press. Sebastien Cramoisy, for example, never had his own press, instead "putting out" his work to other members of the corporation. Martin, "Un grand éditeur parisien," p. 185. For the sixteenth century, see E. Armstrong, *Robert Estienne* (London: 1954).

[53] In 1644, Mazarin and Séguier ordered an inquest into the printing industry in Paris. The following entry is one of 75 listed: "Théophraste Regnaudot, gazettier, demeurant rue de la Callande, sur lequel avons trouvé quatre presses, sur l'une desquelles l'on imprime une *Extraordinaire* concernant la lettre du Roy d'Angleterre [*extraordinaire* of 10 March 1644]. Et a trois compagnons auxquelz nous avons faict les deffences cy-dessus et enjoinct de se retirer en l'Université." (B.N. mss. 18600, f. 671-86; reprinted by G. Lepreux, "Une enquête sur l'imprimerie de Paris en 1644," *Bibliographe moderne*, XIV, 5-36).

The press Renaudot used differed little from the press originally developed 2 centuries earlier. Each press required 2 men to operate it. Working a full 12 to 16 hour day, they could print 1,200-1,500 "feuilles," each "feuille" containing four pages. With four presses, Renaudot could reserve one of them for his *extraordinaires*, and use the other 3 for the regular *Gazette-Nouvelles* "run." For a description of the operation of the press, see L. Febvre, *l'Apparition du livre*, pp. 81-92.

[54] See p. 202.

printed, wherever and by whomever he pleases, all *Gazettes, Relations,* and *Nouvelles,* ordinary as well as extraordinary."[55] This included provincial editions published with Renaudot's approval in Lyon, Rouen, Orleans, and perhaps elsewhere. In addition, Renaudot had to contend with provincial printers producing unauthorized *Gazettes* without the official Bureau d'Adresse rubric. Unfortunately, as was true of most governmental and social matters, technical problems prohibited rapid, immediate diffusion of the *Gazette* in the provinces. As were so many official ventures of the epoch, the *Gazette* was Paris-based and Paris-oriented.

[55] B.N. mss. f.fr. 21832, f. 171r.

CHAPTER V

The Content of the Gazette

RENAUDOT'S numerous critics never lacked a pretext to attack
him, and Renaudot, ever the man of letters, never lacked an
opportunity to plead his case to his readers. He seldom used
the weekly *Gazette* or *Nouvelles ordinaires* for personal reflection, but instead reserved it for the *Extraordinaires*, the
Relations, and the Preface to his yearly *Recueils*. It was here
that Renaudot, sometimes angry, usually misunderstood, always impassioned, discussed the role of the journalist.

Renaudot insisted that his "pen is only the Recorder" of the
exploits and actions of others.[1] As a recorder, the journalist
must maintain faceless anonymity and total distance from the
stories he reports. His articles "must be devoid of all passion."[2]
In a word, the facts were to speak for themselves.[3]

Renaudot said that "henceforth small children will know
that [the *Gazette*] is only the recorder of reputation and
renown [*bruit et de la rénomée*]."[4] Under the most perfect
conditions, all facts could be subject to uncompromising scru-
tiny. Under the chaotic and unstable conditions in which the
journalist was forced to operate, the reliability of such facts was
even more questionable. The newspaperman was a slave to the
news. He could not afford the luxury of time to confirm the
facts, but had to publish the news when and as he received it.
One man's *bruit* was Renaudot's *nouvelles*. "And if the fear of
displeasing their century has prevented great Authors from
touching the history of their age, what must be the difficulty in
writing the news of the week, indeed, of the very day on which

[1] *Requeste présentée à la Reyne* (Paris: 1643), p. 4.
[2] *Extraordinaire*, 12 February 1642.
[3] See pp. 69ff.
[4] *Extraordinaire*, 20 August 1638.

123

it is published? Add to it the brevity of time which our characteristic impatience permits me, and I would be very mistaken
if the rudest of critics could not find something to criticize in a
work which must be done in four hours, which the arrival of
Couriers each week leaves me to compose, adjust, and print
these lines."[5] And elsewhere, he continued in the same spirit.
"The King has well honored me with the public pen: but God
has not given me intuitive knowledge or the mind of the
Prophets, to know more than what I am told, of which I am
but the simple intermediary: and I invoke these two divinities
of Heaven and of Earth against the injustices of those who,
during the ten years that I have thus justified my methods, have
not reformed [their criticism]."[6]

Renaudot was willing to admit that certain stories which he
had published were false, once other reports had reached him.[7]
In certain cases, particularly events in England, he warned his
readers that the news came from a variety of sources and "each
one writes to his own advantage."[8] It was for the reader to
judge whether or not these rumors were acceptable as fact. The
journalist was akin "to the court secretary who records the
pleas of the two advocates and the *arrêt* of the court, without
being more sure of the truth of one than of the justice of the
other."[9] In many cases, what would appear to twentieth century

[5] "Preface," *Recueil de 1631*, p. 6.

[6] *Extraordinaire*, 22 December 1639.

[7] See, for example, the issue of 29 December 1640. Charles Sorel, who
enjoyed ridiculing Renaudot's activities, at least paid tribute to his
integrity as a journalist: "Si on prétend avoir subjet de se plaindre de
ce qu'on y voit quelquefois des choses trop exagérées, & d'autres qui ne
sont pas entièrement selon la vérité, il faut prendre gard que les choses
éloignées ne sont écrites que sur la foy d'autruy, & que de plus il arrive
souvent qu'une *Gazette* corrige l'autre, de sorte qu'on ne peut manquer
à trouver la vérité quand on les void toutes." *La bibliothèque françoise*
(Paris: 1664), p. 326.

[8] *Extraordinaire*, 18 November 1642.

[9] *Requeste présentée au Roy . . . sur le sujet des Gazettes et Nouvelles*
(Paris: 21 September 1640), p. 659.

eyes as *bruit ou rénommée* was presented as unassailable fact. If authorities attested to a faith-healing, no matter how questionable, it was presented as news.[10] To Renaudot, it was a demonstrable and obvious fact. Once given this assumption, the *Gazette* could never devote too much space to the court, for "it is the journal of kings and of the powers of the earth."[11] An analysis of the *Gazette* must begin and end at the court.

One of the first duties of a prince was to act like one, for in pomp and ceremony lay the force of power. "All these ceremonies are only the greater part of the just and reasonable obligation which Frenchmen owe to the Majesty of their Sovereigns: just as God commanded them, they consider and contemplate in this world the principal images and reflections of the Divine Majesty."[12] Richelieu had supposedly promised Louis XIII "to restore his name among foreign nations to the point where it must be." To do this, Richelieu insisted that his monarch must pay greater attention to ceremony, protocol, royal deportment: "foreigners who came to France in my time were often astonished to see a State so well restored and a household so humbled."[13]

But the performance of royalty was not enough. Without being broadcast to others, domestic or foreign, it was ineffective. To glorify the royal reputation was Renaudot's charge, and in 1651 he compared his service for Louis XIII to that which Apelles had performed for Alexander.[14] News of the royal family, their sports and games and health, the ceremonies of court, the ballets and banquets, filled the *Gazette*. In terms of fulfilling Richelieu's hopes, Renaudot outdid himself.

News of French origin did not appear until the sixth issue of the *Gazette* (4 July 1631), but from then on it remained a

---

[10] 21 August 1642.

[11] "Au Roy," *Recueil de 1631*, p. 4.

[12] Thomas Godefroy, *Le cérémonial françois* (Paris: 1619), "Dédication au Roy."

[13] *Testament politique*, L. André, ed., pp. 95, 280.

[14] 10 August 1651.

mainstay of the weekly edition. There were always dispatches from wherever the king might be at the time—Paris, St. Germain, Vincennes, battlefields, provincial capitals.

Royal actions, unlike those of other great men, were always commented upon: since "true and solid praise [is] always being found in virtuous actions, to tell the truth is therefore to praise everything that merits it."[15] All of these stories reflected the superhuman qualities of royalty. The king knew 4,000 persons from memory; he killed a raccoon with a single blow after an entire company of troops had been unable to do so.[16] He performed at ballet "with the delight inseparable from all the activities to which His Majesty applies himself," and his musical ability proved that "one can believe nothing more kingly than the knowledge of everything."[17] Louis XIII's remarkable presence evoked remarkable acts, as when a white dove flew endlessly beneath his window, "sending back to their books those who do not know that the lives of the Caesars are full of things much less remarkable."[18]

Louis XIII's personal life was a catalogue of "all the heroic and Christian virtues" which his subjects should imitate. When he lay on his deathbed, Renaudot wrote of him: "since our sins, rather than those of this good Prince, keep him abed, each of us should devote himself to his prayers with the same dedication which he [Louis XIII] has always employed in the welfare and safety of his people."[19] France was felicitous because it had a felicitous prince, whom God had favored. God's justice never ceased to defend its favorite prince. The execution of Cinq Mars and de Thou "clearly demonstrates the admirable effects of God's justice, and of his protection of the sacred person of His Majesty, and of his State."[20] His thaumaturgical responsibilities most clearly revealed his "heroic and Christian

---

[15] *Relation . . . de Mars 1633*, 1 April 1633.
[16] 29 August 1631; 16 January 1632.
[17] 21 February 1635; 14 April 1635.
[18] 12 August 1634.   [19] 25 April 1643.   [20] 4 October 1642.

virtues." Every major holiday was an occasion for performing the ancient sacerdotal rite. The most Christian King of France touched all men, regardless of their nationality: "on the twenty-sixth of last month, the Day of the Holy Sacrament, the King touched 1,169 ill, of whom 266 were Spanish and the rest of other nations." There are other examples, as when at Amiens on Pentecost 1633 he touched 400, half of them Spanish. Even in January 1643, just weeks before his death, Louis XIII was still healing the ill.[21] His charitable concern for his subjects always came first, as when he left "his beautiful houses at St. Germain and Fontainebleau, his pleasures at Versailles, and even the most tender sentiments of the least of his subjects" to repulse France's enemies.[22]

Louis XIII's health and hypochondria confronted Renaudot with delicate problems. He had to keep his readers informed, yet too much candor, especially in Louis' last years, was politically dangerous. As much as possible, Renaudot drew good news out of bad. After a sad description of the king's weak condition, Renaudot concluded that "the best news that I can give you is that the King is cured, thanks to God, of an intermittent fever from which he suffered several attacks: and now is taking the waters to strengthen his health."[23]

Louis XIII's health deteriorated steadily during the summer of 1642, yet not a word of it appeared in the *Gazette*. On 2 August 1642 a stark note: "the King's health has been greatly strengthened since his arrival at Fontainebleau." Two weeks later, Renaudot tried harder, and reported that the king was "in the strongest and most vigorous condition, thanks to God, that His Majesty has had for a long time."[24] By the end of the year, the king's failing health was common knowledge. From

---

[21] 4 June 1632; 4 June 1633; 3 January 1643. See M. Bloch's study, *Les rois thaumaturges* for the renewed seventeenth century interest in these practices: "Elle forme un des articles de cette foi monarchique qui va s'épanouir en France dans l'absolutisme louisquatorzien" (p. 344).

[22] 20 August 1638.   [23] 14 May 1639.   [24] 16 August 1642.

21 February 1643 on, Renaudot concluded each dispatch from St. Germain with a comment on the king's condition, usually a noncommittal "the King is here in good health, thanks to God." In the *Extraordinaire* "l'Assemblée faite à Saint Germain . . . le 20 Avril 1643: pour entendre la Déclaration de Sa Majesté, sur le gouvernement de ses Estats," Renaudot reported that Louis XIII "carries his concern even to the future, to establish an assured repose and a stability which can never be shaken."[25] Nowhere was his condition mentioned. In the *Gazette* of 25 April, a Paris-dated dispatch reported that constant prayers were being offered throughout the realm, and from St. Germain Renaudot reported that "every day we have new reason to believe that God wishes to have pity on this Kingdom, because His Majesty is much better than he has been before, thanks to God." Five days later, Renaudot devoted an entire 8-page *Relation* to the king's health.[26] The king continued to get worse, and on 9 May Renaudot wrote that "no good news being as important to us as the perfect health of the King, all good Frenchmen and lovers of the peace and goodness of Christianity are obligated to continue their good hopes and prayers to God, as are incessantly offered in all churches of this city, for the complete convalescence of His Majesty." Louis died on 14 May. Renaudot reported the sad news in the regular *Gazette* of 16 May. Along with it apeared an 8-page *Extraordinaire* entitled "La France en Deuil."

Renaudot's admiration for Richelieu was complete and unabashed, and as was true of all of Richelieu's creatures, Renaudot received total and unflinching support from the man to whom he gave his dedicated service.[27] He portrayed the Cardinal within a framework hallowed by tradition, as simply an

[25] 22 April 1643.

[26] "Relation de ce qui s'est passé jusques à present de plus mémorable en la maladie du Roy."

[27] Delavaud, *Quelques collaborateurs*, pp. 20-21; O. Ranum, *Councillors of Louis XIII*, pp. 7-9.

extension of his royal master. From Louis XIII Richelieu received his political power, and the metaphor even extended to
his physical strength: "True it is that the perfect health in
which he left the King is the best medicine he can receive for
his own health."[28] The king visited the ailing Cardinal at
Tarasçon in 1642, when he himself was taking the waters
nearby. "Through the honor and contentment received by His
Eminence his health, which is still improving, has been so
strengthened that he is preparing to take the road to follow
His Majesty."[29]

Renaudot portrayed Richelieu as a specially endowed human
being. The report of Richelieu's 18 January 1634 appearance at
Parlement demonstrates this. Richelieu had gone to promote
the rapid acceptance of Louis XIII's declaration against the
marriage of Monsieur to Marguerite of Lorraine, and the resulting speech was a panegyric to Richelieu's administration.
After describing the attendance, the entrance of the various
officers and notables, Renaudot described the extraordinary
effect Richelieu made: "then the Cardinal Duke . . . took the
occasion to praise the King, dwelling on his glorious actions
in the past and his good intentions for the future. The more
there was to say on this subject, the more difficult it was to
treat: but His Eminence's unequaled eloquence, and the perfect knowledge he had of this material made the discourse so
easy for him, that he spoke for nearly an hour. During which
time one had never seen such attention, with the eyes of the
entire assembly steadily fixed upon him, their ears set upon
every word, and their bodies immobile, these were certain
signs: as their unanimous applause was so far from any suspicion of flattery, it was their state of rapture which made him
so able to gain the hearts of the entire audience."[30] Contrary to

[28] 23 July 1632.   [29] 5 July 1642.
[30] 21 January 1634. Renaudot did not publish an extract or tran-
scription of this address in either the regular *Gazette* or in an *extraor-*

numerous critics of Renaudot's servility, his editorship was hardly a 23-year-long panegyric to Richelieu. Richelieu appeared when the news demanded it, and never otherwise. During the years 1636-1639, for example, the Cardinal is mentioned only a handful of times. Richelieu in the *Gazette* was the same as Richelieu at court, his personality always present, but seldom visible. He styled himself as an extension of the king, and nothing more.

Other court figures were treated likewise, as persons secondary to the king himself. Anne of Austria is a perfect example. The relations between the king and his wife were not the warmest, to say the least, and some have even alleged that Louis XIII used *Gazette* articles to embarrass his wife.[31] In any case, until the death of her husband she appeared very infrequently in the *Gazette*. Her religious predilections were mentioned, as one would expect of any queen, but there was nothing extraordinary about this. After Louis XIII's death, however, reports of her activities fill the *Gazette*. Each weekly edition recounted her daily devotions, her constant trips to Val de Grâce, her interest in Protestant, Muslim, and Jewish conversions to Catholicism. Until 1643 she appeared in the *Gazette* as the crown treated her in life, the wife of Louis XIII rather than the Queen of France.

If Renaudot was the father of the *Gazette*, Marie de Medici perhaps deserved credit as its unwilling midwife. Her 1630-1631 intrigues inspired the royal publicity and propaganda of which the *Gazette* was part. The *Gazette* began its life long after the Queen Mother had left Paris. No matter: for the next 4 years almost weekly dispatches report the ballets, intrigues, banquets, bleedings, and purgings of her court at Brussels, with the same thoroughness as the dispatches emanating from the

---

dinaire. It was published elsewhere, however, and later was treated at length in the *Mercure français* in 1637, on page 4.

[31] É. Fournier, *Les écrivains sur le trône* (Paris: 1865), pp. 7-8.

court at St. Germain or at Paris. Renaudot conscientiously reported the confusion of the meeting of the Estates at Brussels which coincided with her arrival. The meaning was clear: confusion was a part of the Queen Mother's life, in direct contrast to the unity and repose of France reported weekly in the same pages. In spite of her political sins and social indiscretions, Marie de Medici was still mother of the king of France. The *Gazette* of 18 June 1633 reported that Louis XIII sent Riolan and Pietre, "famous physicians of this city of Paris," to Brussels to attend Marie. In spite of all, the relations of mother and son transcended politics. On 19 July 1642, Renaudot published her obituary: "The third of this month, in the afternoon, at Cologne, died the Queen Mother, member of the most-illustrious house of Medici, which in the last century produced eight cardinals and four popes: She was the daughter of Francis of Medici the Grand Duke of Tuscany, and of Jeanne of Austria, born Queen of Hungary and Bohemia, niece, daughter, sister, and aunt of four Emperors: She was the widow of Henry the Great, and mother of the kings and queens who possess the most important crowns of Europe. The sorrow of her death to this court is increased by her absence, caused by following the advice of a few plotting spirits in whom she had too much confidence." The article epitomizes the *Gazette*'s generous and traditional treatment of dissidents within the royal family, never personally culpable, but rather the unfortunate, unwilling victims of bad counsel.

Gaston d'Orleans, Louis XIII's precipitous brother, received similar treatment. Monsieur's half-baked schemes of opposition, his reconciliations and oaths to the king fill Renaudot's weekly publications, but never was his personal ambition or character called into question. Several articles regarding Monsieur were written by Richelieu or Louis XIII himself, and are written in a spirit of magnanimity and royal forgiveness.[32]

[32] These include the *Extraordinaire* of 12 October 1634, concerning Gaston's return to obedience, and that of 26 October 1634, "l'Entreveue

The *Gazette* reflected the major activities of the King of France, waging war and seeking peace. The Thirty Years' War and the English Civil War provided Renaudot with continuing military and diplomatic stories, but no single period so tested the *Gazette* as did the months following the French declaration of war against the Hapsburgs on 19 May 1635. Ever since its founding, the *Gazette* had helped explain royal policy. It would now have a new task: to help mobilize the country for war. The year of Corbie was for Renaudot, as it was for Richelieu and the crown, a year of trial and challenge.

Except for regular news of Rohan's efforts in controlling the Valtelline, Renaudot had few successes to report to his readers during the first year of active French involvement in the Thirty Years' War. Domestic news was no better, and Renaudot made no mention of the serious tax riots in Perigord, Anjou, or Bordeaux, nor of parlementary reaction to the intendants. Although occasional *extraordinaires* would broadcast royal invocation of the *ban* and *arrière-ban*,[33] a *Gazette* reader who had no other source of information might think that all was well.

By the summer of 1636, however, a perspicacious reader would think otherwise. Renaudot had occasionally published transcripts of important speeches and decrees, but now he devoted entire *extraordinaires* to ordinances regulating currency and prices, enlistment, and invocation of the *ban* and *arrière-ban*. In mid-March he published excerpts of 42 of these ordinances, and on 11 August he published another 21. Renaudot could no longer hide the pressure under which he was working, and one notes a surfeit of mechanical errors and corrections in the *Gazette*. Blocked roads and troop movements, causing delays and errors, aggravated the situation.[34]

---

du Roy et de Monseigneur son Frere." See Richelieu, *Lettres* (Avenel, ed.), iv, 622, 624n.

[33] 30 July 1635.   [34] 16 July 1635.

On 15 August 1636 Spanish troops captured the fortress of Corbie, near Amiens. Imperial forces were now only 80 miles from Paris, and scouting parties had been reported in the environs of the capital itself. After 40 years of peace, the walls of the city were in disrepair. Thousands of refugees fleeing the enemy threatened a city hard-pressed to feed its own. Panic and rumor gripped the city. Yet the *Gazette* reader would know nothing of this. All that one reads is the *Extraordinaire* of 16 August publishing ordinances against soldiers and gentlemen away from their units without leave, and ordering each workshop in France to supply able-bodied men to the army.

The first direct indication of a military crisis appeared in the *Gazette* of 6 September, when Renaudot noted extraordinary movement of French troops in the Paris area. On 14 October, two months after the fall of Corbie, Renaudot finally published "Particularitez du blocus de Corbie," written by Louis XIII himself.[35] Subsequent *Gazettes* carried regular stories of Corbie, its fortifications, lists of field commanders, the description of troops deployed. Finally on 17 November 1636 Renaudot published a 4-page *Extraordinaire* entitled "Le reprise de Corbie." The extra appeared only 3 days after the French victory, in sharp contrast to the 2-month silence following Corbie's capture by the Spanish. Success was attributed to the personal presence of Louis XIII and of Richelieu, who accepted the capitulation of the fortress in Louis' name.

By the winter of 1636-1637, the immediate military threat to the monarchy had passed. Renaudot's efforts in controlling the news and helping to mobilize the country were as essential to victory as those of any field commander, diplomat, or bureaucrat. In no small measure, the realm's ability to weather the year of Corbie must partially be attributed to Renaudot's *Gazette*. Richelieu well knew this, and each year the monarchy would make even greater demands upon Renaudot. The *Gazette* had become an integral organ of a government at war.

---

[35] See p. 147.

The age produced a surfeit of military giants—Johan von Werth, Schomberg, Gustavus Adolphus, de Gassion, Tilly, Weimar, Cromwell, the great Condé, de la Force, Cardinal Vallette, as well as Louis XIII and Charles of Lorraine—and Renaudot's readers avidly followed their careers, be they French or foreign. Throughout the campaigns of 1637 and 1638, for example, Renaudot regularly reported the activities of the Bavarian general Johan von Werth. Finally he was defeated and captured by French allies. Renaudot published an *Extraordinaire* the day he received the news: "I cannot keep the good news from you, even stripped of many details which will in time come to you."[36] Three months later, Werth and Enkenfort, another captured general, were taken to Paris. Richelieu met them, and invited them to dine with him. "After dinner and two hours of conversation, the generals Werth and Enkenfort returned in His Eminence's carriage to the forest of Vincennes, where they enjoy as many of the reasonable liberties that important military commanders, in the condition where the fortunes of war have cast them, could desire."[37] Werth was released in January 1641, in exchange for the Swedish Marshal Horn. Before his departure, however, Renaudot reported that Werth first took leave of Richelieu and Louis XIII.[38] To the readers of the *Gazette*, he was an international hero whose exploits and character transcended national allegiances.

When French or allied armies were victorious, Renaudot glowed that "God's works are marvelous everywhere, but he reserves his miracle for France."[39] But when it was impossible to hold back news of French defeat, the reporting demanded more delicate treatment. "It is impossible to give bad news agreeably; but since we profess to report historically what happens—in telling the good, it is not permitted to keep silent on the bad."[40] No matter how monumental the defeat, it was

[36] 11 March 1638.   [37] 19 June 1638.   [38] 26 January 1641.
[39] 15 May 1640.   [40] 13 July 1641.

134

still a defeat, and therefore never worth an *extraordinaire*. After one particularly severe French defeat, Renaudot reported that "the town of Aire has finally returned to Spanish control. They took their advantage in this point, and we thank God that he has also given us ours. The King considered either to save Aire or to destroy the enemy army, ruin their country, and seize some rather important emplacements. By their own confession the enemy lost 10,000 men who died from the illness, misery, and famine within their own fortifications. Fifty thousand peasants are also dead. Lens, La Bassée, and Bapaume were taken during the siege of Aire, and remain in the King's hands. Only the law of God prohibiting the envy of one's neighbor, the French conduct themselves so sincerely that the most zealous among them hope that the Spanish will always enjoy such costly victories."[41] Foreign victories were by definition Pyrrhic victories.

Armies of the first half of the seventeenth century were little more than hordes of organized barbarians, but if one based his opinions only upon Renaudot's *Gazette*, the French and their allies never committed a single atrocity. They might destroy the countryside (as they did after the defeat at Aire), but this was militarily excusable. Enemies, on the other hand, were devoid of all Christian virtue. Their atrocities fill the *Gazette*, and could even inspire an entire *Extraordinaire*.[42] Moreover, "as rare as it is for the enemies of France to surpass her in valor, they must confess that their ruses and plots are much more frequent than hers. And nevertheless, it often happens that these hidden plans (whose strength resides only in their secrecy) being divulged before having produced their effect, turn only to shame the plotters."[43] Renaudot was willing to grant that evil was evil, but only reluctantly. Louis XIII led

[41] 14 December 1641.
[42] The 22 April 1638 *Extraordinaire* was devoted in large part to the atrocities committed by Imperial forces near Aix-la-Chapelle.
[43] 4 March 1639.

135

France to war with a heavy moral responsibility, and "the greatest difference between a just prince and the iniquitous usurper is that the latter wages war to sustain himself while the former does so only to have peace."[44] This self-righteousness pervades every military article in the *Gazette*.

Diplomatic news was printed in article form, or as extracted or complete reproductions of official declarations, treaties, and speeches. These documents seldom appeared in the weekly *Gazette* and *Nouvelles ordinaires*, but instead formed the major content of *Extraordinaires* and *Relations*. These included, as one would expect, decisions directly involving France: for example, the "Déclaration du Roy, sur l'ouverture de la guerre contre le Roy d'Espagne" of 18 June 1635.[45] In 1648-1649 there were publications of the conferences at Münster and Osnabrück. Such publications were just as prominent in French domestic affairs. Harangues and complete discourses of notables were reprinted constantly,[46] as were the capitulations of provinces and towns reentering the service of the king.

But these items were not limited to French affairs alone. The English Civil War, for example, gave Renaudot innumerable chances to publish agreements, treaties, and speeches of the various factions. In this case, Renaudot seems to have been motivated as much by political as by journalistic considerations, for by publishing these items verbatim, he avoided the responsibility of analyzing their significance, leaving that up to the reader.

Just as significant in the *Gazette* as it was in early modern diplomacy is the great attention placed upon triumphal entrances, diplomatic visits, gifts, and appointments. The career of the Duke of Créqui, the French ambassador to Rome, is an

[44] 4 April 1641.
[45] This was published, without date, on either 20 or 21 June 1635.
[46] For example, the 20 November 1643 *Extraordinaire* recording Schomberg's address to the Estates of Languedoc.

136

excellent example. In the 4-page *Gazette* of 23 July 1633, his triumphal entry occupied 2 pages. And if this account left any doubt of French magnificence, Renaudot's conclusion dispelled it: "Also, this Ambassador, returning the salute to all who saluted him, showed the Roman people what difference there is between the pride of some other nations and French courtesy."[47] For the next 4 weeks, Créqui did nothing but receive the lay and religious notables of Rome, and, in turn, repay their visits. These visits were usually reserved for the *Extraordinaires*. Occasionally, Renaudot included not one, but two such events in the same issue: for example, an *Extraordinaire* of 7 December 1637 detailed the arrival of the Moroccan ambassador in London and the French ambassador at The Hague. Renaudot's first large-scale article on English affairs consisted of a 2-page account of Charles I's journey to Edinburgh for coronation as King of Scotland. The list included over 2,000 in the royal party, plus another 5,000 notables and retainers who accompanied the king at their own expense![48]

The *Gazette* reported musical, literary, and artistic news. It is obvious that these activities were seldom possible without the high patronage and approval, either tacit or open, of *gens d'importance*, but Renaudot treated them as reflections of royal, French grandeur rather than as cultural and artistic achievements by themselves. The very first article date-lined from Paris concerned a literary topic: "The beautiful edition of the great nine volume, eight language Bible is continuing here, and will be finished in a year. We invite all the nations to participate, with greater motives than the Sybarites had a year before inviting guests to their feasts."[49] It was a French event first, a literary event second. Renaudot likewise reported the completion of an 8-volume, Greek and Latin edition of Hippocrates and Galen which Richelieu sponsored: the ac-

[47] 23 July 1633.   [48] *Relation . . . de mai 1633.*
[49] 4 July 1631.

137

cent in the story is not upon the edition, but rather the ceremonial presentation of the first copies to Louis XIII and to Richelieu.[50]

Artists and scientists take significance only through their propinquity to persons of power. Rubens was mentioned as a famous painter, but his importance resulted from representing the Queen Mother in England.[51] Galileo's obituary tells us less about Galileo than about the Grand Duke of Tuscany: "Last night [8 January 1641] in his eightieth year, Sieur Galileo Galilei, the most excellent mathematician and one of the greatest philosophers of this century, died not far from this town. A magnificent burial in the Church of the Cordeliers is being prepared for him: the Grand Duke is thereby imitating the affection with which his ancestors have always honored the memory of illustrious persons, having a tomb with his marble effigy built opposite that recently erected to Michel Ange Bonnarota, likewise incomparable in the arts of painting, sculpture, and architecture."[52] Renaudot reported the commission of Biard's equestrian statue of Louis XIII for the Place Royale (today's Place de Vosges). The work was less important than the fact that Richelieu was pleased with it.[53] The statue was dedicated when the king reached the age of 39. Renaudot detailed the panoply of the dedication ceremony, but said almost nothing of the statue itself.[54] Likewise Renaudot's dispatch marking the arrival of Nicolas Poussin in Paris: "The seventeenth of this month sieur de Poussin, excellent painter whom the King summoned from Rome, arrived in this city, and was received by sieur de Noyers, Secretary of State and Superintendent of Buildings for His Majesty, and later by His Eminence, with embraces proportionate to the grandeur of merit and reputation he has acquired in his art."[55] On 6 August

---

[50] 8 January 1639. [51] 5 July 1631.
[52] 1 February 1642. The dispatch originated in Florence.
[53] 5 August 1634. [54] 1 October 1639.
[55] 22 December 1640.

1633 Renaudot's readers learned that the Pope had rewarded "Cavaillier Bernino" 8,000 *écus* for designing and executing the altar of the Holy Apostles at St. Peter's. Except for this dispatch, specifically named artists and works of art did not figure in foreign dispatches.

Renaudot had a special interest in ballet and drama, and the popularity of these art forms, especially ballet, at the French court gave him much opportunity to indulge his fancy. No activity was better designed to show off the grandiose and the grandiloquent. Ballet was dance and ceremony, a homage to the religious and the antique at the same time, a deadly serious hybrid "neither an artistic production nor diversion pure and simple."[56] If the subjects seem frivolous or the performance fantastical, this does not mean that the seventeenth century took the ballet lightly. Its qualities were those upon which the century and the men of the century depended: grace, poise, social presence, musical rhythm, and a sense of the dramatic.[57]

Renaudot often devoted entire *extraordinaires* to these ballets. One, for example, entitled "Le Ballet du Roy, où la vieille Cour et les habitans des Reves de la Seine viennent danser pour les triomphes de sa Majesté," had as its subject "a representation of the vicissitudes of human things." The performance and Renaudot's description of it satisfied the same end: to display the ability of the king. Louis XIII himself danced 3 different times, in different costumes, and according to different styles of dance, "but always with the delight inseparable from all the exercises to which His Majesty applies himself."[58]

These ballets were often topical, and *Gazette* descriptions are valuable records of noble interests and pastimes. In a *Re-*

[56] F. Reyna, *Des origines du ballet* (Paris: 1955), p. 149.
[57] At least two sessions of Renaudot's academy were dedicated to "De la danse" (19 February 1635), and "De la spectacle" (23 July 1635).
[58] 21 February 1635.

lation of 9 March 1634, Renaudot described at length a ballet presented before the king and queen at London. After a procession of physicians, lawyers, etc., there appeared "a windmill against which Dom Guichotte [sic] courageously battled, assisted by his squire Sancho, who carried behind him his lance and arms." A description of a *Ballet des Improvistes*, "invented, produced, and danced in six days" before Louis XIII indicates that Renaudot's activities were well known at the court. The action went something like this: two men set up a used clothing shop, where a number of Frenchmen enter, change their garments, and then dance for the assembly— 2 valets, 4 volunteers "who have resolved to forget the burdens of war," 4 courtesans, 3 students, "4 good townsmen, who learned the place of the assembly through the Bureau d'Adresse," 2 servants, 3 violinists, 2 countrymen, and 2 countrywomen, etc.[59] No wonder Renaudot took such pains to reproduce the entire ballet for his readers.

The birth of the future Louis XIV prompted many celebrations and ballets, and Renaudot devoted 12 pages to describe "Le Ballet de la félicité sur le sujet de l'heureuse naissance de Monseigneur le Dauphin: dansé à l'Hostel de Richelieu, et à la Maison de Ville."[60] Such news increased as Louis XIV reached maturity. If such pastimes were a duty for Louis XIII, they were a delight for his son.

Religious news, complained Renaudot, demanded the most delicate treatment, since it was susceptible to hate, rancor, and anger at the same time.[61] But religion was too important to be ignored by the *Gazette*. Much of the religious news reported the devotions and ceremonies performed by the royal family. But along with this, Renaudot published religious stories, not only from elsewhere in France but from throughout the world.

[59] 19 February 1636. [60] 12 March 1639.
[61] 12 February 1642.

A large number of stories concerned converts to Catholicism. They may be of notable Frenchmen, as Renaudot reported in the *Gazette* of 11 December 1638. "Last week, Sieur Talmand, Counselor in the Parlement of this city [Paris], brought up in the so-called reformed religion, accepted the Catholic faith, between the hands of the Bishop of St. Flour." Even juicier stories were those of non-Christians who accepted the faith: "the papal nuncio baptized a Rabbi here [at Vienna], well-respected among the Jews; the King of Hungary was the godfather."[62] And again, another dispatch reported the baptism of 3 Turks at Paris.[63] These stories would increase steadily after 1643, as Anne of Austria became more prominent in the *Gazette.*

Religious news was always well received, always topical, and always available whenever Renaudot needed copy. He could devote an 8-page *Extraordinaire* to "Le cruel martyre d'un Evesque, de deux Pères Capucins François, et d'autres religieux dans l'Ethiopie."[64] There was always a miracle "straying from the ordinary course of nature" to report.[65] At one point Renaudot published the miraculous cure of a 35-year-old man by the Holy Virgin. He admitted his reluctance to publish the story, but justified it by publishing testimony from a physician, a surgeon, and the Bishop of Maillezais authenticating the miracle.[66] These statements took Renaudot off the hook, his reporting no longer subject to doubt but, through these certifications, "truth."

Renaudot published news of natural calamities if the event directly affected someone at court, or it carried a greater political or social portent. A fire in a stable, for example, was hardly newsworthy. It became news, however, if the stable belonged to Richelieu.[67] A flood was reported for several

---

[62] 5 February 1639.
[63] 25 October 1642.
[64] 23 January 1642.
[65] 29 December 1634.
[66] 21 August 1642.
[67] 14 November 1631.

weeks, because the flood struck the court while in passage near Narbonne.[68] It was the presence of the ladies-in-waiting, and not the torrential rains, that made the event noteworthy.

Unnatural events were worthy of attention, but their significance was left to the discerning reader. Renaudot's German correspondents in particular took great stock in strange happenings, and Renaudot published them with a sense of awe and wonder. The reports of the various German campaigns were full of bleeding trees, comets, and other strange phenomena.[69] An entire *Extraordinaire* concerned "Les prodiges arrives en plusieurs lieux arrivé cette année, contenus en une lettre de Francfort, en datte du 10 Avril 1642."[70] But Renaudot did not use these stories only as fillers when hardcore news was unavailable. This *was* hardcore news. Without exception, these stories concluded with the correspondent's uneasy suspicion that the event demanded varying interpretations from the reader. One such account, from Leipzig, concluded that "we have not yet seen the last of our evils."[71] Another dispatch described a fireworks display at Milan celebrating the death of Wallenstein. A rocket went awry and set a church tower on fire. The tower fell on the crowd, killing 12 and injuring another 100, "letting it up to each one to conjecture," ominously intoned the conclusion, "the consequences of that sign."[72]

It is difficult to ascertain if Renaudot's medical background had any influence upon his treatment of medical stories in the *Gazette*. There was the regular round of royal bleedings and royal purgings, and complete *extraordinaires* devoted to Louis XIII's fatal illness.[73] Medical stories per se, however, were much less frequent than one would expect of an editor who

---

[68] 29 October, 5 November 1632.   [69] 22, 29 August 1631.
[70] 30 April 1642.   [71] 5 July 1643.
[72] 22 April 1634.
[73] "Relation de ce qui s'est passé jusques à present de plus mémorable en la maladie du Roy," 30 April 1643; "La France en Deuil" included a long account of his illness from 30 April through his death (published 16 May 1643).

was first of all a physician. Medical stories were treated as were other interesting wonderments; as today, it was the strange disease that made the headlines. He devoted part of an *extraordinaire*, for example, to "La merveille escrit d'Aragon d'un espine croissante en l'estomach d'un berger."[74] Perhaps the cure was strange and "marvelous," as Renaudot himself admitted, but he justified its publication by reproducing the testimony of several recognized "experts" who attested to its truth. Another time, he recounted the birth of Siamese twins in Provence. This was not hardcore news, but nonetheless worthy of the reader's attention. Renaudot explained that he wished "to lighten your spirits and bring them back from the anxiety of combat to the repose which one finds in contemplating the wonders of nature."[75]

News of weather was steady and regular, if not frequent. As with other topics, they usually had a larger significance, but sometimes the sheer magnitude of the event justified the report. Certain stories were continuing. During the spring of 1638, there were weekly dispatches from Naples, concerning severe earthquakes. Likewise there were descriptions of the flooding of the Danube, "which has never happened in the memory of man."[76] Often these meteorological calamities had severe economic effects. For example, earthquakes at St. Gallin in 1638 were as devastating as those of 3 years earlier, frightening all who remember "that the barrenness [was so horrible] that many died of hunger."[77]

Renaudot's treatment of economic news was highly *engagé*. The Dutch challenge to French economic interests was a major preoccupation of the post-Louis XIII era, but already in Renaudot's *Gazette* were constant reminders of the economic superiority of these traders to the north. From the *Gazette* of 11 August 1640: "Eight ships from Fernambouc arrived this week at Texel, two from Guinea charged with 1,900 gold

---

[74] 20 January 1638.
[75] 4 August 1639.
[76] 9 January 1638.
[77] 20 February 1638.

marks, quantities of ivory, 3,400 cases of sugar and great quantity of other costly goods. Seven ships have also arrived from the Straits with rich cargoes, and 50 from the Baltic Sea, which should soon be followed by 200 more from the rest of the North. No one can remember ever having seen so many riches enter this country at one time; since the cargo of these vessels is valued at 20 millions." The challenge to France was clear, and reports from Holland remained steady and pointed. Stories of trade and commerce increased through 1639 and the early 1640's, reflecting Richelieu's interest in developing foreign and internal trade.[78] Renaudot celebrated the first barges to use the new canal from the Loire to the Seine between Briare and Montargis: "Paris will receive a great influx of all sorts of commodities."[79] The *Gazette* reported the formation of New World trading companies and one of the longest economic articles was a glowing account of the wonders of "le Royaume de Lacadie." "Those who try to support themselves, or spend their lives embroiled in the courts over an *arpent* of land, will find it cheaper there; and if those in this Kingdom who are hounded by misery and need would open their eyes to this expedient they could, by the change of climate, break the course of their bad fortune. This enterprise is to be valued above all by relieving us, we hope, of all the able-bodied beggars in France."[80] Renaudot's *Gazette* played an essential role in publicizing Richelieu's economic policies. Throughout its his-

[78] The *Extraordinaire* of 26 November 1639 included a transcript of the declaration of 19 November 1639: "Restablissement du Commerce par mer et par terre, en tous pais estrangers, de toutes sortes de denrées et marchandises."

[79] 30 March 1638.

[80] 16 January 1632. Those who wished to take advantage of these attractions could direct themselves to the Bureau d'Adresse for more information on the subject (20 December 1634). This was the first time in 3 years of publication that Renaudot mentioned his other activities. The *Gazette* was hardly, as W. H. Lewis had alleged, founded to provide an advertising outlet for Renaudot's other activities (*The Splendid Century* [New York: 1953], p. 183).

tory the pages of the *Gazette* were full of economic laws and regulations. Renaudot needed little encouragement to broadcast these items: as we have indicated elsewhere,[81] he was personally committed to the revitalization of France's economy.

Richelieu's influence in the *Gazette* ranged from making theoretical suggestions, to assigning specific articles to specific individuals, to writing and editing complete dispatches himself. Much of this direction is difficult to ascertain. Richelieu's seventeenth century critics considered Renaudot the Cardinal's spineless puppet, the *Gazette* "corrected and seasoned according to His Eminence's taste."[82] Richelieu's nineteenth century admirers were equally misled. They so accentuated his talents that, basing one's opinion solely upon their analysis, the Cardinal conceived, founded, wrote, printed, and distributed the weekly *Gazettes* singlehandedly.[83] Specific examples of Richelieu's control are difficult to pinpoint and, as a result, his influence is easily misinterpreted or exaggerated. There are enough isolated examples, however, to suggest the range of the Cardinal's influence upon Renaudot.

Aubéry, one of Richelieu's "approved" historians, wrote that "he sets everything working to arrive finally at the end he wishes, and does not believe that anything can be neglected in the conduct of the State, where the least spark often causes the greatest conflagration. That is why the Cardinal himself

---

[81] See pp. 89ff.

[82] *Catolicon françois* (S.l.: 1636), p. 1. This long political tract is apocryphally attributed to Renaudot, but the style is not his. Moreover, the servility is so overstated that it serves to ridicule Renaudot. At one point he is portrayed waiting to be admitted to the Cardinal's presence, saying "à la porte du cabinet des paternostres de singe" (p. 119).

[83] In a 266-page treatment of Richelieu's political writers, L. Delavaud (*Quelques collaborateurs de Richelieu*) devoted half a paragraph to Renaudot, consisting of no more than an often-reproduced quote from the *Catolicon françois* that Richelieu once called Renaudot "le plus fidel amy et le plus capable de tous mes Conseillers" (p. 88). And when Gabriel Hanotaux discussed Richelieu's entourage of writers and pamphleteers, Renaudot was not mentioned (*Histoire du Cardinal Richelieu*, IV).

does not disdain from sending *mémoires* or private dispatches to Renaudot for insertion in the *Gazette*, and is most demanding of others who supply him with public news, so that in this way he can stop the course and effect of rumors, themselves resembling the contagious air that one breathes, normally corrupting the most sincere and well-intentioned minds through their false impressions."[84] If he glossed over Richelieu's motivation in glorifying the Cardinal, Aubéry at least did note the direction, both personal and intermediate, which Renaudot maintained over the *Gazette*.

Richelieu, as has been suggested, already had had personal experience in writing and publishing *relations*.[85] The same attention to detail Richelieu demanded in his other writings he demanded of those intended for the *Gazette*. His orders were followed in toto, down to the last comma. Louis XIII's letter (4 August 1642) to his ambassadors and provincial officers regarding the arrest of the Duke of Bouillon and Cinq Mars was to be published in the *Gazette*. Richelieu wrote to Sublet de Noyers and Chavigny, both of whom he often employed as

[84] Aubéry, *Histoire du Cardinal-Duc de Richelieu* (Paris: 1660), II, 383. Also see the Preface to H. Griffet, *Histoire du règne de Louis XIII* (Paris: 1758), p. xi, to which Renaudot's biographers often referred for similar information. In 1643, Renaudot publicly admitted the control that the crown and its advisers wielded over him. To those who accused him of servility, he replied: "Chacun sçait que le Roy defunct ne lisoit pas seulement mes *Gazettes*, et n'y souffroit pas le moindre défaut, mais qu'il m'envoyoit presque ordinairement des mémoires pour y employer. Ce que d'ailleurs son Conseil me dictoit, ce que sa Majesté approuvoit, et où elle ne trouvoit rien à rédire, me doit-il estre aujourd'huy réproché après une suite de tant d'années? . . . Ce qui s'appelloit servir le Roy, comme d'y resister, crime de leze Majesté" (*Requeste présentée à la Reyne*, pp. 5-6).

[85] J. LeLong, *Bibliothèque historique de la France* (Paris: 1719), attributed at least two *relations* to Richelieu: *Relation de ce qui s'est passé depuis le vi Febvrier, jusques à present; Relation de ce qui s'est passé pendant le sejour du Roy à Dijon, et depuis qu'il en est party, jusqu'au 8 Avril 1631.* These consist of laws, letters, etc., joined together with commentary, quite similar to the *relations* and *extraordinaires* which Renaudot would continue to publish.

146

intermediaries to the *Gazette*, that "it is most important to give Sr. Renaudot the letter you have sent to the provincial officers and ambassadors. I beseech you to give it to him so well written and so well punctuated that he will print everything necessary, without a single error."[86]

Richelieu often received these news items first, but correspondents were sometimes instructed to send their dispatches directly to Renaudot. Renaudot valued the direct reports of French captains in the field. The *relations* and *extraordinaires* depended upon these first-person accounts since Renaudot "never found a better expedient . . . than to let others speak."[87] Renaudot believed that the testimony of the officer directly involved in the event was less suspect than that of a private person. Their obvious partiality was never at issue. Much more significant to Renaudot was that the military or state figure was always more authoritatively respected, by virtue of his public role, than the uninvolved impartial bystander: "Nothing is better able to rectify false rumors than the letters of commanders who have done the exploits in question."[88]

These men provided Renaudot with constant problems. Most of them seemed to consider writing dispatches for Renaudot a time-consuming nuisance. He was often forced to appeal to them publicly to send news to him.[89] Evidently such pressure was not enough, for Renaudot publicly brought the matter to the king: "Sire, Your Majesty too much loves the truth not to protect that which I try to broadcast all the days to your peoples. . . . Many years ago I addressed myself, in public and private letters, to the commanders and officers of your armies, so as to be informed by them of what happened and to keep the public informed, according to the charge which it pleased Your Majesty to confer upon me: but so few among them, even until now, have cared to satisfy my wish, that I am often forced either to keep silent many things which merit

[86] Tarasçon, 13 August 1642. Richelieu, *Lettres*, VII, 91-92.
[87] 3 January 1642.   [88] 15 July 1639.   [89] 21 October 1636.

147

being known, or to report them on the testimony of private individuals, usually partial and selfish, who appear more suspect than the public persons in charge and, consequently, informed." What was even worse, continued Renaudot, was that these same commanders and officers found it easier "to condemn my writings after they have been given to the public. ... I do not demand a polished discourse from them, but only the simple dates and names of persons, places, and actions."[90] Renaudot complained to his readers of constant difficulty in securing fresh, accurate news. After the death of Richelieu, his informants became even less reliable. In 1651, they were indignant that Renaudot, in an economy move, had stopped sending them their free copies of the *Gazette*.[91]

In particularly delicate situations, news stories automatically went through Richelieu's hands before reaching Renaudot's printshop. These editorial considerations account for the varying delays between events and their final appearance in the pages of the *Gazette*. For example, Richelieu wrote to Chavigny on 15 September 1638, regarding the heroic death of de Roches in a naval battle near Genoa: "I ask you to inform Renaudot to print nothing of this action until I send him who among the captains of our galleys have been wounded."[92] Two days later, he wrote again: "I am sending you the relation of the battle of our galleys, as it must be given to Renaudot; I have had corrected certain things which wounded all the captains in general, without excepting those who came out better."[93] Finally, on 20 September, it appeared in the *Gazette* as "Le furieux

[90] *Requeste présentée au Roy . . . sur le sujet des Gazettes*, pp. 657-60. The phraseology of this excerpt suggests Renaudot's preference for testimony from involved, public figures rather than the uninvolved, private bystander.

[91] "l'Apologie du Bureau d'Adresse contre ceux qui se plaignent de ce qu'il ne leur peut plus donner gratuitment les Gazettes," 9 June 1651.

[92] St. Quentin, 15 September 1638. Richelieu, *Lettres*, vi, 175-76.

[93] St. Quentin, 17 September 1638. Richelieu, *Lettres*, vi, 176-81.

combat des Galères de France et d'Espagne, arrivé près de Genes: où il est demeure cinq à six mil hommes." Even the king, perhaps especially the king, was subject to the same treatment from Richelieu. There exists at the Bibliothèque Nationale a notebook of articles and *relations* which Louis XIII wrote on the battlefield, and which subsequently appeared in the *Gazette*.[94] One of these, for example, was an account of the return of Monsieur to the royal fold. The *Gazette* accounts of 14 and 21 October 1634 reprint in substantially the same form the original entries in Louis' notebook. There are important corrections, however, and only the Cardinal could have authorized or made the changes himself.

Renaudot could expect editorial changes from Richelieu right up to the last minute. In one case, the *Gazette* of 4 June 1633, half of the copies had already been printed and distributed when, early that morning, Richelieu sent Renaudot an article for insertion in that issue. Renaudot hastily deleted the original story, and published the new version in the still-to-be printed issues.[95] This particular incident would become important 10

[94] Several reports of the battle of Corbie came directly from the king. Several of these *extraordinaires* appear in the manuscript (B.N. mss. f.fr. 3840): "Particularitez du blocus de Corbie: ses forts, redoubts, et autres travaux" (14 October 1636); *Extraordinaire* of 18 October; the dispatch in the 25 October *Gazette* "du camp devant Corbie"; "Continuation du Journal de Corbie . . . depuis le 22 de ce mois" (29 October 1636), etc.

[95] The article sent by Richelieu which Renaudot published in the remaining issues is as follows: "Fontenbleu, 3 Juin: Le Sieur de Lafemas, Intendent de la Justice es provinces et armées de Chapagne, est arrivé depuis trois jours en ca lieu, et a fait amener avec luy plusieurs prisonniers d'État: entre lesquels est le sieur Dom Jouan de Médicis, lequel fut luy arresté à Troyes, venant de Bruxelles en habit desguisé, se faisant nommer Marquis de S. Ange. On tient qu'il estoit chargé de plusieurs papiers importans, et particulierement de plans de villes et places de ce Royaume, et de lettres tendantes à descrier le Roy et le gouvernement de son Estat, dont on ne sçait pas les particularitez. Mais ce qui se peut sçavoir, est que par l'une desdites lettres on supposoit que le Roy envoyoit à Rome pour trois choses, aussi malicieuses

years later, when Renaudot was in the midst of his battle with the medical faculty. In another case of having to change articles in the middle of a press run, Renaudot publicly apologized to his readers. For example, in the 17 November 1640 *Gazette*, he wrote that "the office of Grand Panetier de France has not changed hands: the *mémoire* which was given to my correspondents and employed in some copies, in the last article of the most recent *Gazette*, having been discovered false, has been removed from all other impressions and *recueils* which are made throughout the year."

The Cardinal maintained control of the *Gazette* through a number of intermediaries. This has often been described as "an editorial committee, composed of men devoted to the monarchy."[96] The terminology suggests something typical of a large modern daily, but such formalized committee structures are inconsistent with what we know of royal administration under Louis XIII and Richelieu. Committees and councils were not formal "dress-up" affairs, and the term *conseil* in seventeenth century usage designated any group of minister-councilors working together on any state business. The nu-

---

qu'elles sont esloignées de tout apparence: à sçavoir: Pour repudier la Royne; Pour faire declarer Monsieur le Duc d'Orleans inhabile et incapable de succeder à la Couronne; Et pour avoir liberté de proteger les Lutheriens."

Ten years later the medical faculty cited this as an example of Renaudot's perfidy, of his attempt to make Louis XIII an enemy of God and a protector of Lutherans (see *Examen de la requeste présentée à la Reine par le Gazettier*, p. 22). Renaudot replied: "Ce qui s'appelloit servir le Roy, comme d'y resister, crime de lèze Majesté" (*Requeste presentée à la Reyne*, pp. 5-6).

[96] W. H. Evans, *l'Historien Mézeray et la conception de l'histoire en France au XVIIe siècle* (Paris: 1930), p. 62. Typical of many writers, Evans derived this information from Hatin and Gilles de la Tourette, both of whom describe the committee as a rigid, formal affair. L. André and E. Bourgeois, *Les sources de l'histoire de France: XVIIe siècle* (Paris: 1924), repeated the same information and, in turn, suggested that the committee was highly formalized.

merical composition of the various councils—*Conseil des Affaires, Conseil des Dépêches, Conseil Secret, Conseil de Cabinet,* or the inclusive term *Conseil d'en Haut* used regularly after 1643—was always fluid. Overlapping of functions was common and usual, and most members of Richelieu's team filled a variety of offices. While any number of men might work together in a common function on a single council, their power derived as individuals from the crown, and it was as individuals that they reported back to the king.[97] It is within this light that one must view the several individuals who acted as intermediaries between Richelieu and Renaudot.

Père Joseph, who had introduced Renaudot to Richelieu, helped supervise the *Gazette.* He had long been editor of the *Mercure françois,* which Renaudot would edit after Père Joseph's death in 1638, and was a keen propagandist. His correspondence with Capuchin missions abroad provided Renaudot's readers with news of Abyssinia, China, Japan, and India. Indeed, the variety and intensity of non-European sources declined noticeably after Père Joseph's death. Specific examples of his influence upon Renaudot, however, are difficult to find. When Richelieu was not in Paris, Leon de Bouthillier, le Comte de Chavigny, was entrusted with direction of the *Gazette.* Chavigny was Secretary of State, charged with foreign affairs. At least Chavigny's duties are specifically mentioned in Richelieu's correspondence:[98] the activities of other overseers of the *Gazette* are much more difficult to pinpoint. Pierre d'Hozier, Juge d'Armes de France and author of *l'Armorial général,* brought his Europeanwide communication network to Renaudot's benefit. According to d'Hozier's son, "his many correspondents informed him of everything that was

---

[97] See O. Ranum, *Councillors of Louis XIII,* esp. Chapter 1; and R. Mousnier, "Le Conseil du Roi de la mort de Henri IV au gouvernement de Louis XIV," *Études d'histoire moderne et contemporaine* (1947-1948), 29-67.

[98] B.N. mss. f.fr. 9354 (letter of 5 September 1638).

done, said, and written. [d'Hozier] communicated all of his news to Théophraste Renaudot, his friend; and it was by the aid which he furnished in this great work that the idea of the *Gazettes* was formed and followed with such success."[99] Other commonly mentioned overseers included the pamphleteer Mézeray, author of *l'Histoire de France*, and Abbé de Masle, Sieur de Roches, who was perhaps Richelieu's oldest, most-trusted personal attaché.[100]

The poets La Calprenède and Voiture, members of the Académie Française, were supposedly involved in the *Gazette*, as was Guillaume Bautru, Master of Ceremonies at the court. Bautru was known to his contemporaries as one of the few men permitted to joke in His Eminence's presence.[101] When Riche-

[99] L-P. d'Hozier, *Armorial général ou registres de la noblesse de France* (Paris: 1763-1768), III, 540.

[100] G. Gilles de la Tourette, *Théophraste Renaudot* (Paris: 1884), p. 204; M. Deloche, *La maison du Cardinal Richelieu* (Paris: 1912), p. 103. Renaudot served as physician to de Roches, but according to Guy Patin, not without problems: l'Abbé "se servoit autrefois du gazetier pour médecin, lequel en fut ignominieusement chassé pour lui avoir donné un purgatif trop violent . . . qui en augmenterent fort: au lieu du gazetier, il prit un de nos médecins, dont il s'est toujours servi depuis. Enfin, en ayant été heureusement assisté, avec le conseil de quelques une de nos anciens, il s'est résolu, avant que de mourir, de faire un coup d'un habile homme, et qui fera parler de lui, qui est donner à la Faculté de Médecine la somme de dix mille écus comptant pour la faire rétablir, sans nous demander ni nous obliger à chose aucune." (Patin to Spon, 28 March 1643.) When he died in 1662, he left the money instead to the Hôtel Dieu: "Il auroit bien pu nous faire davantage de bien, mais il se mécontenta de nous sur le refus que nous lui fimes de rompre nos statuts pour plusieurs particuliers qu'il nous recommandoit trop souvent, et cela n'alloit qu'à ruiner notre Faculté." (Patin to Falconet, 29 February 1662.)

[101] Of the three, Voiture is best remembered, and only then as a versifier of the second rank. (A. Adam, *Histoire de la littérature française au XVIIe siècle*: [Paris, 1948.] p. 387.) He was an habitué of the Rambouillet circle, and after 1639 was *Maître d'Hôtel du Roy*. His relations with Renaudot might have exceeded that of literary adviser, for one of his numerous mistresses was Renaudot's daughter. His 1648 death prompted J. F. Sarasin, one of his imitators, to write "La

lieu died, Bautru transferred his loyalties to Mazarin, and continued to oversee the *Gazette* until his death.[102] Mazarin also charged Gabriel Naudé, the *studieux mécreant* who was his librarian, with similar responsibilities.[103] Naudé distributed copies of the *Gazette* to the Cardinal's entourage "by order of Mr. Renaudot." "When Sieur Renaudot was ill two years ago [1647] with the paralysis which thought to play a bad trick on him, he charged me with the distribution of the *Gazette* each Saturday to the Cardinal's household, and sometimes even, I presented a couple of gold-leafed copies to His Eminence [a task] which from time to time earned me a few *pistoles*."[104] Naudé was the most intellectually sophisticated of these several men, and from the tone of his remarks, appears to have been deeply involved in the *Gazette*, less as Renaudot's overseer than as his colleague. Shortly before the outbreak of the Fronde he and Renaudot parted ways. The break appears to be consistent with Naudé's general skepticism regarding the power of human rationality. "I will tell you the truth: Monsieur Renaudot is a very fine man, and was never offended to have someone work

---

Pompe Funebre de Voiture." The third chapter recorded this love affair: "Comme Vetturius [Voiture] arriva en l'Isle des Mensonges, où il s'amourache de la belle Extraordinaire, fille de Nazin de Gazette, Dinaste du pays. Commes les archives lui en furent monstrées, où il ne vit qu'Histoires Hebdomadaires, qui ne contenaient que billevesées." (*Oeuvres* [Paris: 1926], p. 453.) Renaudot dedicated the *Troisiesme Centurie* of his conferences to Bautru.

[102] Tallement des Réaux wrote: "Il avait du reste, depuis quelques temps, l'inspection sur les *Gazettes* et sur les *Extraordinaires* de France, et l'on pretent que c'était lui qui se chargeait de rédiger les éloges qu'elle addressait à l'administration et au charactère de Mazarin, en sorte que s'il ne tint pas l'épée pour l'Éminence, il fit au moins la guerre de plume à son service." (Cited by R. Kerviler, *Guillaume Bautru* [Paris: 1876], p. 70.)

[103] The phrase is Pintard's. *Libertinage érudit*, I, 155-72, 306-10. Also see J. V. Rice, *Gabriel Naudé* (Baltimore), 1939.

[104] *Jugement de tout ce qui a esté imprimé contre le Cardinal Mazarin, depuis le sixieme Janvier, jusques à la Déclaration du premier Avril mil six cens quarante-neuf* (S.l.n.d.), p. 271.

with him, but he could not stand my criticism of the *Gazette*, and my attributing to him a part of the evils which have troubled us for some time: because it makes the people too knowledgeable in their own affairs as well as their neighbors' . . . it does not seem appropriate to me for the least of the population to have too much news: what good is it to inform them so punctually of the revolts of Naples, the seditions in Turkey, of the horrible crime in England, and they hardly need to be told the details of the tumults in Moscovy. Certainly one would not publish such contagious news at Rome, or at Venice, because these two cities are much better policed than Paris: Now as this discourse must not have pleased Monsieur Renaudot and since he recognized in me the verity of the proverb *Namen expellas furca, tamen ipsa recurret,* he quite politely asked me to retire."[105]

With the exception of Père Joseph and Chavigny, these men were less government officials or administrators than literati or personal servitors of the Cardinal. The bulk of their duties, considering their place at the court, was to make sure that the news reached Renaudot and to help perfect the *Gazette*'s style. Editorial decisions were made at the top, with these men acting only as intermediaries.

In spite of his contacts at court, in spite of the pressure upon generals and officers to keep him informed, Renaudot was often forced to appeal directly to his readers for news. No situation was more extraordinary to France, nor to the *Gazette*, than the birth of the future Louis XIV, "l'enfant donné de Dieu."[106] Renaudot published an ecstatic *Extraordinaire,* "l'Heureuse naissance de monseigneur le Daufin" on 5 Septem-

[105] Naudé, p. 380. From the tone of his remarks, Naudé evidently helped Renaudot only during his illness. The collaboration could not have been very long since Naudé had just returned from Italy in January 1647. Rice, pp. 26-27.

[106] The term first appeared in the *Gazette* on 28 April 1638, in the *Extraordinaire* "l'Heureuse nouvelle de la Grossesse asseurée de la Reine."

ber, the day of his birth; "Particularitez de la naissance de monseigneur le Dauphin, et ce qui s'est passé en suite à S. Germain et à Paris" on 10 September; and "Les Feux de joye et autres Magnificences faites à Paris par la Naissance de Monseigneur le Dauphin" on 17 September, all in addition to reports appearing regularly in the *Gazette*. But such a story demanded even more attention, so Renaudot encouraged his readers to send descriptions of local celebrations so that he could publish them for the enjoyment of all.[107] These collected reports filled the *extraordinaires* of 14 October and 27 October.

Renaudot's foreign news originated from a greater variety of sources than did his domestic news. As one would expect, most of his informants appear to be French. These included military dispatches from the Swedish armies in Germany.[108] The greatest bulk seem to have been regular French diplomatic sources, both ordinary and extraordinary embassies. Particularly thorough were the dispatches from Rome, and for good reason. Seventeenth century Rome was "the most corrupt of administrative capitals," in a word, a newspaperman's goldmine.[109] From the arrival of the Duke of Créqui as Louis XIII's ambassador in 1632, dispatches from Rome remain the most consistent and thorough of any in the *Gazette*. But much of the news datelined at Rome occurred elsewhere. Rome was the French listening post for news of the Swiss Confederation; during the 1637-1638 Franco-Spanish tensions, Spanish news, both domestic and foreign, appeared in the *Gazette* as it came to Paris—from Rome. There were events from as far away as

---

[107] 14 September 1638.   [108] 6, 13 June 1631.

[109] G. De Santillana, *The Crime of Galileo* (Chicago: 1955), p. 117. Renaudot published very little personal scandal, but the juiciest exception to this rule was a dispatch from Rome. It concerned a Roman gentleman madly in love with a nun. After spreading the rumor that he was going to be away from Rome for a week, he had himself locked into a large chest. He had earlier instructed his valet to deliver it to the nun. The valet, however, went on a drinking binge and delivered the chest four days late. The nun opened it to find her lover had died of hunger. 18 August 1635.

China, which filtered back to St. Peter's and thence to Renaudot's readers.[110]

The *Gazette*'s diplomatic function was most noticeable in its early years. Reports which came to Richelieu went directly to Renaudot, usually without the slightest changes in the interest of journalistic style. They were completely epistolary in format. Correspondents used the first person singular, and often responded to specific questions which they had been asked before.[111] As the *Gazette* matured, this stylistic crudeness became less blatant, but the diplomatic function of Renaudot's correspondents remained.

In addition to translating articles from foreign journals, Renaudot often relied, as did the government, on private persons for foreign news. Some individuals seem to have been attached regularly and over a long period of time to the *Gazette*. In addition to these semi-permanent French sources abroad, Renaudot relied on letters and dispatches from foreign nationals. In a series of dispatches from lower Saxony and Leipzig, the correspondent spoke of "our elector."[112] Direct epistolary accounts were primarily from Germany, and occur during the first 2 years of the *Gazette*. These were probably some of the contacts of Louis Epstin or Pierre d'Hozier. There were first-person reports during the same years from "Alep in Syrie" speaking of "the pilgrimages which we are going to make ... for the happy deliverance of Pasha Vizir Azan," and from "Maroc" speaking of "our King of Maroc."[113]

[110] A dispatch in the 29 August 1631 *Gazette* from Rome reported that the Jesuits had baptized the king and court of the kingdom of Monomotapa, located in present day Rhodesia: "on mande aussi de la Chine que plusieurs Mandarins qui sont les Docteurs de leur loy ont embrassé le Christianisme avec le permission du Roy qui tesmoigne luy-mesme une grande affection à la foy Catholique. Aussi faut-il qu'en la plenitude des temps plus éloignez de l'Eglise s'en approchent."

[111] A correspondent in Languedoc, following the activities of Monsieur, wrote: "pour le second poinct que vous requirez de moy, voicy la liste des forces de Monsieur." 30 July 1632.

[112] 11 July, 31 August 1631.   [113] 18 July, 8 August 1631.

No matter what was the nationality of his correspondents, Renaudot published a striking number of reports from distant places. Much of this news must be attributed to Père Joseph's Capuchin correspondents. The *Gazette*'s first years saw news directly from "Hispan en Perse" of the mercy of the Shah, giving hope, said the *Gazette*, "of his conversion to the Catholic faith." The same correspondent continued that "from Nagasaki we have been written that the Emperor has by edict ceased persecuting Christians, after seeing a cross and hearing the words '*in hoc signo vinces*,' which long ago restored the battered courage of Constantine the Great."[114] News from eastern sources reached Renaudot by roundabout ways. A correspondent in Antwerp, for example, wrote to Renaudot of famines in Portuguese India: he had received the news from Lisbon.[115] An *Extraordinaire* published 7 September 1634 reproduced an "Extraict d'une lettre escrite du Jappon à Rome, le 5 Septembre 1633" which included, among other things, the ghastly murder of Christian missionaries in Japan.

News from the New World was steady, if not frequent. There were continuing reports of naval battles in "Fernambouc," for example. These stories were often treated as *extraordinaires* and as fillers. Renaudot justified publishing "Les exploits et logement des François dans l'Isle de Gardeloupe," for example, because the winter season had "prohibited great deeds as it did plants from growing in this climate."[116] Most often, however, they appeared in the *Gazette* or *Nouvelles ordinaires*. News of Nouvelle France appeared very infrequently, usually no more than a short statement of an arriving ship from Canada.[117]

The first article in the first issue of the *Gazette* was dispatched from Constantinople: "The King of Persia, with 15,000 horsemen and 50,000 infantry laid siege to Dille [i.e., Hille], two days' march from the city of Babylon: where the Grand

[114] 22 August 1631. [115] 12 February 1633.
[116] 27 February 1638. [117] 19 February 1633.

Seigneur has commanded all his Janissaries to report, under
pain of life: in spite of this diversion, he still wages a harsh war
against tobacco users, whom he has suffocated by smoke."[118]
News from Constantinople appeared so regularly that it is
perhaps misleading to characterize it as exotic.[119] These dispatches were the source of news of the Balkan principalities, as
well as occasional news of the Holy Land. But even more than
this, French readers could indulge their fancies in the flam-
boyant entrances, ceremonies, and banquets, as well as the intrigues and scandals of the seraglio.[120] These articles may have
been strange and glamorous, but they appeared as frequently
as news from other European capitals, if not more so. News
from Kiev and Moscow was infrequently published, and then
usually via reports from Danzig or Warsaw.

Not until the twenty-eighth issue (28 November 1631) did
news dispatches from England appear in the *Gazette*, and then
simply noting that "The Duke of Vendôme arrived here on the
thirteenth. The Queen of England gave birth on the fourteenth
to a daughter, prematurely we believe." For the next several
years, dispatches were few and far between. The English government prohibited all newspaper publication from 1632 to
1638,[121] and Renaudot was forced to rely on an occasional
private letter or diplomatic dispatch. During this period, Renaudot reported two or three sentences every month or month-
and-a-half, usually on the ceremonial activities of the royal fam-

---

[118] Without date, but published on 30 May 1631.

[119] As Mandrou (*Introduction à la France moderne*, p. 316) has
indicated, much of the travel literature of this period concerned the
Levant and mid-East, rather than the New World or Africa. The *Gazette* likewise reflected this greater fascination with the Levant and
mid-East. See Martin, *Livre, pouvoirs, et société*, pp. 208-11, 853-54.

[120] These often consisted of complete *Extraordinaires*: "La Magnificence du Grand Seigneur en sa marche, contre le Roy de Perse," 5 July
1638; "l'Entrée du Grand Seigneur au Constantinople," 1 September
1639.

[121] J. Frank, *Beginnings of the English Newspaper 1620-1660* (Cambridge, Mass.: 1962), p. 14.

ily. With the resumption of newspaper publishing in England, Renaudot again had a steady stream of news, and short dispatches begin to appear regularly in the weekly *Gazette* and *Nouvelles ordinaires*. On 7 August 1638, Renaudot's correspondent observed that growing tension between Charles I and his Scottish subjects "seems to be straining to open war." The *Gazette*, nonetheless, reported the news simply and without undue excitement. In many cases, up to 2 pages of the 12-page weekly publication were devoted to dispatches from London, in addition to frequent dispatches from Scotland and Ireland.

But this was not enough, and in 1639 Renaudot began to devote *extraordinaires* to the problem. His readers were so hungry for news that he had little choice over whom his sources were. As a result, these dispatches were packed with rumor: "Everyone has been able to remark how soberly I have spoken of the disturbances of Great Britain: that discretion resulting from the uncertainty of rumors variously scattered by minds affected by the same."[122] The affairs of Great Britain were unimaginable and unique to the French court, and the *Gazette* reflects their doubt and disbelief. Problems increased for Renaudot as English affairs intensified. His news sources became more and more varied: publications, letters of private individuals, speeches of various leaders, treaties and agreements between the factions. Renaudot, to an extent never before seen in the *Gazette*, constantly warned his readers of the partiality of these sources. As early as 18 July 1639, for example, he prefaced a discussion of Scottish events with the notice: "While the King of Great Britain has published today, in a book just printed in London by his printer Robert Young, the motives and progress of these troubles, I would be criticized if I do not assign them at least some small corner in the vast tableau of events of this era."

In 1640 English problems fill the *Gazette*: rumors of the English fleet at Edinburgh (19 May); the end of Parliament at

[122] 18 July 1639.

London (26 May); mobs of lackeys and apprentices pillaging the Archbishop of Canterbury's palace in London (9 June); desertions of Royalist forces to the Scottish banner (18 August); members of the nobility calling for a meeting of Parliament at York (20 October). For the rest of the decade, English affairs were without question Renaudot's major news story, often earning more space in the *Gazette* than French domestic events.

Reports from England often occupied 3 to 4 pages of the 12-page weekly *Gazette-Nouvelles ordinaires* during 1641 and 1642. For example, 4 pages of the 25 January 1642 issue consist of the London dispatch, covering events day by day from 17 December 1641 through 4 January; more than 3 pages of the issue of 1 February 1642 were devoted to a 12 January dispatch from London, including transcripts of Charles I's harangues to Parliament in December 1641 and January 1642, as well as treason charges against "Mandevill, Pim, Hambden, Hazebrig, Holles et Stroode." Likewise, the number of *extraordinaires* increased dramatically. Renaudot published 65 *extraordinaires* during 1642, at least 27 devoted exclusively or preponderantly to English affairs. An English correspondent could not contain his wonder that "the affairs of this Kingdom have never been as confused or in such an unfortunate state as they are at present."[123] And the problem for Renaudot, as he confided to his readers, was that "each [of the parties] writes of it to its own advantage."[124] He followed the advice and pattern of his correspondents, and published news from both sides. For example, the "Journal des affaires d'Angleterre," published on 3 December 1642, contained news drawn from Royal sources, and from a recently published Parliamentary tract. Throughout this time, he had published these accounts without comment. Finally, on 1 January 1643, Renaudot broke his silence and publicly gloated that "England, after having its merchants

[123] 9 August 1642.   [124] 18 November 1642.

160

profit from commerce prohibited to its neighbors, today expends more than it gained: finding itself enveloped in civil war, so disastrous that its King, victorious or vanquished, must in any case remain even weaker, it still pursues an adventure where it can gain nothing but lose everything." This was the first time he commented directly on the events in England. Almost without exception, Renaudot would continue to let dispatches from England "speak for themselves," because their message was clear enough.

By publishing stories about the chaos in England, Renaudot was by contrast silently extolling the social and political calm at home. Much of this calm, however, was illusory. As the 1640's wore on, France would experience royal death, ministerial change, aristocratic and parlementary independence. All of these events colored the pages of the *Gazette,* and—just as indelibly—Renaudot's personal career.

161

CHAPTER VI

The Faculty of Medicine

If Renaudot is remembered primarily as father of the French press, his activities were no less significant in the realm of medicine. Medicine was always the center of his life's work. His first public title was *Médecin du Roi*; his first published works were on medical topics; it was as physician that he aroused the anger and jealousy of the Parisian medical community, leading eventually to his defeat.

The University of Paris considered itself the eldest daughter of Crown and Papacy.[1] From the outset, this double-edged temporal and spiritual-preeminence colored its existence. Its doctrinal and theoretical authority had the strength of religious orthodoxy and its corporate influence was encrusted with layer upon layer of political privilege and exemption. If the university of the seventeenth century cast only a shadow of its former vitality, its medical faculty was still the most important in the world. If innovation and discovery was occurring elsewhere in Europe, tradition and reputation continued to look to Paris for approval.

In spite of the faculty reforms of 1598, ancient practices were as firmly established as ever. Candidates for the baccalaureate in medicine had to have the Master of Arts degree, either earned within 4 years at the University of Paris, or within 8 years if earned elsewhere.[2] During the first 2 years,

---

[1] The Faculty claimed that the University was begun under Charlemagne. *La Défense de la Faculté de Médecine contre son Calumniateur* (Paris: 1641), p. 43. In the seventeenth century the rector of the University stood to the left of the Archbishop of Paris, and in front of the papal nuncio, during ceremonial occasions. Fr. Olivier-Martin, *l'Organization corporative de l'ancien régime* (Paris: 1938), p. 31.

[2] For the organization of the University, see the works of A. Corlieu, and C.M.G. Jourdain, *Histoire de l'Université de Paris au XVIIe et*

novices followed the lectures of 2 or 3 professors. According to the statutes, "lecturers will explain only Hippocrates, Galen, and the other princes of medicine: they will read the texts of these authors and comment upon them with care." Lectures were divided into the 3 traditional divisions of (1) things natural (anatomy and physiology), (2) things unnatural (hygiene and diet), and (3) things contra-nature (pathology and therapeutics). Each morning students attended sessions taught by older colleagues who had already earned the baccalaureate; they offered little more than glosses on the lessons they had heard earlier from the professors. All classes, indeed all activities of the faculty, were conducted in Latin.

Once every 2 years, in March, students were examined by 4 doctors. When the student had passed the baccalaureate (after also having his moral status certified by 3 members of the faculty), he attached himself to a doctor-regent, observing his practice, writing down his diagnoses and prescriptions, and perfecting his understanding of the classic texts. As Bachelor of Medicine, he commented on the classics to the first and second year students. In effect, then, he passed the first 2 years as student pure-and-simple, his second 2 years as both student and teacher and as apprentice to his doctor-regent. In the winter of his second year, the bachelor performed a dissection before the entire faculty. Shortly thereafter he was examined; if successful, the student was then licensed to practice medicine. Most students, however, would wish to receive the doctorate for eventual admission to the faculty. Six weeks after the licentiate, the student publicly swore to uphold the principles of medicine, to maintain the traditions and reputation of the Faculty of Paris. By this act he was admitted to the faculty as a Doctor in Medicine.[3]

XVIIIe siècles (Paris: 1862-1866), esp. pp. 19-24. The 1598 statutes of the faculty were published by M. Thèry, *Histoire de l'éducation en France* (Paris: 1858), ii, 372-88.

[3] Statutes of the medical faculty.

The medical faculty of the University of Paris consisted of all of its doctors, and not only those actively involved in teaching. Until 1634, there were only 2 professors, one teaching the courses in things natural and nonnatural, and the other the things contra-nature. All doctors, i.e., all members of the faculty, could serve as professor, the professorate lasting only about 2 years. The dean, elected for a 2-year term, did not teach, but served as chief administrator and examiner.[4] His obligations as spokesman for the faculty were so demanding that, after 1640, a 9-man committee was appointed to aid him in his official functions and ceremonies.

This, then, was the basic organization of the Parisian faculty. Its internal organization was as traditionally oriented as its teaching methods. Members of the professional medical community were also members of the educational community. In effect, all social and political conflicts were potentially educational and doctrinal conflicts, and vice versa. There was no division between what went on within its classrooms on the rue de la Boucherie and the activities of its physicians when they participated in the political and social life of Paris.

The faculty member interpreted all of his responsibilities toward the ancient art of healing in corporate terms. In medicine's primeval origins, the priest and the physician were the same man, and seventeenth century medicine still had about it a religious aura. "A Deo est omnis medicina": the physician was God's intermediary, always conscious of his partnership in the divine art of healing. To be admitted to this hallowed profession, one had to be morally clean and physically untainted. The acolyte physician took vows as binding and as demanding as the vows of those entering religious orders. The medical faculty of the University of Paris was the corporate

---

[4] According to the preface of E. Bachot's *Apologie . . . pour la saignée* . . . (Paris: 1646), there were 122 doctors of the faculty in Paris in 1646.

embodiment of this latterday priesthood. What affected one member of the faculty affected all, for there was no distinction between the private interests of the individual physician and the interests of the entire faculty.

The medical faculty at Paris had clothed itself as the embodiment of medical truth. Its physicians had the right to practice within Paris and throughout the realm. The Papacy had considered the University of Paris its eldest and most faithful daughter, and the precedence of its theology and law faculties over other European universities likewise applied to its medical faculty. As part of the first University of France, the medical faculty jealously insisted that only its graduates could practice throughout the realm; graduates of other French faculties were limited to the cities where they had been trained. Centuries of tradition and litigation had solidified this precedence. To practice in Paris, foreign-trained physicians had to be approved by the Faculty of Medicine, otherwise risking criminal action.[5] Imperfect judicial and administrative procedures made it difficult to police these malpractitioners, but the hard-pressed faculty never relented in hounding them.

As was true of all privilege in the ancien régime, exceptions existed. All physicians attached to the court could practice in Paris, regardless of where they had been trained. Royal appointments were easy to get: "by means of a few *pistoles* [one could buy] some letter-patent of physician to the king from some royal secretary: but these titles are laughed at in this world and in the next; nevertheless, in the countryside fellows with these imaginary bulls really think highly of themselves."[6] The price of these royal appointments, whether paid in money or in servility, was well invested to keep the faculty off one's back.

The major rival of the Faculty of Paris was the University

[5] Statute 59.
[6] Patin to Belin, 28 May 1635.

of Medicine of Montpellier.[7] The southern faculty had long welcomed non-Catholic students. Heretics in religion and in medicine, these Montpellierians were unworthy practitioners of religiously sanctified medicine, according to the Parisians. There was evidence that Montpellier maintained two different standards: one standard, parallel to the traditional standards of the Parisian faculty, for those who would practice in Montpellier and throughout the realm; and another, less-rigorous one for physicians who would leave Montpellier after their training and never practice there. To the Parisians, this was a source of ridicule and shame.

The University of Medicine of Montpellier considered itself as the legitimate daughter of Church and State also. During the Avignon papacy, the nearby faculty was virtually a papal institution, providing her physicians. Citing statements by Urban V and Martin V, Montpellier claimed for its graduates the right to practice *hic et ubique terrarum*, the privilege which the University of Paris claimed for its graduates alone. The involvement of the two faculties in the Renaudot affair revolved around this issue. For centuries the Crown had often bypassed the Parisian faculty and chosen its royal physicians from Montpellier.[8] The majority of non-Parisian physicians practicing in Paris, legally or illegally, were from Montpellier.

Doctrinal and theoretical matters aggravated this rivalry. The University of Medicine at Montpellier had offered lectures in botany and chemistry long before the University of Paris had done so. Its support of chemical medicine had allied the faculty with Montpellier's apothecaries. The southern

[7] The Montpellier body styled itself as the "Université de Médecine de Montpellier," while the Parisian group referred to itself as the "Faculté de Médecine de l'Université de Paris."

[8] This was particularly true of Henry IV and Louis XIII. The Paris faculty was sensitive to this, and always reminded everyone that "si l'on excepte le feu Roy Henri IV, les Rois precedans ont presque tous eu des premiers Médecins de nostre Eschole." *La Défense de la Faculté contre son Calumniateur.*

166

faculty was instrumental in recognizing the interdependence of medicine and surgery. Although it maintained the surgeon-physician distinctions common to the age, Montpellier experienced less of the antagonisms which marked medical-surgical and medical-apothecary relations at Paris.[9]

At Paris, discord between the faculty and the surgeons and the apothecaries was usual and traditional. During the medieval period, the Christian physician was first of all a cleric. For a man of God to bloody his hands or touch the sexual organs was taboo: "Ecclesia abhorret a sanguine."[10] Physical operations were corrupt intrusions upon the sacred art of healing, and manual tasks were therefore performed by persons who had not taken religious and medical vows, such as barbers, masseurs, or bathhouse attendants. Those among them who ceased to cut hair or run bathhouses, who developed their skill as the physician's right-arm, became the core of the surgical profession. All maladies which called for the use of instruments, bandages, or cupping were surgical maladies.[11] In spite of their importance, surgeons remained handmaidens to the medical faculty. Surgeons had to be certified by the medical faculty, and were not permitted to touch a patient without a physician in attendance. During all operations and dissections, the surgeon was prohibited from speaking, and he could not begin operating without a signal from the attending doctor.

Their proficiency made the surgeon's traditional subservience all the more odious. Surgeons were responsible for many of the great changes in early modern medicine, and younger physicians were increasingly eager to study with these men. The faculty repeatedly prohibited surgeons from giving private lessons or dissections, because many of the faculty's students were sneaking away to study procedures which the

[9] R. Chancerel, *Les apothecaires et l'ancienne faculté de médecine de Paris* (Dijon: 1892), and the collected essays of A. Germain.

[10] Regulation 11, Fourth Lateran Council.

[11] Corlieu, *l'Ancienne faculté de médecine de Paris*, p. 133.

faculty considered heretical. The faculty did all it could to treat surgeons as second-rank technicians, teaching them in French while reserving pure Latin for its own students. Prospective medical students had to renounce all manual crafts, and according to a 1607 faculty ruling, surgery was one of these.[12] Not until 1634 did the faculty finally give in and establish a chair in surgery. Relations between the physician and the surgeon were marked by professional pride, jealousy, and the condescension of a master to his servant.

Professional animosity was mirrored on the corporate level, between the college of surgeons and the faculty of medicine. Surgeons had organized the religiously oriented Confrerie de St. Côme, and the physicians opposed all further organization as attempts to create a rival faculty. In 1544 Francis I granted the College of Surgeons rights and privileges enjoyed by other adjuncts of the University. They were permitted to teach, certify their students, and oversee the practice of surgery in Paris. Likewise, they were permitted to wear their own regalia, the long robe, distinguishing them from barbers of the short robe.[13] Nevertheless the medical faculty still considered them second-rank technicians. In spite of their growing scientific importance, surgeons suffered from their corporate structure as much as from theoretical and practical considerations. Their rivals, the barbers of the short robe and the physicians, were under direct royal surveillance via the first barber and first physician of the king. Both groups enjoyed the status that royal recognition brought.[14] Not at all allied to the state, surgeons were little different from carpenters or bakers, a craft community and nothing more. Moreover, the medical faculty read Guy de Chaliac and other authorities to the barbers, and

[12] Statutes 24, 51, 56.

[13] Barbers of the short robe, unlike surgeons, were not permitted to administer laxatives.

[14] J. Rigal, *La communauté des maîtres-chirurgiens jurés de Paris au XVIIe et au XVIIIe siècle* (Paris: 1936), pp. 27-35.

used them as foils against the surgeons of St. Côme. The physicians never let the surgeons forget, reputation and skill notwithstanding, that the surgeons formed a college and not a faculty. As the seventeenth century wore on, the faculty constantly flaunted its corporate superiority. Relations were easily aggravated and always explosive.

The third branch of the medical profession, the apothecaries, likewise occupied a position subservient to the faculty. Since 1485, apothecaries were joined to the *épiciers* as one of Paris' six *corps des marchands*. The functions of the two groups had long been confused and confounded. By the seventeenth century it was recognized that apothecaries were charged with all medications prepared from the distillation of mineral waters, through infusion, and all preparations derived from honey. *Épiciers*, on the other hand, had exclusive right to produce medications distilled from aromatic waters, derived from preparations brought from abroad (they were, after all, originally retail and wholesale spice merchants), or from oils obtained by pressing. In spite of their medical role, apothecaries were still formally allied with the *épiciers*, who were first of all tradesmen. This group was no different from any of the other five corporations involved in the city government: the furriers, drapers, mercers, goldsmiths, and hatters. All apothecary shops were subject to an annual inspection by the medical faculty, and certain important drugs could be prepared only in their presence. Apothecaries were prohibited from dispensing medications without a proper prescription from a certified physician. There is no doubt that such safeguards were necessary, but it is also true that the faculty used these considerations to glorify itself at the apothecary's expense. Not until 1777 were the apothecaries officially separated from the *épiciers*. Until then they operated with the stigma of common tradesmen attached to their name.[15]

[15] R. Chancerel, pp. 13, 48, 70.

169

This, then, provided the all-encompassing power of the medical faculty within Paris. Not only did it oppose certain procedures and theories jealously supported by its subordinates, but just as important to the litigious seventeenth century, it dominated their political and social existence. Theoretical and doctrinal squabbles were ultimately political and social. All members of the Parisian medical community—physician, surgeon of the long robe, barber of the short robe, apothecary—operated within a fragile maze of legal and political entanglements. Without appreciating this intricately woven world, Renaudot's career is incomprehensible.

As we have seen, Renaudot provided weekly free medical treatment at the Bureau d'Adresse as early as 1632. By 1641, treatment was available from 10:00 A.M. until noon, five days a week.[16] Renaudot drew his staff from those whom the Faculty of Paris had branded nonpersons: graduates of non-Parisian faculties, Protestants, heretics, advocates of chemical medicine. The faculty, jealous of its *hic et ubique terrarum* privilege, argued that these pariahs could not practice in Paris. Renaudot ignored their argument. As *Commissaire Général des Pauvres*, he was empowered to establish at his Bureau whatever he saw fit. As part of the Bureau d'Adresse, these men were exempt from the faculty's ban.

The majority of Renaudot's confederates appear to have been fellow-graduates of the University of Medicine of Montpellier. Not only, therefore, were they members of a foreign faculty within the sacred precincts of the University of Paris, but just as important, they were exponents of chemical cures anathema to Parisian orthodoxy. These included opium, quinine, and antimony, the latter condemned by the Parisian faculty in 1560.

---

[16] *La présence des absens* (Paris: 1642), p. 3. In his *Response . . . au libelle fait contre les consultations charitables*, written in 1641, Renaudot said that he had been offering consultations at the Bureau for more than 10 years.

For over a century, the European medical community had
been divided on the use of antimony. Until Paracelsus and
Valerian Basil, who wrote the first treatise on antimony at
the end of the fifteenth century, there had been no controversy.
According to Paracelsus, antimony was *mercurius vitae*, able
to expel impurities from gold and silver. If man was the
measure and reflection of all things, why could antimony not
have similar purifying effects in the human body? A number
of broadsheets joined the battle in the middle of the sixteenth
century. To Pierre Sevarin (*Idea Medicinae*, Basle, 1571),
antimony speeded up the three normal aims of medicine: *vo-
mere, cacare, sudare*.[17] Advocates of antimony favored purgation over bleeding, which traditionalists favored. As Guy
Patin, the most irrepressible traditionalist in the Parisian
medical establishment, affirmed, "Long live the grand method
of Galen and the beautiful verse of Joachim de Bellay: *'O
bonne, O saincte, O divine saignée!'* "[18] The trouble with
vomiting and purging was that they could, and usually did,
have violent effects. "Bloodletting has been the most popular
of all remedies, because only it embodies all of the desired
properties of the perfect remedy: it cures surely, gently, and
promptly. Only it among the powerful remedies heals with
the least number of accidents, and it permits the physician to
stop or continue the treatment whenever he finds it advanta-
geous. As to the gentleness of its action, there is no medication
which operates with less ill effect upon the sick."[19] Chemists
sought to introduce an untried element into the body, while
bloodletting required no such risk. In spite of its attributes,
antimony was a dangerous poison, much too dangerous to
employ.

[17] A. G. Chevalier, "La guerre de l'antimoine," *Revue Ciba* (1959),
pp. 21-25; M. Emery, *Renaudot et l'introduction de la médication
chimique* (Montpellier: 1888), pp. 13-35; A. G. Debis, *The English
Paracelsians* (New York: 1966), pp. 30ff.
[18] Patin to Falconet, 26 December 1662.
[19] L. Savot, *Le livre de Galien* (Paris: 1603), Preface, p. 7.

The University of Paris' 1560 condemnation, and the rationale behind it, remained operative throughout the following century. During this period, however, numerous pamphlets and treatises praised antimony and other chemicals, at the expense of traditional medical methods.[20] In 1615 the Faculty prohibited apothecaries from selling the chemical, thus indicating how unsuccessful the faculty injunction had been. The major advocates of antimony and other chemical cures included surgeons, apothecaries, and physicians from foreign faculties, with those of Montpellier leading the pack. The Parisian faculty rigidly upheld the tried-and-true three S's, "Saignée, sirop, séné." Advocates of antimony "have insisted that antimony is good in many situations, provided that it is well-prepared and carefully given. It is the same with all remedies, and with poisons even: sometimes it's necessary to give opium, no matter that it is certainly a poison; it is that we have no better nor more certain narcotic, but we do have many other purgatives better than antimony. . . . I might be able to swear that all the most dangerous poisons are good and useful remedies, providing that they are well prepared and carefully given, including *sang d'aspic*, the *sublime*, etc. But the point is preparing and mixing them well; we still cannot do that with their antimony, which has been so roundly discredited by the deaths that it has caused that they no longer dare prescribe it in their own families."[21] Faculty rigidity became more and more difficult to maintain as many of its own members adopted chemical treatments themselves.

To make the issue more embarrassing, a commission had included antimony in the official faculty codex of approved medications. Hardouin St. Jacques, dean in 1638, had evidently railroaded approval of the publication against the wishes of

[20] Including Renaudot's *Description d'un médicament appellé Polychreston* (Loudun: 1619).

[21] Patin to Belin, 7 September 1654.

172

most of the faculty's older and more conservative members.[22] Chemical treatment during this decade was a source of controversy and chaos, both as a doctrinal issue and as an intramural political matter. When Renaudot established his charitable consultations with a staff drawn almost exclusively from advocates of these controversial practices, the "hundred years' war" of antimony once again entered a hot phase.

Not only were Renaudot and his fellow *chymiques* placing great confidence in apothecaries for preparing these cures, but Renaudot's physicians even prescribed to them in Latin.[23] The faculty was scandalized: it had always addressed apothecaries and surgeons in French, the vulgar language, rather than sullying the purity of a Latin reserved for physicians alone. Renaudot was elevating apothecaries to the status of the physician! This was not an argument of nit-pickers and obscurantists, but rather an issue which could undermine the entire hierarchical order of medical practice.

Renaudot had encouraged heretics from Montpellier by giving them a place to practice, he had dared to discuss these new chemicals in his public conferences, he had made apothecaries the intellectual equals of physicians by prescribing to them in Latin. Finally on 2 September 1640 the Cour des Monnaies granted Renaudot permission to establish laboratories at the Bureau d'Adresse, "since a part of the experiments which are done concern remedies drawn from plants, animals, and

---

[22] "Notre école n'a jamais approuvé ni reconnu pour sien cet antidotaire que St. Jacques fit imprimer de son doyenné: aussi est'il trop chétif et fautif, et tout-à-fait indigne de l'aveu de notre Faculté" (Patin to Belin, 16 December 1652). Patin was never one to forget an issue: in 1658 he was still referring to the St-Jacques' as "charlatans, fauteurs et valets de charlatans, *ne dicam pejus.*" Patin to Belin, n.d. (edition Reveillé-Parise, I 259). See E. Krieger, *Une grande querelle médicale: histoire thérapeutique de l'antimoine* (Paris: 1878), p. 66.

[23] *Defense de la Faculté . . . contre son Calumniateur*, pp. 23-25; *Advertissement à Théophraste Renaudot . . .* , pp. 31-32; *Remarques sur l'avertissement. . .* , p. 25.

minerals: for the preparation of which he is obliged to keep all sorts of furnaces, alembics, receptacles, and other vessels and instruments of chemistry, or alchemy, to extract by the operations of the aforesaid art all sorts of waters, oils, salts, prescriptions, extracts, quintessences, limes, tinctures, metallic antimony, precipitates, and generally all the other effects of the aforesaid art of chemistry which are useful to the healing of illnesses, when they are methodically administered according to the precepts of medicine."[24] In addition to preparing medications, Renaudot's associates could now dabble publicly with the secrets of physical matter. Those afraid that Renaudot's *vents-à-grâce* controlled all the money in Paris had additional fears: he had persuaded the mint to give him permission to erect furnaces just like theirs.[25] Cheap loans, free medical treatment, and now alchemy.

With the popularity of his charitable consultations, the Maison du Grand Coq—combination pawnshop, medical clinic, employment office, lecture hall, chemical laboratory, and publishing bureau—was more inadequate than ever. By 1640 Renaudot had drawn up plans for a new facility abutting the city ramparts in the tenement-packed Faubourg St. Antoine, housing all of his medical facilities under one roof. The king had sweetened the project by granting Renaudot 200,000 *écus* to put it into effect.[26] Renaudot's permission was quite extraordinary, as property development on the ramparts was normally prohibited for reasons of town security. Town ramparts were special and holy, and were to remain eternally inviolate.[27]

---

[24] Reprinted in *Consultations charitables*, pp. 11-12.

[25] Renaudot's eldest son, Théophraste *fils*, had been a councillor of the Cour des Monnaies since 1638. Drouault, "Notes inédites," p. 8.

[26] *Commentarii Facultatis Medicinae*, XIII, f. 172r.

[27] Renaudot said that Louis XIII sent the patents to Parlement in February 1643. They were opposed by the Duke d'Uzes and his wife, who owned land adjacent to the proposed site. The letters were never registered; Louis XIII died on 14 May and the *Maison des consultations charitables* died with him.

The Parisian medical establishment had never been so critically threatened in its history. Renaudot now had all of the elements necessary to establish a rival faculty. This faculty consisted of foreign-trained physicians, licensed and certified to practice throughout France by virtue of their affiliation with the Bureau d'Adresse. His teaching staff consisted of these physicians, discussing the theories of the new medicine in the weekly conferences and their practical application in the equally public consultations. He certainly had no difficulty in attracting students from the medical faculty in the rue de la Boucherie. At his weekly conferences they found active discussion of the chemical topics which the Parisian doctors chose to ignore and could even join in the discussions themselves. He had established chemical laboratories to produce the drugs his doctors and apothecaries were dispensing. Moreover, the public consultations were in fact a teaching clinic, providing practical knowledge which the faculty did not yet provide.

Renaudot had the active and voluntary support of the surgeons and apothecaries, "none among them who would not voluntarily offer to contribute his efforts and industry" to the Bureau.[28] The faculty could extract similar cooperation only through the pressure of formalized writ and rigid tradition. The faculty had maintained its orthodoxy at the expense of these two ancillary groups, and Renaudot was clearly receiving their enthusiastic cooperation. He was extending his operations throughout the realm, and the faculty feared that he wished to establish national licensing standards through his commissioners, at the faculty's obvious expense.[29]

There was further indication that he was offering his activities to those unable to attend the consultations in person. In 1642 he published *La présence des absens*. This was, according to Renaudot, "a formulary for the use of *malades absens*, so

[28] *Consultations charitables*, p. 9.
[29] J. Riolan *fils, Curieuses recherches sur les escholes en médecine de Paris et de Montpellier* (Paris: 1651), pp. 3-4.

175

simple that not only the country apothecary or surgeon or those who might have the least knowledge of illnesses and their forms, but also simple peasant women [*femmelettes*] and their children, provided that they can read, will be able to indicate the condition of the sick person, of his malady, and of all the symptoms and circumstances [so that we may] treat him as methodically and well as if he were present." The blue-covered, 60-page pamphlet sold for 5 *sous* and had a very complete index, its format and price indicating it was intended for a wide audience. It consisted of diagrams of the human body upon which the *absen* could mark the location of the malady, and extended lists of possible symptoms from which he could select those that applied. He then sent the filled-out formulary to Renaudot's staff for evaluation. Such long-distance diagnosis would force everyone, those describing and those at the Bureau d'Adresse evaluating, to be "more exact in the recognition and discernment of maladies, and of the description of their cure."[30] With his enthusiasm for chemical medicine, Renaudot's clinic attracted a large number of syphilitics.[31] *La présence des absens* permitted those with "shameful" (*honteux*) maladies to use the Bureau's services without appearing there in person. A portion of *La présence des absens* is reproduced in the Appendix.

This little publication indicated the heights of Renaudot's optimism, his grand confidence that his physicians could effectively serve not only Paris, but the entire realm. To the medical establishment, *La présence des absens* was a lewd affront: imagine crediting simple *femmelettes* with the ability to indicate the sensible symptoms of illness! No wonder Guy Patin wrote that *La présence des absens* "isn't worth the devil, or

[30] *Présence des absens* (Paris: 1642), pp. 5, 8-9. Also see A. Hahn, *Histoire de la médecine et du livre médical* (Paris: 1962), p. 246, and Mandrou, *Culture populaire*, pp. 64-66.
[31] *Inventaire des Adresses*, p. 24.

even its author: it isn't worth the blue paper it's covered with."[32]

The faculty responded to Renaudot's challenge by mounting an all-out pamphlet and litigation war. This struggle was significant far beyond its immediate effect upon Renaudot's career, for it provided a focus for questioning standards and practices basic to the political and social life of the ancien régime itself. What was the power of royal patronage before the power of parlementary sovereignty? How viable were traditional concepts of private charity and medical practice when threatened by Renaudot's conception of social welfare? The struggle likewise suggests how a variety of disparate arguments and interests—corporate, religious, commercial, medical, and parlementary—could coalesce against him.

Three weeks after Renaudot received permission to establish furnaces at the Bureau, the faculty informed him, through the civil authorities at Châtelet, of the 1598 faculty injunction against foreign physicians at Paris.[33] On 3 November 1640, Guillaume du Val replaced Simon Bazin as dean of the medical faculty. Du Val was a no-nonsense traditionalist. His first act as dean was to appoint commissioners to investigate the large number of *empyriques* in Paris, especially Renaudot, "a man of extraordinary audacity, who provides a haven . . . for foreign-trained physicians, vagabonds, *exotiques*, and under the pretext of illegitimate charity (illegitimate because it is without jurisdiction, and moreover goes against the laws and jurisdiction of the Academy of Paris . . .), has instituted consultations with his physicians."[34] Renaudot published two small pamphlets opposing the faculty appeal to Parlement and to Châtelet, restating prior *arrêts* in his favor.[35] At the same time,

[32] Patin to Spon, 2 March 1643.   [33] Statute 59.
[34] *Commentarii*, XIII, f. 107.
[35] *Factum de l'instance de TR . . . contre les doyen et docteurs de l'Ecole en Médecine* [*demandeur en lettres patentes du 7e December*]

177

he published the keynote of his defense, *Les Consultations Charitables*. It was dedicated to M. Sublet de Noyers, Secretary of State. By invoking Sublet de Noyers' name, Renaudot had thrown the gauntlet before those who would challenge the privileges he had received through faithful royal service. The *Consultations Charitables* included the entire text of his 2 September 1640 privilege, since Renaudot felt obliged "to enlighten" those seduced by his enemies' propaganda.[36]

Immediately the dean and two of his colleagues appealed to Sublet de Noyers and Bouvard, the king's physician, to advance their case against Renaudot at the court.[37] If these appeals had no effect, the faculty had another opportunity to pressure Renaudot. Renaudot's sons Isaac and Eusèbe had been students of the medical faculty since 1636. When the brothers applied for their baccalaureate in 1638, the faculty made them swear before a notary that "having the honor of being certified as bachelors of the aforesaid faculty and other degrees thereof, in which they trust and to which they have petitioned, they will not perform any of the functions of the Bureau d'Adresse, in that manner devoting themselves exclusively to the practice of medicine."[38] This was probably very difficult for Renaudot *père* to swallow, but realizing better than most the importance of a doctoral bonnet from the University of Paris, he condoned his sons' actions. Renaudot was seeking the active participation of the faculty at his consultations, and certainly knew that compromise was necessary. But the faculty found cause to attack Renaudot through his sons; on 26 January 1641 it informed the brothers that they were barred from their ap-

---

(S.l.n.d.): *Factum du procez d'entre maistre TR . . . demandeur en requeste présentée au Conseil Privé . . . 30 Octobre 1640 . . .* (S.l.n.d.).

[36] *Consultations charitables*, pp. 10-11.

[37] *Commentarii*, xiii, f. 123 included the payments on 21 March 1641 to the dean, Cusinot, Morlet, and Moreau to cover the expenses of their journey to St. Germain en Laye.

[38] 28 March 1638, *Commentarii*, xiii, f. 46.

proaching doctoral exercises "as a result of the grave injuries caused by their father."

Renaudot quickly appealed to Richelieu. Richelieu had a special interest in the case, as Eusèbe was already attached to his household as a physician. After a fruitless exchange of intermediaries, Richelieu summoned du Val (14 May 1641) and told him that he had ordered Chancellor Séguier to cut off all the Faculty's legal efforts against Renaudot. The cardinal reminded the dean of the Biblical injunction that "sons should not carry the burden of their father's sins"; in other words, readmit the brothers and call off the attack. Du Val promised to use all of his influence to persuade his colleagues, and Renaudot was convinced of the dean's sincerity.[39] His faculty, however, would have none of it. In their 17 May assembly they not only commended those who had thus far written pamphlets against Renaudot, but also insisted upon pursuing the case against him![40] Patin confided to a friend that "if the gazeteer were not supported by His Eminence, as *nebulo hebdomadarius*, we would institute criminal proceedings against him, after which there would be the tumbril or the hang-man or, at least, a full apology; but we must bide our time."[41]

The pamphlet war intensified when Guy Patin entered the lists. Patin was a dyed-in-the-wool medical traditionalist who, with "a good lancet and a *livre* of senna" claimed to cure more sick people "than the Arabs, with all their syrups and opiates."[42]

---

[39] *Commentarii*, f. 116f. Renaudot acknowledged du Val's sincerity in *Response . . . au Libelle fait contre les consultations charitables.*

[40] *Commentarii*, XIII, f. 153.

[41] Patin to Belin, 15 May 1641. See P. Triare, "Richelieu et Guy Patin," *La France médicale* (1905), pp. 21-24.

[42] Patin to Spon, 29 May 1648. Patin offered, among others, the following "préceptes particuliers d'un médecin à son fils": "Soyez homme de bien, ayez le crainte du Dieu devant les yeux et la charité chrestienne en vostre coeur. Visitez vos malades gayement et avec plaisir. N'attendez point de contentement d'eux, mais de Dieu et de vous mesmes. S'ils sont pauvres ou incommedez en leurs affaires, ne prenez rien d'eux qu'ils ne soient devenus riches. Scachez et tenez

His life-long duty, pure and simple, was to rail against the false
gods of superstition and confusion. To Patin, *dévotés* of medical novelty worshiped both. Patin hated Richelieu and Mazarin,
the "red devils," and he attacked their surrogate Renaudot with
all the venom he could muster. In the anonymous *Avertissement à Théophraste Renaudot* he appealed to Bouvard to
cleanse Paris of the charlatans who have "established themselves in Paris under the pretext of charity, which is really a
means of introducing great confusion into medicine, great
profits to Renaudot, and certain ruin to the public." Patin
marshaled all the traditional arguments: the precedents of
those prosecuted for practicing without faculty permission; the
claim that the University of Paris was older than the University of Montpellier; the fact that charitable treatments existed
in Paris long before those at the Bureau d'Adresse. Renaudot's
training was assailed: how much medicine could a 19-year-old
physician possibly know? The only reason Renaudot prescribed
in Latin was so that his apothecaries could better bilk the
public. The only end his public consultations served was "to
amuse the simple people and get money from the spectators
who have come to see the histrionics."

Even Renaudot's publishing came under fire. Patin said that
Renaudot did not invent the gazette, but that they had existed
in Rome some 40 years before. Instead of being an honorable

pour certain que vous devez votre paine aux pauvres sans aucun
salaire . . . Les pauvres sont membres de Dieu et nous sont recom-
mandez de Dieu; mais gardez vous de leur importunité, à quoy ils
sont fort sujets et plus que les riches . . . La pharmacie est une pierre
d'achoppement et de scandale à un medecin, dont il se doit sagement
garder. Ne faites jamais rien contre vostre conscience et l'honneur de
vostre profession en faveur d'un apothecaire . . . [their profession]
n'est entrée en credit que par la connivence de quelques medecins et
par la sottise du peuple qui veut estre trompé. Un medecin ne scauroit
beaucoup ordonner chez un malade sans luy faire tort et à sa conscience aussi, et mesmes le plus souvent il se damne et tue son malade."
R. Pintard, ed., *La Mothe le Vayer, Gassendi, Guy Patin* (Paris: 1943),
pp. 63, 67.

historiographer, Renaudot was instead a gazetteer who would publish any story, true or false, as long as it sold copies. Patin's conclusions left no doubt of the mission at hand. "Since Renaudot, from a roomful of junkmen [*frippiers*] and usurers, wished to erect a synagogue of physicians within the University, each of the physicians of Paris has the right, staff in hand, to rout these physicians, companions of junkmen and usurers, who profane and prostitute the beauty and chastity of Medicine. And if we wished to use our authority, we would send our students to wreck all the vessels of these new Alchemists, as Hesiod did in the shop of a potter who had profaned the lovely verses he had composed about human work. Here then is my intent, and the purpose of this writing."[43]

Four days later, Renaudot responded in *Remarques sur l'avertissement à Théophraste Renaudot . . . par Maschurat.* Few polemicists could equal Patin, but in this pamphlet Renaudot rose to the challenge and came as close as he ever did to being Patin's acerbic equal. He addressed him as Maschurat, a sly dig at Patin's student past when he had supported himself as proofreader. He referred to Patin as "this young doctor," a criticism Patin had first leveled against Renaudot. *Remarques sur l'avertissement* was a step by step rebuttal of the preceding pamphlet. The faculty had attacked Renaudot for prescribing in Latin: Renaudot attacked them for prescribing in French, expecting no more training of an apothecary than one would expect of "a servant girl just arrived from the country, whom one wouldn't trust to boil an egg." The Paris faculty would rather prescribe an enema or bloodletting, some senna or cassia than "list on paper a succession of other good remedies, in the exact description of which appears and exists the proof of a physician's ignorance or ability."[44] There was nothing irreligious about Arab, i.e., chemical medicine. If "our proofreader" reasoned that Hip-

[43] *Avertissement . . .* , pp. 7, 31-32, 35, 58.
[44] *Remarques sur l'avertissement . . .* , pp. 10, 38.

pocrates and Galen could have been good Christians, why not also Arab physicians, and by association, the physicians of Montpellier? Renaudot published these documents independently and as part of the *Gazette* of 25 July 1641.[45] He was now at the height of his power.

Its civil and parlementary recourses ineffective, the faculty could do nothing but sit back and watch Renaudot bask in Richelieu's protection. Soon, however, it took advantage of Richelieu's absence from Paris. On 1 February 1642 the faculty requested the royal council to abolish Renaudot's privileges. There was another reason why it chose to take advantage of Richelieu's absence. In spite of numerous delays, Renaudot's sons were now candidates for the doctoral bonnet. Candidates were presented in the order in which they had passed the licentiate; if a candidate were not present, he had to wait for the entire list to be accepted and passed before he could again present himself.[46] The faculty often made concessions for candidates unable to follow this order, but Eusèbe was with Richelieu serving as one of his physicians, and it had no intention of waiving the requirements for a Renaudot. Anticipating this, Richelieu wrote directly to du Val requesting that they reserve Eusèbe's place until his return to Paris.[47] The faculty acknowledged the letter of 13 March, and thanked Richelieu for sending it. But they were not finished. In the meanwhile, they sought to prevent Eusèbe's brother Isaac from passing the vesperies, the public elocution preparatory to the doctorate. On 30 August they offered to stop obstructing the brothers, if they would again renounce the Bureau d'Adresse. Renaudot must have been furious by this reminder of the distasteful statement his sons had signed in 1638. On 6 September Renau-

---

[45] *Extrait des registres du Conseil privé du Roy* (S.l.n.d.); *No. 85. Arrests du conseil donnez en faveur des consultations charitables* (Paris: 25 July 1641), pp. 445-53.

[46] Statute 34.

[47] Gilles de la Tourette, *Renaudot*, pp. 182-83.

dot and his sons secured a parlementary *arrêt*, evidently through the influence of Mathieu Molé, ordering the faculty, "in the accustomed manner," to admit the brothers within two weeks; if not, "at the end of the elapsed period, the present *arrêt* will serve as their doctoral title." The *arrêt* was read to the faculty on 15 September. Ever the casuists, they decided that the "accustomed manner" meant a *senatus-consultum* of the faculty. In fact, they could delay the brothers' admittance as long as they wished, since they had never passed their examinations![48] The faculty knew that Richelieu was very ill, and that time was on its side. The correspondence dragged on: Richelieu appealed to du Val through Citoys, his chief physician. On 20 October the faculty agreed to Richelieu's request to admit the brothers to the vesperies and the doctorate, "but that they humbly beseech the Cardinal to attempt to silence the faculty's rude Calumniator, their father, and to use his authority to prohibit the gazeteer from sullying the doctors of this flourishing School, who shall sing the praises of His Eminence if he would agree to these proposals."[49] On 23 October, Richelieu consented. Four days later the faculty agreed "that the two brothers would be admitted, thanks to His Eminence."[50]

Meanwhile, Renaudot had become embroiled in another issue. In 1641, René Moreau, a former dean, sponsored a new edition of the works of Daniel Sennert, the Wittenburg professor whose writings sought a *via media* between orthodox Galenists and advocates of the new chemicals. The Latin preface, otherwise undistinguished, spoke of Moreau's efforts "against some rascals [*nebulonem*] who, claiming false piety and insincere charity, have been unsuccessful in introducing their novelties into the city."[51] The preface was signed by the printers, but in fact had been written by Guy Patin. Patin

---

[48] *Ibid.*, p. 192.   [49] *Commentarii*, XIII, f. 142.

[50] *Ibid.*, f. 153 records payment of 30 *sous* for the two new transcriptions of renunciation which Eusèbe and Isaac had to sign.

[51] *Operum* (Paris: 1641), Preface.

acknowledged his authorship, but refused to identify who his specific target had been. Renaudot was certain the remarks were intended for him. Louise de la Brosse, sister of Guy de la Brosse, founder of the Jardin des Plantes, thought that Patin was attacking the memory of her dead brother, whom Patin despised almost as much as he despised Renaudot.[52] Renaudot, joined by de la Brosse's sister, initiated a private libel suit against Patin. On 14 August 1642 they confronted Patin before the *Maître des Requêtes*, demanding that Patin deny their charges. This was a tactical error. Not only did they lose their case, but the occasion gave Patin a golden opportunity to attack his accusers. For an hour and three-quarters, in a packed auditorium, gloated Patin, "I spoke *sur-le-champ*, without having practiced or even written a single word: two barristers who came to plead against me, one in the name of the gazeteer and the other in the name of de la Brosse, made me eager to outdo them and to say better things. Neither the one nor the other was able to prove that '*nebulo et blatero*' were injurious terms . . . their feeble arguments served as well to vindicate me as all the eloquence in the world, and my innocence obtained for me so favorable an audience, that I had the entire assembly of judges for me."[53] Meanwhile, on 2 December 1642, the faculty finally permitted Isaac to defend his thesis for the vesperies. He was asked to discuss the topic "Must a person bitten by a mad dog be bled?"[54]—a topic calculated to embarrass the son

[52] Patin wrote to Belin on 4 September 1641, soon after de la Brosse's death: "Comme on lui parla ce même vendredi d'être saigné, il repondit que c'était le rémède des pedants sanguinaires (il nous fasoit l'honneur de nous appeler ainsi), et qu'il aimoit mieux mourir que d'être saigné; aussi a-t-il fait. Le diable le saignera en l'autre monde, comme mérite un fourbe, un athée, un imposteur, un homicide et bourreau public, tel qu'il était." Some authors have incorrectly believed Louise de la Brosse to be Guy's daughter. See E. T. Hamy, "La famille de Guy de la Brosse," *Bulletin du Muséum d'Histoire Naturelle*, vi (1900), 13-16. I wish to thank Rio Howard for bringing this article to my attention.

[53] Patin to Belin, 12 August 1643, 22 August 1647.

[54] Gilles de la Tourette, *Renaudot*, p. 195.

of a *chymique*. By this act, the faculty had satisfied at least part of its responsibility under the *arrêt* of 6 September. But any hopes of triumphing against the faculty would be short-lived. On 4 December 1642, Richelieu died.

The faculty immediately reversed its position. On 30 December it declared that Isaac would not be admitted to the doctorate because during the vesperies he had responded rudely to his dean. With Richelieu dead, the faculty reopened the attack on Renaudot's charitable consultations. Bouvard now assured the faculty that he would use his influence to prohibit the Grand Conseil from verifying the letters patent: "as long as I live, I shall be your strongest support."[55] On 2 April 1643, Michel de la Vigne, newly elected dean, enlisted the University against Renaudot. This broadened the issue tremendously. Now the entire Parisian educational establishment—all of its faculties, colleges, and auxiliaries—was involved, and not the physicians alone. With their newly found strength, with Renaudot devoid of Richelieu's and Louis XIII's support (the king had died on 14 May 1643), the faculty went in for the kill. On 16 July the faculty appealed directly to the Conseil du Roi, instead of using the civil and parlementary channels it had always used before. Not only had it enlarged its support, but also now its target. It demanded injunctions against not only the charitable consultations, but against all of Renaudot's activities. Also attacked were the "many foreigners, without titles, degrees, letters, or approval, [who] shamelessly attempt the said practice [of medicine] under the pretext of the assemblies and charitable consultations at the Bureau d'Adresse, by which they abuse the credulity of common people to the prejudice of the public. [Since] the petitioners have felt themselves duty-bound to bring this to the attention of the *prévôt* of Paris, legitimate judge of the parties to whom jurisdiction of these police matters pertain, he should be in agreement to subpoena M. Théophraste Renaudot, author of these disorders

---

[55] *Commentarii*, XIII, f. 162v.

and patron of this entire cabal."[56] The faculty argued that since this case was within the *prévôt*'s jurisdiction, Renaudot's *arrêts de conseil* of 4 June and 9 July 1641 should be ignored.

On 7 August 1643, the Conseil judged that Renaudot's activities fell within the jurisdiction of the *prévôt* of Paris, completely reversing its policy of the past 25 years. "The King in his Council, referred and still refers the dean and doctors in Medicine of the Faculty of Paris, their litigation and circumstances related thereunto, to the *prévôt* of Paris, to be judged and effected."[57] For all practical purposes, Renaudot had lost his case.

He realized the desperation of his position in *La requeste présentée à la Reyne*. His only recourse was to servility: "The sweetness by which your regency has begun suffices to give me boldness to throw myself to Your Majesty's feet, and implore your favor." Renaudot invoked the memory of the dead king, reminding Anne that she could have no higher calling than to continue his good works. To criticism that Renaudot spoke "according to the times," he replied that "everyone knows that the dead king not only read my *Gazettes* and did not permit the least blemish in them, but sent me *mémoires* to use there almost every day." His conclusion was direct and candid, perhaps too candid. How sad, he said, that the royal council could destroy his philanthropic and medical activities in so cavalier a fashion while continuing in good conscience to exploit his *Gazette*.[58]

The faculty, eager to silence Renaudot, bought 300 copies of his *Requeste*.[59] At the same time Patin continued the offensive by writing *Examen de la requeste présentée à la Reyne par le Gazetier* (4 November 1643). Patin never referred to the gaze-

---

[56] *Ibid.*, f. 179.
[57] Quoted by Gilles de la Tourette, *Renaudot*, pp. 207-08.
[58] *Requeste presentée à la Reyne*, pp. 1, 5, 7-8.
[59] *Commentarii*, XIII, f. 180.

teer by name, since "one must not befoul paper with his name, a name which will be odious and execrable to posterity." He attacked Renaudot's effrontery in reminding the Queen of her duties, his presumption in asserting that the Bureau d'Adresse was the only charitable medical outlet in Paris. What kind of a man was this, asked Patin, who would sully the ancient ramparts of the city with his hospital? Why did Renaudot need a magnificent building and a large staff when the faculty of Paris had none, when Louis XIII—without staff or facilities—could cure thousands in the courtyard of St. Germain through the power of his touch alone? The gazeteer's consultations were a place of disorder, where libertines, Huguenots, and heretics babbled endlessly, where younger physicians showed no respect to their elders. There were no teachers to interpret the Masters. As a result, Renaudot's disciples might know theories, but knew nothing of specific cases. And that was not all: Renaudot of the *Gazette* was as culpable as Renaudot of the Bureau d'Adresse. Patin referred to a *Gazette* article of 4 June 1633 in which Renaudot supposedly made Louis XIII "the enemy of God and the protector of the Lutherans."[60] What could one say of the protector of Huguenot physicians, defiler of Christian charity and of the reputation of the most Christian king of Europe, provider of annual masses for the soul of a wife "who died in Huguenotism?"[61]

Patin's appeal to the Queen, revealing Renaudot's religious sins, hit the mark. On 9 December 1643 Renaudot and his associates were ordered to cease all of their activities. A short time later the Dean and several colleagues inspected Renaudot's premises, and ordered a commission to inventory all that they found there.[62] Renaudot desperately reappealed to the council, arguing that enforcement of the 7 August 1643 *arrêt* in favor of

[60] See p. 149, n. 95.
[61] *Examen de la Requeste. . .* , pp. 7, 16, 18, 22-23. See pp. 10, 18.
[62] *Commentarii*, XIII, ff. 210-11.

the faculty would denigrate the reputation of royal council and destroy the hallowed tradition it had earned under Louis XIII.[63]

In a final *Response à l'examen de la requeste présentée à la reyne par Théophraste Renaudot . . . par Maschurat*, Renaudot attempted to reverse the forces which were sweeping him aside. He reminded his readers that, in addition to his efforts, he gave 2,000 *livres* each year to the poor. Sovereignty was not communicable; therefore jurisdiction of the charitable consultations belonged to the royal council in which it originated, and not the lower court to which the faculty constantly appealed. Examining patients by committee, as he did at the Bureau, was much more effective than examining them by one man, as the faculty insisted. How dare they criticize him for treating so many patients when their doctors claimed to treat 1,500 ill each day at the Hôtel Dieu. His lifelong mission, he said, was self-dedication to the principles and practices of Christian charity.[64]

After several days of arguments from 5 lawyers representing Renaudot, his sons, the University of Medicine of Montpellier, the medical faculty of Paris, and the University of Paris, final statements were offered on 1 March 1644 in a public session of the Parlement. The parties recapitulated all of the issues of the pamphlet war, but in some cases with a new emphasis. In a room packed to the rafters, facing members of the faculty, the Parlement, the six *corps des marchands* in full array, Renaudot listened to the arguments which would either abrogate or vindicate his life's work.

The faculty attacked Renaudot on the basis of medical incompetence, moral and religious character, and usurpation of the role played by the University of Paris.

Chenvot, the faculty advocate, insisted that no matter how effective new chemical cures might be in theory, there was no

[63] *Factum du procez d'entre TR . . . et médecins de l'eschole de Paris* (S.l. 1643).
[64] *Response à l'examen. . . ,* pp. 9, 21, 30, 71.

stronger argument for categorically condemning them than the death of one or two chemical patients. As chemical exponents themselves agreed, the new medications at best accomplished no more than what traditional methods did in their own good time. The efficacy of chemical cures was hardly an issue: to the faculty, what was most important was not their potential value, but the actual danger of poor refining and overdosage. Encouraging these cures was reprehensible and irresponsible. Since time immemorial the same ends had been accomplished much more surely, if less quickly, through bloodletting. This remained the faculty point of view, always.

Chenvot argued that Renaudot received a second-rate education at Montpellier. He never attacked Montpellier directly, choosing instead to discuss Arab medicine, *circulateurs*, etc. Not only had Renaudot been seduced by dangerous and unproven theories, but he held Montpellier's cheap degree, rather than the thorough degree similar to that granted at Paris. Moreover, he had been graduated at the age of 19, much younger than the 22 years of age required by the Parisian faculty. In a word, he was unfit to practice medicine. Citing his activities as journalist, educator, pawnbroker, lecturer, chemist, and employment counselor, the faculty insisted that Renaudot could not have practiced medicine with the dedication it deserved. This allegation was a backhanded compliment to Renaudot's virtuosity, but a telling argument, nonetheless. To the faculty, medicine was a full-time responsibility, seriously assumed and rigorously practiced, demanding total dedication at the expense of all other responsibility. Either one practiced medicine, or one did not. Renaudot's own career was confused and chaotic, and in such a situation, medical expertise could not flourish unsullied.

Renaudot had committed the unpardonable sin of creating disorder in the medical profession itself. At his charitable consultations and in his writings, he had granted equality to surgeons and apothecaries, and in so doing, destroyed the traditional hierarchy of responsibility and authority upon which the ancient art thrived. To question the social relationships between the physician and his surgeons and apothecaries could not help but question the authority of traditional medical methods over surgical and pharmaceutical methods. If any science must remain orderly, it was medicine, dedicated to the proper maintenance of order in the human body.

Renaudot's personal life provided his opponents with ample ammunition. From the outset, they assailed his Protestant origins, the fact that his first wife was Protestant, that a large number of his colleagues were Protestant. And even though they recognized his conversion to Catholicism, they insisted that he did so for politics and Richelieu, rather than out of any burning zeal.

He was born in Loudun, "where the devils have established their residence." He had been a party to their secrets and "deceits."[65] Renaudot was known to have associated with Urbain Grandier while at Loudun, and perhaps had used his influence defending Grandier's excesses. At the least, Renaudot had printed the absolute minimum on this most notorious scandal of the decade; at the most, he may even have published an eulogy after his friend's execution.[66] Chenvot reminded the court that there were two methods by which those in league

[65] *Arrest de la cour de Parlement . . . contre TR* (Paris: 1 March 1644), p. 6.

[66] The *Gazette* of 26 August 1634 contained this dispatch from Loudun: "Hier [18 August] fut icy bruslé vif Urbain Grandier Curé de l'Eglise S. Pierre du Marché de cette ville, natif du pais du Maine, apres avoir fait l'amende honorable nud en chemise: pour Magie et autres crimes énormes; par jugement du sieur Lauberdemont Conseiller d'Estat et 12 autres Commissaires à ce deputez par Sa Majesté." This is hardly the eulogy which G. Legué (*Urbain Grandier*, p. 22n) said appeared in the *Gazette.* Dumoustier de la Fond said that the separately-published *Oraison funebre* "sur la mort d'Urbain Grandier, n'a d'autre mérite que d'avoir eté publiée dans un temps où il falloit croire que Grandier avoit eté coupable du crime de magie." (*Essais sur l'histoire de Loudun*, p. 123). I have not been able to locate this eulogy. See Mandrou, *Magistrats et sorciers*, p. 211n.

with the Devil impressed the unwary, by carrying news from afar and by conjuring up strange potions for the ill. "To the rank of Gazeteer [Renaudot] wishes to join that of the Empiric, under the title of *Médecin charitable*."[67] The accident of being named Théophraste, "which promises nothing less than divine and supernatural actions," was nearly as incriminating as the accident of his Poitevan birth. His first name was the same as one of the classic authorities on personality and bodily traits. What *hubris*, said the faculty, for Renaudot to assume that they were equal![68] Even more telling was the comparison of "Cacophraste" Renaudot to another Théophraste: Philippus Aureolus Theophrastus Bombastus von Hohenheim, the infamous Paracelsus.[69] Considering the hermetic and mystical topics discussed at the Bureau d'Adresse, his laboratories and inventions, Renaudot's enemies had good reason to fear him as a dangerous *magus*.

Even Renaudot's physiognomy conspired against him. The noble art of medicine, so the faculty argued, demanded nobly formed practitioners. "At the University of Louvain, they admit no one to the doctorate in Medicine, nor to its practice, who has a facial deformity. Lanfranc hoped that no Surgeon would be ugly. Hippocrates desired that a Physician should be a healthy, well-formed man, *Distortum vultum sequitur destortio morum*. A deformed man must not be admitted to the exercise of Medicine, because he could trouble the imagination of pregnant women, who might give birth to monsters who resemble these physicians. Moreover, such a horrible face

---

[67] *Arrest de la cour...*, p. 6. One of the inventions considered by the 1634 conferences was a method for sending information a distance of 50 miles, without employing cannons or bells. See Appendix B.

[68] *Arrest de la cour...*, p. 15.

[69] This was one of Patin's favorite sobriquets for Renaudot, "l'infame menteur et imposteur *Théophraste*, ou plutôt *Cacophraste* Renaudot, ce vilain nez pourri de gazetier (Quand le savant philosophe et bon médecin Thomas Erastus, parle contre le roi des charlatans, il l'appelle *Cacophrastus*)." Patin to Falconet, 4 December 1665.

191

frightens the ill, and can cause their death, as happened to
Phaillus, in Pausantas, who so intently gazed at the bronze
skeleton which Hippocrates had consecrated at the Temple of
Esculape, that, later dreaming of the hideousness of the skeleton, he became ill and died. Those who had a broken nose
were not admitted to the Priesthood, as it says in Leviticus,
so that they would not frighten women who, seeing such a
priest at the altar and later remembering his appearance, might
retain that memory and give birth to monsters."[70] Guy Patin
was proud of his own sharp well-formed nose, and detested
flat-nosed men, "almost all of whom are reeking and stinking
fellows [*puants et punais*], like the gazeteer Théophraste
Renaudot."[71] To an age which believed that superior physical

[70] Riolan *fils, Curieuses recherches*, pp. 280-82.

[71] Patin to Spon, 16 August 1650. In the same letter, Patin remembered his triumph on 14 August 1642, when Renaudot and Louise
de la Brosse unsuccessfully accused him of defamation of character.
"Aussi me souviens-je qu'en sortant du palais [du Justice] ce jour-là,
je l'abordai en lui disant: M. Renaudot, vous pouvez vous consoler, car
vous avez gagné en perdant. Comment don? Me repondit-il. C'est, lui
dis-je, que vout étiez camus lorsque vout etes entre ici, et que vous en
sortez avec un pied de nez."
Patin celebrated the 1 March 1644 decision in a 4-page *Le nez
pourry de Théophraste Renaudot*. An example of Patin's verse:

> Un pied de Nez serviroit davantage
> A ce Fripier, Docteur du bas Etage,
> Pour fleurer tout, du matin jusqu'au soir;
> Et toutesfois on diroit à le voir,
> Que c'est un Dieu de la Chinoise plage.
>   Mais qu'ay-je dit: c'est plustost un fromage,
> Ou sans respect la Mite a fait ravage;
> Pour le sentir, il ne faut point avoir
>   Un pied de Nez.
> Le fin Camus touche de ce langage,
> Met aussi, tost un remede en usage,
> Ou d'Esculape il ressent le pouvoir:
> Car s'y frottant, il s'est vu recevoir
> En plein Senat, tout le long du visage,
>   Un pied de Nez.

form reflected moral superiority, such arguments were telling indeed.

If Renaudot practiced charity, he did not practice Christian charity. He sought his own reward, instead of thinking first of the recipient of his charity. True Christian charity was performed quietly and privately, completely contrary to the way Renaudot, with his publishing, posters, and consultations in public, offered it. His *vents-à-grâce* were private money-making institutions, bilking the public and reestablishing usury in Paris. Chenvot's remarks here represented the sentiments of the six *corps des marchands* of the city, who had long opposed Renaudot's *monts-de-piété* and were currently engaged in preventing further banking activities in Paris.[72] It likewise reflected the strong, diffuse religious and moral opposition to low-interest loans.

Finally, the faculty attacked Renaudot for usurping its traditional and legal rights. To prove Renaudot had no right to practice in Paris, they marshaled lists of Montpellierans who earlier had been banned from practice. Chenvot argued that Parisians expected and received similar treatment when they wished to practice in Montpellier, even though the University of Paris had precedence over Montpellier as "the oldest daughter of the kings, and the mother of other universities."

---

[72] Balthasar Gerbier received letters patent on 3 September 1643 for the "Direction et Intendance général" of *monts-de-piété* in Paris and throughout France, under the protection of the Duke of Orleans and the Prince de Condé. It has been suggested that his lobbying was responsible for the revocation of Renaudot's patents. (G. H. Turnbull, *Hartlib, Dury* and *Comenius*, p. 57.) In spite of appeals to Church and civic powers, Gerbier was unsuccessful in getting parlementary approval, and in 1648 his patents were revoked. See his arguments in *Remonstrance tres-humble . . . à monseigneur l'illustrissime Archevesque de Paris. . . .* (Paris: 1643) and *Exposition . . . à messieurs les docteurs en theologie de la Faculté à Paris. . . .* (Paris: 1644), both reprinted in *Archives curieuses de l'histoire de France* (2nd series), VI, pp. 215-26, 233-42. B.N. mss. f.fr. 17438, f. 80r; Thoisy 148, ff. 350-77.

All arts, crafts, and communities had a certain place to occupy, unique to them alone. "It is appropriate for natural bodies to reject everything which is of a foreign substance: and therefore, we show ourselves as a *Faculté expultrice*, in order to purge the body of excrements and evil humors. Why do foreigners come to harvest the fruits of our labors? Is the University so sterile that she must call others to her aid? . . . The faculty is a mother, obliged to raise and support her legitimate children, to disavow any of her illegitimate children, to suffocate any forgeries or miscarriages, to expose these counterfeit seeds, these inanimate moles, these superfetations which come to life only from corruption and rotting compost; to cut to the quick these superfluous, supernumerary parts which grow upon the body and which serve only to inconvenience it and make it more hideous and monstrous. [They] would build a new University, erect altar against altar, faction and party, in the Capital."[73]

These remarks were not simply empty rhetorical flourishes. Order, unity, place, station, simplicity, legitimacy: these values cut across every dimension of the case. Without these, the universe falls apart, society cannot thrive, the human body cannot exist, medicine cannot heal, Christianity cannot bring salvation. If Renaudot were permitted to mock these values, everything the faculty represented would be destroyed— Christianity, Medical Truth, Professional Morality. The issues were as broad as the attack, the stakes as high as the rhetoric. To a faculty and a university which had absorbed one humiliating defeat after another, be it Richelieu's attack upon their immunities or libertine ridicule of their scholasticism or declining incomes, the victory against Renaudot was necessary for their psychic survival. We do the faculty an injustice if we see the events of 1 March 1644 as simply a vendetta against one Théophraste Renaudot. It was that, but much, much more.

[73] *Arrest de la cour* . . . , pp. 11, 14.

The faculty recognized in principle that royal physicians could practice in Paris. It insisted, however, that Renaudot had never fulfilled the office to which he was named in 1612. He was not paid, was not called upon to serve, nor did he serve *par quartier,* i.e., he was not attached directly and actively to the royal household.[74]

In Chenvot's deposition, the faculty did not repeat the accusations it had earlier made regarding Renaudot's other titles. Elsewhere, it said that the title of *Commissaire Général des Pauvres, Maître et Intendant Général des Bureaux d'Adresse de France* was an empty title, "Intendant" being reserved for financial officers.[75] Also, the so-called duties for the poor which he would perform were already being performed by the *Aumônier de France,* as head of the royal and national charities.

Questioning Renaudot's titles was a particularly fruitful approach. Whether as a purely private or completely public figure, on the most essential level Renaudot had exposed the conflict between private charity, as traditionally conceived, and secularized public welfare. Renaudot's programs ran counter to traditional private charity, both in conception and execution. If one could question Renaudot's offices, if one could prove that he was a private individual, one could thereby prove that he had usurped roles performed by long-established corporate individuals, the faculty, and the Church. The age may have been able to make a mental distinction between public and private, but still could not separate them emotionally; confusion, in Mousnier's phrase, "vivait encore dans les sensibilités."[76] Renaudot had little defense against these accusations. Clearly, the title that he had assumed had not existed before, and it was difficult to speak of his position as

---

[74] *Ibid.,* p. 8.

[75] *Défense de la Faculté de Médecine de Paris contre son Calumniateur,* p. 7.

[76] R. Mousnier, *La venalité des offices sous Henri IV et Louis XIII* (Rouen: 1945), p. 409.

an office, in modern terms. He was a royal appointee, a private individual with royal protection and encouragement, regardless of how "national" the title sounded. Without royal support behind him, the title meant nothing, and as a result the faculty could successfully attack the title and destroy it.[77] The content of the new office of *Commissaire Général des Pauvres* was superfluous, and the title was so vague as to be meaningless.

Bataille, Renaudot's lawyer, built his defense upon two major points: the question was less judicial than scientific in nature, and secondly, it should not even be discussed in Parlement as it fell instead within the jurisdiction of royal council.[78]

Renaudot always argued that the faculty was more threatened by his medical and scientific ideas than by this legal and judicial issue. Why else, then, would the faculty have directed so much abuse against his sons, and against the University of Medicine of Montpellier: "*Voilà*, gentlemen, the state of the controversy which you must judge: in which it seems that one might be able to treat this problem, to overcome this difficulty which pertains more to the School than to the Bar: to know if Medicine is a science which has principles and proofs; if its employment is absolutely useful and necessary; or if it is a casual and arbitrary art, a fortuitous and uncertain knowledge."[79] That Renaudot claimed to stand for a science "which should

[77] The term "intendant" was used for financial officers in general, but not until Colbert's ministry did the title imply a specific and continuing office existing apart from the individual officeholder. G. Pagès, "Essai sur l'évolution des institutions administratives . . . ," *Revue d'histoire moderne* (1932), 49, and G. Zeller, "l'Administration monarchique avant les intendants," *Revue historique* (1947), passim.

[78] It is difficult to identify Renaudot's advocate precisely, as there were three Batailles attached to the court during the period. C. E. Holmes believes it was Gilles Bataille (admitted to Parlement in 1617), who had a long tradition of speaking for Richelieu, and who enjoyed a greater reputation than did the two younger men (Étienne, admitted in 1643; Jacques, admitted 1637). *l'Éloquence judiciare de 1620 à 1660* (Paris: 1967), p. 138n.

[79] *Arrest de la cour* . . . , pp. 20-21.

have principles and proofs" more than did the University of Paris is perhaps interesting, but in terms of the trial itself, insignificant. More important, by taking this stand Renaudot hoped to show how ill-suited this question was to judicial settlement. If the faculty were so worried about Renaudot's medicine, why then did it pursue the attack by quibbling over legal technicalities?

And this stance led to the second element in Renaudot's defense, the superiority of the Conseil du Roi over lesser courts. On this point, in a strictly legal sense, Renaudot had a stronger case. The lower courts could deliberate, but only at the behest of higher jurisdictions. Lower deliberations were always liable to an *arrêt*, quite literally a "stoppage," from a higher jurisdiction. The king in his councils was supreme, and as his prior *arrêts* had stated, lower courts had no jurisdiction over matters pertaining to Renaudot's Bureau d'Adresse. But the Conseil du Roi could undo as well as do, as it did on 7 August 1643 when it referred Renaudot's affairs to the *prévôt* of Paris and the Parlement. Renaudot knew not to question council's prerogative to refer cases to lower jurisdictions; instead he stressed the fact that this contradicted the policies Louis XIII had established and maintained. The Bureau d'Adresse was born in the Conseil du Roi, and there its fortunes should remain.

The strength of this narrow, legalistic interpretation for Renaudot through 1642 was also the source of his downfall in 1643-1644. Without the support of a Richelieu or a Louis XIII in the Conseil du Roi, Renaudot had no recourse before the power of ordinary, parlementary sovereignty. The *parlementaires* eagerly took advantage of the lack of leadership and the fluidity of membership and organization in the council of 1643-1644. Renaudot's important friends, Sublet de Noyers and Chavigny were both disgraced, and Louis XIII and Richelieu dead.[80] His immunity and the antagonism he had engendered

[80] R. Mousnier, "Le Conseil du Roi de la mort de Henri III au gouvernement personnel de Louis XIV," *Études d'histoire moderne et*

197

derived from their patronage. But with these men gone, Renaudot had to stand defenseless before the groups which he had antagonized with their encouragement: the university, the corporations which ran the city, the publishing interests, and a Parlement disgusted by Richelieu's usurpation of its traditional powers. Renaudot could not have had a more powerful patron than Richelieu. He could not have incurred a more formidable group of enemies than those, implicitly and explicitly, arrayed before him in Parlement on 1 March 1644.

With all of these enemies, Renaudot needed strong friends. Mazarin's attitude toward Renaudot differed from Richelieu's. Although Mazarin inherited Renaudot, and Renaudot quickly enough transferred his services to Mazarin, never did he receive Mazarin's total support. Part of it was personal. Renaudot was Richelieu's creature, and for 30 years owed and gladly rendered him his sincere and total loyalty. In exchange, Richelieu created and defined the public Renaudot. Without him, the public Renaudot did not exist. Richelieu needed Renaudot's *Gazette*, but he also eagerly defended Renaudot's other activities. Mazarin, on the other hand, could not have cared less about Richelieu's creature. While he was eager to use Renaudot's presses, he was unconcerned with defending his other interests.

If Mazarin was lukewarm toward Renaudot, Anne of Austria was openly hostile. Renaudot suffered from his total identity with Richelieu, Anne's nemesis. Through Richelieu's control, she seldom appeared in the first 12 years of the *Gazette*; one can sense a change of regime in mid-1643 simply by noticing her increased presence in the *Gazette*. Some have suggested that Louis XIII himself may have used news suppression as a way of embarrassing his wife.[81] In any case,

---

contemporaine (1947-1948), 54, 62-67; O. Ranum, *Councillors of Louis XIII*, pp. 99, 112.

[81] Fournier, *Écrivains sur le trône*, pp. 7-8.

Renaudot was caught in the middle. The faculty took advantage of this antipathy. They reminded her of Renaudot's effrontery in *Requeste présentée à la Reyne* when he wrote that the queen could do no greater good than to continue the good works of Louis XIII's reign.[82] This was a horrible tactical error on Renaudot's part, reminding the queen to be more like her dead husband! Faculty attacks upon Renaudot's career were tailor-made to turn the queen against him. The piously superstitious Anne had no sympathy for a man characterized as a libertine, Huguenot, charlatan, Jew, and sorcerer, a man who represented the antithesis of her good work. Every faculty appeal to the queen used this as its major weapon.

Given the situation, the outcome was inevitable. The court rendered its verdict. Renaudot was ordered "to present to this court the letters patent addressed to it obtained by Renaudot for the establishment of the Bureau and permission for his *vents-à-grâce*: in the meanwhile [the court] very expressly prohibits him from either selling or lending on interest in the future, regardless of anything the court may have previously ordained. The officers of Châtelet shall go to Renaudot's premises to draw up an inventory of all the goods found at his establishment, in order to return and distribute them to whomever they belong."[83] Except for his publishing, all of Renaudot's activities were effectively stopped. He would continue to use his titles as *Maître et Intendant Général des Bureaux d'Adresse de France*, but for all practical purposes without meaning to them.

The 1 March *arrêt* ordered the faculty, "within a week, to assemble and consider . . . a system of charitable consultations for the poor, and then report back to the court for its approval."[84] Long before, in March 1639, the faculty had attempted to establish consultations parallel to Renaudot's. Their efforts were poorly received, and two years later they had to

[82] *Requeste présentée à la Reyne*, p. 3.
[83] *Arrest de la cour . . .* , p. 33.   [84] *Ibid.*

solicit the aid of parish priests to publicize their Saturday consultations.[85] The *arrêt* of 13 May 1644 finally organized their charitable consultations. Every Wednesday and Saturday morning, 6 members of the faculty would be available for medical advice: "they will examine diligently and exactly the maladies of each of the poor people [who come there] and prescribe the proper and necessary remedies . . . so that the illnesses of no poor person should be neglected; if there are any persons in the city who cannot walk and whose wounds are not dressed as they should be, the dean of the faculty, being advised thereof, will order that each of them shall be visited by a physician and an apothecary."[86] Faculty-sponsored consultations began on 4 June 1644. Renaudot had provided the faculty with its model.

[85] Renaudot, *Response au libelle* . . . , p. 17f.
[86] *Commentarii*, XIII, ff. 223-24.

CHAPTER VII

Last Years: 1644-1653

WITH his patents revoked and hopes of expanding his Bureau d'Adresse stifled, Renaudot's last years showed little of his characteristic experimentation and enthusiasm. There were still journalistic battles to be fought and victories for the state to be won, but these were internecine and sordid compared to the international battles which Renaudot had fought under Richelieu. He continued to serve the crown through its new chief minister, but less fervently than before. His defeat in Parlement and the pressures of age would take their toll, and the Renaudot of this decade was a sorry shadow of the confident Renaudot of the Richelieu era.

In a society which characterized a 40-year old man as "barbon," Renaudot was a very old man when his patents were revoked. He was 58 in 1644, and the pressures of age and poor health had caught up with him. Ill health prompted rumors of his death. He had contracted syphilis, understandable enough considering the large number of syphilitics he treated at the Bureau d'Adresse. It was also possible, if we believe his enemy Patin, that he contracted the infection from a woman of easy virtue.[1] In any case, scars pockmarked his face. His flat nose, long the butt of ridicule, was considerably worn away by 1644. Renaudot's 1631 portrait suggests that he may have habitually breathed through his mouth, and he probably had respiratory problems as the syphilis damaged his nasal passages. He suffered a number of strokes by 1649, as the worsening infection affected his cardio-vascular system.[2]

---

[1] "Le gazetier n'est pas mort. Il est vrai qu'il a été longtemps malade et enferme sans être vu de personne. On dit qu'il a sué la vérole trois fois depuis deux ans, et je sais de bonne part qu'il est fort paillard." Patin to Spon, 2 June 1645.

[2] Renaudot's condition, as far as we can determine, followed the

Isaac and Eusèbe were increasingly brought into active journalistic partnership. They handled many of the mundane reportorial tasks which earlier Renaudot had done himself. But Renaudot *père* was still in control. In 1648, when Naudé broke with the *Gazette*, he did not mention the brothers at all.[3] By the outbreak of the Fronde, however, Isaac and Eusèbe were expert enough to edit the *Gazette* in Paris when their father followed the court to St. Germain.

Renaudot was no longer as active at court as he had been during Richelieu's ministry. Under Richelieu, everyone paid courtesies and compliments to Renaudot. No matter he was bourgeois, no matter he was tight-lipped and unattractive: he was one of Richelieu's favored men, and privy to state secrets. At the cardinal's behest, Renaudot could make or break reputations. Much of this changed when Richelieu died. Anne of Austria's party had little tolerance, if not outright contempt, for a man whose *Gazette* had opposed them on every score. Doors which had always been open to him now stayed closed. Secretaries were less diligent in replying to his requests for information. Ushers were less punctilious when presenting him to government officials. Except for Bautru, there were few friends still active at court who shared with Renaudot the memories of serving Richelieu. Patin once observed that "the steps of the Louvre were very slippery, and one had to be resolute to stay there very long."[4] Renaudot knew this as a fact.

Richelieu had hardly treated Renaudot with kid gloves; Mazarin, on the other hand, cared little for Renaudot one way or the other. Clearly the events of 1643-1644 indicate Mazarin's

---

classic pattern of syphilitic infection, and in all likelihood his strokes reflected the infection in an advanced stage. Conversations with Dr. Mutya Sanagustin helped the author clarify his assumptions on Renaudot's health.

[3] Naudé, *Jugement* . . . , p. 380.
[4] Patin to Falconet, 31 August 1660.

lack of interest in Renaudot's personal fortunes. He was Mazarin's functionary, but never Mazarin's man. Renaudot dedicated the *Recueil* of 1644, published in January 1645, to Mazarin. By the beginning of 1647, Renaudot consistently styled himself *Historiographe du Roi*, a purely honorific title. The term indicated no new attitude toward news or journalism. It signified only that Renaudot had nominally, but effectively, been rewarded for his public transfer of allegiance to Mazarin.[5] A year later, he moved to the Louvre. Henceforth all *Gazettes* carried the rubric "du Bureau d'Adresse, aux Galleries du Louvre."

As the decade wore on, accounts of Anne and of her pet religious activities, the coming and going of royal hangers-on filled the dispatches. Mazarin's nieces appeared regularly, and the *Gazette* earned a reputation as a Mazarin family mouthpiece. The anonymous complaint of *Le Commerce des nouvelles restably* was true by 1648: "Mademoiselle Flattery got along well with that sly dog [*Gazette*]: they were two heads in the same bonnet, the one never going anywhere without the other; and when *Gazette* could not cast some *Relation*, Flattery was always alongside to whisper in her ear the expression she should use."[6] The content of the *Gazette* underwent subtle, but noticeable changes, as attributable perhaps to Mazarin's attitude as to Renaudot's. As a holdover from the prior ministry, as an unwelcome but necessary reminder to the Queen of her lowly position under Louis XIII, Renaudot could not

[5] Renaudot was not listed as royal historiographer "couchez sur l'Estat" (B.N. mss. f.fr. 23045, f. 126), or one of the authors "qui ont escrit de l'histoire de la France par commission des princes sous la Regne de qui ils vivoient" (B.N. mss. f.fr. 14127). There seemed to be a cloudy distinction between *Historiographe de France*, which was a single office, and *Historiographe du Roi* (which Renaudot claimed to be), innumerable and revocable at royal pleasure. The distinction was not at all clear in the seventeenth century. E. Roy, *La vie de Charles Sorel* (Paris: 1891), p. 350.
[6] *Commerce des nouvelles restably*, p. 8.

command the respect he had enjoyed under Richelieu. Perfunctoriness is as obvious in the post-1644 *Gazette* as attention to detail had been before. Conrart, the secretary of the Académie Française, noted this in a letter to a friend in 1647: Renaudot was "less rigorous and less careful than he used to be in making sure that everything he says is true."[7] The personal control and interest which Richelieu had maintained in the *Gazette*'s correspondents fell apart under Mazarin's ministry. Royal officers were less ardent in sending dispatches to Renaudot.[8] Postal rates increased as postal services worsened during the decade, compounding Renaudot's problems.[9] This increased the amount of "filler" material, of news of banquets, religious ceremonies, and ballets. True, this was still of the stuff of royal cultism, but too much royal incense is potentially asphixiating.

Mazarin's basic indifference to the *Gazette* affected far more than Renaudot's personal career. During the 1640's, the *Gazette* was the most complete source in France for news about England, publishing Parliamentary tracts as enthusiastically and uncritically as it published Royalist propaganda. While such candor meant increased circulations for Renaudot, it was bad politics for the Crown. As Naudé had complained, it was politically unwise and morally wrong "for the least of the population to have too much news" of civil wars abroad.[10] Foreign affairs could present pattern and precedent for dissidents at home. Mazarin recognized in the English disturbances

---

[7] Quoted by R. Fournier, *Écrivains sur le trône*, p. 9.

[8] One of the few times Renaudot appeared in A. Chéruel's edition of Mazarin's correspondence, the Cardinal wrote that lieutenants were not sending him the news as they had been instructed (8 January 1653). Another time Mazarin complained that Renaudot printed details of battles without thinking ahead of the implications (21 August 1644).

[9] E. Vaillé, *Histoire générale des postes françaises* (Paris: 1950), III, 159, 164ff.

[10] Naudé, p. 380. See p. 154.

certain elements dangerously similar to those existing in France,[11] but he did not have the feeling for, or the mastery of censorship which his predecessor had. Mazarin was by no means solely responsible for the explosion of antistatist criticism before and during the Fronde, but he was singularly unable or unwilling to commit his propaganda machine to oppose it. His policy toward Renaudot's *Gazette* reflects this laissez-faire attitude.

Through 1646 and 1647 the *Gazette* occupied itself with typical concerns: news from England, the German wars, "l'Heureuse Convalescence du Roi" from a severe smallpox infection.[12] Indications of the domestic tensions between Parlement and the regency were nonexistent. Finally, however, in the *lit de justice* of 15 January 1648 the regency submitted 12 new judgeships for sale, in effect devaluing the offices held by members of Parlement. The following day, Parlement stubbornly refused to grant approval, as it had always done before. With this rebuff, Anne refused to continue the Paulette, which was then due for its renewal. On 13 May the Parlement declared its union with the three related *compagnies* of the Grand Conseil, the Cour des Comptes, and the Cour des Aides, and on 30 June Anne reluctantly agreed to their union. This act drew the battle lines of the Parlementary Fronde. Throughout it all, the *Gazette* characteristically did its work. Renaudot dutifully described the entrances and ceremonies of the *séance* of 15 January and then noted that "while the first President and the other Presidents stood in their ranks and paid homage to their Majesties, the first President delivered an harangue worthy of his important charge."[13] Renaudot did not record that following Mathieu Molé's remarks, Omer Talon, the advocate-general, criticized the Queen and her government for

[11] See P. Knachel, *England and the Fronde* (Ithaca: 1967), esp. pp. 40-53, 184ff.
[12] 29 November 1647.   [13] 20 January 1648.

governing France, "where men are born free," with methods more suitable to "Scythians or other barbarians."[14] On 11 July Renaudot reported that de Meilleray had replaced d'Emery as Superintendent of Finances, and that "everyone roundly applauds this choice." He did not report that Parlementary opposition to d'Emery had led to that change. The dissent and doubt became too great for even Renaudot to ignore, and he finally acknowledged it, begrudgingly, by blaming it upon France's enemies: "the rumors which the enemies of this State broadcast everywhere, of great divisions and disorders which they have imagined, have until now served to reveal their evil intentions."[15]

The regency had been unable to dampen Parlement's self-confidence. Condé's magnificent victory over the Spanish at Lens, however, on 20 August provided a chance for Anne and Mazarin to seize the offensive. Following the *Te Deum* in Notre Dame on 26 August, they attempted to arrest several outspoken leaders of the Parlement. In the sordid scenes that followed, pro-Parlementary crowds nearly succeeded in preventing their arrests. Renaudot reported none of this, nor of the three days of subsequent rioting.[16] According to the *Gazette*, the regency sought only peace and tranquility, and France's enemies "would be poorly served by their spies if . . . they feel obliged to take false measures, and, believing in our so-called divisions, obstinately continue the war."[17] The Parlement finally forced the regency to limit much of its arbitrary power, to admit the existence of abuses in its tax methods, even to abolish the hated *lettres de cachet*. In the *Gazette*, these were not defeats for royal power and prerogative, but instead the deeds of a magnanimous ministry seeking the

[14] Quoted by J. B. Wolf, *Louis XIV* (New York: 1968), p. 31.
[15] 25 July 1648.
[16] The best treatment of the riots is R. Mousnier, "Quelques raisons de la Fronde: les causes des journées révolutionaires parisiennes de 1648," *Dix-septième siècle* (1949), pp. 33-78.
[17] 5 September 1648.

"ordering of the justice, police, finances and welfare of His Majesty's subjects."[18] An uneasy truce had been established, but the poor faith in which the promises were made gave them little substance. For Renaudot, as for others, events had reached an impasse, with the crown, Parlement, and aristocracy separating in their own private interests. The *Gazettes* of late 1648 testify to a deceptive tranquility; beneath the surface, however, no one was satisfied.

The scene changed immediately after the new year. Early on 6 January, Mazarin whisked Anne and her sons away from Paris to the royal enclave at St. Germain en Laye. A laconic sentence in the *Gazette* of 9 January reported that "their Majesties and the entire court arrived here [St. Germain] from Paris on the sixth of this month, at nine o'clock in the morning." Partially paralyzed, "in the rudest season of the year," Renaudot followed the court to St. Germain. He established presses at the Orangerie of the palace, and served as a sort of publicity officer for the regency. A variety of anonymous broadsheets left his press, and were secreted into Paris and clandestinely distributed.[19] The author of at least 8 of these pamphlets, distinguished by the label "à S. Germain en Laye," is Renaudot himself.[20]

Renaudot's pamphlets and *Gazettes* during this period reflect his unflinching devotion to the values of royal order and authority. Mazarin's particular ministry was the occasion, and not the cause, of these sentiments. Renaudot was not simply

[18] 31 October 1648.

[19] At the end of a manuscript copy of *Lis et fais*, an anonymous pamphlet distributed in Paris early in February 1649, is the following note: "Le roi ordonne au Sr. Regnaudot de faire imprimer l'escrit cy-dessus qu'un bourgeois de Paris zele pour le bien de l'Estat a envoyé à sa Majesté. Et ce sans y apporter le nom de l'imprimeur ni le lieu de l'impression nonobstant toutes ordonnances à ce contraires. Fait à St. Germain en Laye le 27 Janvier 1649. [signed] De Guenegaud." B. N. mss. f.fr. 10225, ff. 101-03; f.fr. 3854, ff. 49-51.

[20] C. Moreau, *Bibliographie des Mazarinades* (Paris: 1850-1851), I, 284.

another nameless, faceless pamphleteer, mouthing current royalist platitudes, but rather an earlier victim of the same forces he now saw tearing France apart.

To Renaudot, social discord derived from the inversion of normal sovereignty and authority. The power of the monarch had been established by God, justified and hallowed by history. Social rebels were slaves of pride, believing that they could wield powers vested in the monarch. Renaudot warned his readers not to expect "anything other than my own sadness at seeing my fellow citizens obstinately set to their own ruin. . . . They wish to constrain the superior powers and take the law from them; who would then be their masters?"[21] Be they the city and Parlement of Paris, the House of Commons in England, or distracted members of the nobility in France, those who opposed the monarch worship false gods. Lesser sovereignties derived their essence from the Crown, and only in a state with a flourishing monarch obeyed and trusted by all do these lesser constituent parts thrive. During this period the *Gazette* was always favorable to the Parlement, at least in appearance. Such favor was consistent with traditional theory. The inversion of loyalty and authority inevitably led to warfare and bloodshed. Here Renaudot was much more resigned and pessimistic than he had been when describing warfare during the 1630's and 1640's. Military conflict justified nothing by itself; there was no glory in this bloody craft. "Less bloody victories are the most complete, especially those involving civilians. It is in this respect that the victory [of the chateau and town of Brie-Comte Robert] is most pleasing to Their Majesties, because they have lost few subjects; their goodness and reason prohibits that they should gain by their loss."[22] Renaudot was distraught by how general war had become, and how universally war reflected man's foolish wish to destroy natural social order. War raged in England, France, and

---

[21] *La prise de Charenton*, p. 1.
[22] *Prise de la ville et chasteau de Brie-Comte Robert*, p. 1.

even in China, he reported to his readers;[23] why did men feel such an overwhelming compulsion to destroy themselves? The tone of his work was quite different from the tone in which he had described France's victories at Rocroi, Casals, and Nordlingen. In 1640 Renaudot had written that "God reserved his [military] victories for France."[24] Not now: warfare served no purpose save to expose human weakness before the chastising, yet healing hand of God. "At the imitation of God, who draws good out of evil, [we should] learn from our past evils to enjoy the repose which is now come to us."[25]

All of France's problems, post-1648, resulted from members of the body politic seeking selfish ends while hypocritically swearing allegiance to the Crown. Renaudot had used the same argument in Parlement in 1644: "Believing firmly that the Crown is the image of God on earth, to submit oneself to the King's Council is to obey God."[26] And again, one should obey the Crown and its chief ministers at all times: if not, "what then would become of royal authority, of royal council, and of the Magistracy?"[27] Renaudot saw little difference between the rebels of the Fronde and his opponents of 1643-1644. Both were motivated by the same pride, the disobedience to royal sovereignty: they sought the same end, the inversion of the social order.

During the blockade of Paris, Isaac and Eusèbe Renaudot published the *Gazette* in Paris, even though their father had followed the court to St. Germain. The inability of the government to police the hundreds of anonymous, illegal publications, the hunger of the Parisians for any news, made it essential to continue publishing the *Gazette* for fear its readers would be seduced to other journals.

[23] "La grande révolution du puissant Royaume de la Chine et autres affaires de l'Orient," 11 September 1648.
[24] 16 May 1640.   [25] *La Paix en France*, p. 8.
[26] *Factum du procez d'entre TR . . . et Médecins de l'eschole de Paris* (1643), p. 8.
[27] *Response à l'examen de la requeste présentée à la Reyne*, pp. 63-64.

Its chief competitor was the *Courrier françois*, which appeared each Friday from 5 January until 7 April 1649. This blatantly pro-Frondeur, anti-Mazarin journal was attributed to Renaudot's sons by Celestin Moreau in his three-volume *Bibliographie des Mazarinades*: "Renaudot, obliged to follow the court to St. Germain in order to continue his *Gazette* and to guard his privileges, left his sons in Paris with orders to publish a pro-Parlementary gazette: this was the *Courrier françois*. He was therefore gazeteer of the king and of the Fronde at the same time."[28] Renaudot's subsequent biographers accepted Moreau's judgment.[29] Moreau made the attribution on the basis of his reading of three Mazarinades. By themselves, they permit the interpretation that the newspaper was a Renaudot production. The *Commerce des nouvelles restably* said the *Courrier françois* was published "de son logis chez l'Imprimeur," probably a printer who had formerly been employed by Renaudot.[30] The author of *La conference secrete du Cardinal Mazarin avec le Gazetier* had Renaudot accuse himself and his family of playing a double role: "all those who give me information are honorable people, and know everything that happens day and night: I have my children at Paris who see the best companies, who produce the gazette for Parlement."[31] And another Mazarinade, *La guerre civile en vers burlesques:*

> Il n'est pas jusqu'au Gazetier
> Père, et fils d'un mesme mestier
> Dont l'un à saint Germain ne crie
> Contre nos bons convoys de Brie,
> Et l'autre en faveur de Paris
> Ne face de contraires cries.[32]

[28] Moreau, I, 249. See Grand-Mesnil, pp. 49-60.
[29] Hatin, *Renaudot*, p. 107; and his *Bibliographie de la presse*, pp. 13-14, for example.
[30] *Commerce des nouvelles restably*, pp. 12-14.
[31] Quoted by Grand-Mesnil, p. 56.
[32] Republished by Moreau, I, 250.

None of these citations conclusively proves Moreau's argument that the *Courrier françois* was a Renaudot family publication. In fact, they may indicate the opposite.

The *Gazette* maintained solid editorial support for the city and Parlement of Paris while at the same time minimizing antimonarchic activities. Articles were never critical of the crown. Antiroyalists were characterized as "le parti contraire."[33] When the Parlement of Rouen joined with the Parlement of Paris, they did so not in opposition to the crown, but "to act in concert for public tranquility."[34] Likewise the Prince de Conti's union with the *parlementaires* was motivated in hopes of "a general peace, the relief of the people, and the conservation of this city" of Paris.[35] In this respect, the *Gazette* remained "the gazette for Parlement" and "in favor of Paris." The *Courrier françois*, so different from the *Gazette* in its politics and its bourgeois rather than aristocratic readership, was published by someone other than the Renaudot family. The Renaudots were not engaged in a fascinating conspiracy to oppose Mazarin in one publication in Paris while defending him in pamphlets published at St. Germain. The actual situation was much more prosaic than Moreau thought. Renaudot had continued to publish a royalist *Gazette* in Frondeur Paris without being too obvious about it.

The end of the blockade forced the *Courrier françois* and its fellow journals out of business. "The *Gazette* had him [*Courrier françois*] arrested and taken by the scruff of the neck when he was at the printers, and led him to the Palais as a rebel to her privileges and patents. . . . He was then condemned high and low . . . and obliged to take Mademoiselle Gazette by the hand and escort her back to the high station that he had tried to usurp."[36]

Even though he could now return to Paris and his *Gazette,* Renaudot's editorial problems continued. He tried marking

[33] 27 February 1649.   [34] 6 February 1649.   [35] 27 March 1649.
[36] *Commerce des nouvelles restably*, pp. 12-14.

211

each edition with a different pseudo-oriental design, so his readers would not be fooled by counterfeiters. He likewise fought the economic pressures facing all printers of the period. Postal rates became prohibitive, and Renaudot informed his readers that no one would henceforth receive free copies.[37]

Renaudot reestablished his loans and address directory in 1647, but the disorders of the Fronde and renewed opposition from civil and ecclesiastical authorities killed his activities by the middle of 1648.[38] For a man living on a fixed income, the inflation of the 1640's was devastating, and by 1651 Renaudot was in severe financial straits. His yearly pension of 800 *livres* was suspended during Mazarin's exile, and Renaudot petitioned the court to reconsider its action. His public *Apologie du Bureau d'Adresse* was the most pathetic piece of his career. He reminded the court that he spent his miserable pension broadcasting the *Gazette* throughout Europe, "and is probably the only writer at the present time who still combats the pernicious libels of evil-minded writers." The court should not forget "the great expenses he incurred in obeying their command and following them to St. Germain, in spite of his extreme age and paralysis," expenses of 2,000 *livres* for which he has not been reimbursed. "Since he is nearing the end of his career," the petition concluded, it would be sad if Renaudot were reduced to total poverty.[39] His appeal had no effect, for two months later Renaudot again publicly lamented his problems. This time, he could not mask his bitterness. "Strange it is that while France abounds with more great men than all other kingdoms, there has been none since the death of the great

[37] "l'Apologie du Bureau d'Adresse contre ceux qui se plaignent de ce qu'il ne leur peut plus donner gratuitement les Gazettes," *Extraordinaire*, 9 June 1651. See E. Vaillé, III, 164ff.
[38] *Le Renouvellement des Bureaux d'Adresse* (Paris: 1647); *Causes d'opposition que mettent pardevant vous Nosseigneurs tenans la Cour de Parlement à Paris* . . . (Paris: 28 November 1647).
[39] 9 June 1651.

Cardinal Duke de Richelieu, the first protector of this invention of mine (which has been imitated by all the other states of the world) who might have wished to be recognized as Maecenas and ask himself how [the *Gazette*] has survived through so many years: but that honor must still be reserved for me alone, since the ancient service I have rendered to the king, the magnates, and to the public, has not been mercenary.

"I believe that, just as Vespasian said that an emperor must die on his feet, my fate is to die seated, and still writing . . . this fidelity is not incompatible with the zeal and hereditary affection which I have devoted to the other heads of this state."[40]

In spite of these appeals, Renaudot did not see his pension reinstated. At the end of the year, Chancellor Séguier offered him the position of director *des imprimeries suivant la cour*. Renaudot would have nothing to do with it. He considered the title a disguise hiding old injustices. A memorandum addressed to Séguier tells it all. Renaudot considered the position "more importune and onerous than profitable," having already spent in excess of 2,000 *livres* above his income in following the royal family to St. Germain en Laye. "For him to accept this charge, which he does not value above his other pursuits or, indeed, even their equal, it would only be by the zeal that he has always borne to the service of the king . . . that if Monsieur the Chancellor would not think it worthy, the charge should be conferred on someone who could perform it better than he, since experience has well proven that it was a necessary one: it is enough for him to have been the first to have had the honor of operating a press while following the court, during the rudest season of the year, when all the others were working against the present government."[41] Renaudot's pension was reduced to nothing. Even though he probably enjoyed some

[40] "l'Avertissement au Lecteur," *Extraordinaire*, 10 August 1651.
[41] B.N. mss. f.fr. 17391, ff. 220-24.

income from his original patrimony of 20,000 *livres,* he died "as poor as a painter," according to Patin.[42]

Even a final attempt at some personal happiness—and the possibility of a lucrative dowry—failed him. We do not know when his second wife, Jeanne Baudot, died, but on 20 October 1651, at the age of 65, Renaudot married Louise Mascon, a 16-year-old widow. May and December marriages were not rare in Renaudot's Paris, but this match was particularly notorious. His family was embarrassed by the old man's affair, for the wedding, at the church of St. Louis en l'Île, was witnessed by only a parish priest and the parish sacristan.[43] The family's shame became compounded when the honeymoon turned sour. Renaudot, broken by several strokes, *camus*-nosed, pockmarked by syphilis, was a sorry mate for his teen-aged wife. The story was a favorite in *La muze historique,* a weekly verse gazette which Jean Loret prepared for Madame de Longueville. Loret recounted how "dame Discorde/Parmy leur hymen se foura:"

> Ne luy donnoit plus de louange,
> Ne dizoit plus: "Mon coeur, mon ange,"
> Mais quelquefois pis que son nom,
> Et l'appelloit souvent: "Guenon!"
> Elle pour prendre sa revanche,
> En metant la main sur la hanche,
> Dizoit, "Voyez ce beau nazeau!
> Voyez ce plaiszant damaoizeau!
> Voyez ce faizeur de gazettes!
> Il luy faut des femmes bien faites!
> Il luy faut des jeunes beautez
> Auprez de ses propres côtez!
> Il luy faut d'aimables visages
> Qui soient doux comme des images!

[42] Patin to Belin, 12 November 1653. Renaudot referred to his patrimony in *Response à l'examen de la requeste présentée à la Reyne,* p. 61.
[43] B.N. mss. f.fr. 8622.

214

Il luy faut des objets rians!
Il luy faut des morceaux frians!
Il luy faut des lèvres sucrées
Qui ne soient qu'à luy consacrées!
Il luy faut des belles Philis,
De beaux teintes d'oeillets et de lis,
Des tétons et des gorges pleines!
Il luy faut ses fievres quarteines!"
Le sage monsieur Renaudot
Le plus souvent ne disoit mot;
Mais, lasse de tant en entendre,
Dizoit quelquefois pis que pendre.

Renaudot and his young bride were divorced:

A la fin, leurs communs parents,
Ayans peurs que leurs diferens
Apres leur amitie detruite,
Eussent une éternelle suite,
Ont jugé tres-fort à propos,
Qu'il les faloit metre en repos:
Si bien que, par leur entremize
Les messieurs de la Cour d'Eglize
En ayans eté fort priez
Les ont enfin demariez.[44]

For the first time, "le sage monsieur Renaudot" was a worthy news item himself. Unfortunately he had become a subject of salon conversation at his own personal expense.

Renaudot continued his activities at the *Gazette* as much as his failing health permitted. But the editions of 1652, as the title page of the *Recueil* of that year indicated, were "printed and published by order of M. Théophraste Renaudot." It is doubtful if Renaudot was actively engaged in the *Gazette*. Even though Isaac and Eusèbe assumed major editorial re-

[44] *La muze historique*, 8 September 1652.

sponsibilities, there was no internal evidence of any change. *Gazette* style and content remained the same as it had been under their father's direction.

Renaudot had suffered strokes in 1649 and in July 1652, aggravated if not caused by his syphilis. Finally, on 25 October 1653, at the age of 67, he suffered his last. His obituary appeared in the *Gazette* of 1 November 1653: "On the twenty-fifth of October, in the fifteenth month of illness and the seventieth [sic] of his life, died Théophraste Renaudot, counselor and royal physician, and Historiographer of His Majesty; so commendable to posterity, which learned from him the names of the great men in these journals, that one must not keep silent about him. As celebrated by the great knowledge and ability that he showed in fifty years of the practice of medicine as by the other beautiful products of his mind, so innocent that having them all destined to the utility of the public, he was ever content to have received its homage." He was buried in the parish church of the Louvre, St. Germain en Auxerrois, before the altar.[45] Jean Loret, who had gotten so much mileage out of Renaudot's marriage, was among those who saw him to his grave. Loret wrote a touching eulogy to Renaudot in *La muze historique*, the tone much different from the description of his ill-fated marriage. It concluded:

> Maintenant il est en repos
> Car on peut pieuzement croire
> Qu'il fit icy son purgatoire.[46]

The patents for the *Gazette* remained in the Renaudot family. Renaudot's eldest son, Théophraste *fils*, a councillor in the Cour des Monnaies, continued to publish the *Gazette*, even though his brothers Isaac and Eusèbe performed most of the

[45] E. Renaudot, "Journal des principalles affaires de ma vie," B.N. mss. f.fr. 14348, f. 9r.
[46] 1 November 1653.

editorial responsibilities. When the bachelor Théophraste *fils* died in 1672, the patent passed to Eusèbe. Eusèbe gave it to his son, François, a member of the chapter of Ste. Genéviève, who then turned the patent over to his elder brother, Eusèbe *fils*, in 1679.[47] Eusèbe *fils* was the most famous of the Renaudot progeny, a member of the Académie Française, confidant of Colbert and Bossuet, an expert on oriental languages, and a fierce defender of Catholic orthodoxy. He was the last direct descendant of the founder to hold the patent. In 1720, on his death, the patent passed to his nephew Eusèbe-Jacques Chapoux de Verneuil, a royal secretary.[48] Finally, in 1762, after having changed hands twice, the patent was retired when Louis XV attached the *Gazette* directly to the Departement des Affaires Étrangères. Its name was now the *Gazette de France*. Its subsequent fortunes are not our concern, but it survived the Revolution and the nineteenth century until the First World War, a strongly conservative journal.[49]

Except for its brief resurrection in 1647, Renaudot's Bureau d'Adresse died in 1644. The idea, however, was a proven one. Repeatedly outlines for bureaux d'adresse in Paris appeared, but repeatedly, they failed to be instituted.[50] Finally in 1691 Nicolas Blegny published *Le livre commode*, a listing of all the addresses and information one could possibly need in Paris; schedules of court sessions, weather forecasts, addresses of officials, physicians, teachers, etc. Blegny's efforts were short-lived, opposed by sentiment similar to that which Renaudot had encountered.[51] Even though no single bureau d'adresse con-

[47] B.N. mss. f.fr. 21741, ff. 220-21.

[48] B.N. mss. f.fr. 21741, ff. 199-202.

[49] Hatin, *Bibliographie . . . de la presse*, pp. 8-10.

[50] See É. Fournier's introduction to N. Blegny, *Le livre commode* (Paris: 1878). B.N. mss. f.fr. 21741, ff. 208-15.

[51] *Le livre commode, contenant les addresses de la ville de Paris, et le trésor des almanachs pour l'année bissextile 1692. . . .* (Paris: 1692); also B.N. mss. f.fr. 21741, f. 229v.

tinued through the eighteenth century, a number of publications and clearinghouses provided the information which Blegny, and Renaudot before him, had furnished.[52]

If the reapplication of Renaudot's ideas was delayed in France, social thinkers tried to apply them in England during his lifetime. Throughout 1646-1648, Samuel Hartlib examined various schemes for the advancement of Christian knowledge as well as social amelioration. He wrote to friends in Paris for information about Renaudot's bureau, and for copies of Renaudot's *Renouvellement des Bureaux d'Adresse*. Even though Hartlib's *Further Discovery of the Office of Publick Adress for Accommodations* duplicated all of Renaudot's arguments, Hartlib's petition to Parliament in 1647 stressed its potential, "through the harmelesse Advancement of Divine and Humane Wisdome," as a vehicle of Protestant ecumenism. Parliament did not grant his petition, although the plan was enthusiastically promoted by his friends John Dury and Henry Robinson. Numerous schemes for "Offices of Enteries," "Offices of Intelligence," and "Places of Encounters," were bruited about.[53] In 1650 Robinson established an Office of Addresses in "Thread-needle Street over against the Castle Tavern, close to the Old Exchange," where the poor could find jobs. In later writings, Robinson also advocated low-interest loans. Except for lasting a few months, there was no proof that Robinson's Office of Addresses was any more successful than Hartlib's.[54] Even though these adaptations did not thrive, Renaudot's English contemporaries were quick to appreciate the way in

---

[52] Introduction to É. Fournier's edition of *Quinziesme feuille du Bureau d'adresse*, published in *Variétés historiques et littéraires* (Paris: 1859), IX, 51-61.

[53] G. H. Turnbull, *Hartlib, Dury and Comenius* (London: 1947), pp. 57-61, 80-87; Turnbull, *Samuel Hartlib* (London: 1920), pp. 53, 63; W. K. Jordan, *Philanthropy in England 1480-1660* (London: 1959), pp. 213ff.

[54] Jordan, *Men of Substance* (Chicago: 1942), pp. 250-53.

which he had applied humanitarian dedication to economic realities, human knowledge to visionary as well as practical ends.

Renaudot had enjoyed the bittersweet satisfaction of seeing the Faculty of Medicine provide charitable consultations when his were suspended in 1644. He had less satisfaction regarding his sons' graduation. Patin in 1645 had gloated to a friend that they "haven't been admitted to our faculty, and perhaps may never be."[55] The faculty did all it could to put them off, but in 1647 and 1648 Isaac and Eusèbe were finally granted the doctoral bonnet. Eusèbe, especially, became a successful and respected physician, and in 1672 was appointed first physician to the Dauphin.[56] He was the major advocate battling faculty opponents to antimony. He wrote *l'Antimoine justifié* in 1653, the most judicious and effective of the many books in this drawnout and sometimes silly controversy.[57] Renaudot's Preface contained the endorsement of 60 fellow faculty members. But this had little effect upon the more orthodox members of the faculty. Jacques Perreau, author of *Rabbat-Joye de l'antimoine triomphant* would not let his readers forget who the father of Eusèbe was.[58] Patin, elected dean in 1650, characterized Renaudot's treatise as "a malicious book and a miserable

[55] Patin to Spon, 2 June 1645.

[56] B.N. mss. f.fr. n.a. 7484, ff. 137, 138. In fine bourgeois fashion, Eusèbe trafficked in Hôtel de Ville *rentes* and landholdings south of Paris (M. Venard, *Bourgeois et paysans au XVIIe siècle* [Paris: 1957], pp. 36-37). His brother Isaac invested in the newly developed Île St. Louis in Paris (M. Dumolin, "La Construction de l'Île St. Louis," *Études de topographie parisienne* [Paris: 1931], p. 241). A plaque on a building on the Quai de Bourbon indicates that it was owned by the "fils de Théophraste Renaudot."

[57] H. Metzger, *Les doctrines chimiques en France du debut du XVIIe à la fin du XVIIIe siècle* (Paris: 1923) characterized Renaudot as "un brillant défenseur de ce nouveau rémède," p. 222.

[58] *Rabbat-Joye de l'Antimoine triomphant, ou Examen de l'Antimoine justifié de M. Eusèbe Renaudot, etc.* (Paris: 1654), Preface. Perreau's publication carried the endorsement of 70 faculty members.

galimatias."[59] The publication war continued, with no clear-cut victories for either side.[60] Antimony did receive some new adherents in 1658, when it helped cure Louis XIV. Nevertheless, it was not until 1666 that the faculty, by a vote of 92 to 10, approved the remedy.[61] Two years later, non-Parisian physicians were finally permitted to practice in the capital, if their credentials were registered with the crown. These physicians would be under the surveillance of the first physician of the king and would enjoy the same rights as members of the Parisian faculty.[62]

Patin, of course, was one of the 10 members who voted against antimony, and vehemently opposed foreign-trained physicians in Paris. To him, as to the rest of the medical community, the two issues were related: "I console myself because there must be heresies so that the good can be tested, but I have never been inclined to worship the Golden Calf, nor to consider Fortune as a goddess. I am content with my own mediocrity. *Paix et peu.* As soon as the winds change, all these champions of antimony will vanish like smoke from their furnaces. *Ipsi peribunt: dii meliora piis. Vale.*"[63] Patin died in 1672, outliving Renaudot by 19 years. His last years must have been unpleasant for him, seeing the eventual triumph of medical ideas which long had been associated with his arch-enemy.

---

[59] Patin to Spon, 21 October 1653. He wrote Spon on 25 November to tell him that Renaudot's book was selling very poorly!

[60] In addition to Renaudot and Perreau's works, one should also see the following publications in this controversy: I. Chartier, *La science du plomb sacré des sages* (Paris: 1651); Claude Germain, *Orthodoxe ou l'abus de l'antimoine* (Paris: 1652); Étienne Carneau, *La Stimmimachie* (Paris: 1656). Also see Maurice Cauchie, "Le rôle des poètes dans la seconde querelle de l'antimoine 1651-1656," *Revue des sciences modernes*, 1955, pp. 401-06.

[61] Chevalier, "La guerre de l'antimoine," *Revue Ciba*, 1959, p. 25.

[62] R. Fauvelle, *Les étudiants en médecine de Paris* (Paris: 1889), p. 168.

[63] Patin to Falconet, 30 July 1666.

Conclusion

THÉOPHRASTE RENAUDOT's career was more than the simple sum of its parts. It often seems, however, that there were three or four Renaudots, each an entity unto itself. The ability to discuss Renaudot the physician distinct from Renaudot the journalist, for example, attests to the breadth of his abilities and contributions. In spite of this, the several Renaudots do coalesce into a multidimensional whole. All of Renaudot's innocent inventions employed refinements in communication and social intercourse to accomplish their goals. Low-interest loans and the *inventaire des addresses* would make existing capital and talent more flexible and fluid; the *Présence des absens* would send Parisian medical expertise to every village in the realm; the *Gazettes* and conferences would harness the power of information and apply it to social and political ends. This reliance, indeed, faith in communication flowed pervasively through his career, joining all of his disparate activities into an organic whole.

Existing propaganda, medical and public welfare, and popular education methods, as Renaudot interpreted them, had revealed their ideational and institutional bankruptcy. The most successful of Renaudot's experiments, at least in terms of a lasting institutional life, was the *Gazette*. His other experiments seem to have died in Parlement on 1 March 1644. Yet they, too, in other guises and through the efforts of other men, reappeared after him to vindicate his efforts. What is important is the general tone of these efforts taken together. Public medicine, popular education, diffusion of technical and scientific knowledge, information from the government—these are all now recognized as indispensable to modern life. We take them for granted, yet it is impossible to conceive of life in a modern state without any of them. Renaudot by no means blueprinted a modern socially conscious state, yet he did at

221

least recognize its responsibilities and the necessity of improved institutions to satisfy them. His career reflects a sincere, if not totally articulated, feeling that existing methods were woefully inadequate in a century forced to deal with new social realities but still saddled with psychological and institutional frameworks from the past. The broad opposition he encountered from the corporate powers of Paris attests to his significance certainly as much as the short-lived success of his activities in the 1630's and early 1640's. Attacks upon him were generalized within his enemies' minds and on the pages of their libels. This broadly based reaction, emotional as well as legal and institutional, attests to the fact that he had exposed the hopelessness in which existing social welfare, educational, and medical methods wallowed.

Renaudot was singularly able to offend and alienate a host of corporate interests within Paris. These particularized powers maintained their independence at the expense of all cooperative actions, making meaningful civic action virtually impossible. Renaudot's career indicated the extent to which one man could ignore corporate pressures if he had the active support of a Richelieu. It would be misleading to see a premeditated, blueprinted scheme between the Cardinal and his bourgeois surrogate to humble the traditional corporate interests, but Richelieu did take characteristic advantage of Renaudot's abilities to further his own program. In Renaudot, the cardinal-minister found an emotional compatriot, a willing and eager colleague. Richelieu cared for his creatures in all their activities, as long as their service to the state warranted it. Renaudot's career is a case in point. It was only during Richelieu's ministry that all of Renaudot's inventions functioned in concert. The multi-dimensional Renaudot outlived his creator by only a few months. When Richelieu died, the ancient corporate interests vehemently flaunted their autonomy, and only Renaudot the state propagandist was allowed to survive. The bitterness of the attacks upon Renaudot suggests that service in the ancien régime seldom brought its own reward, especially when that service was protected by Richelieu.

Renaudot was eager to attack corporate attitudes. He viewed the poor as individual men with individual problems, rather than as a conglomerate, corporative body. He roundly scored the Faculty of Medicine for enervating professional life in the name of its own corporate priorities. One might argue that by establishing the Bureau d'Adresse, Renaudot wished to erect a corporation of his own apart from that of the medical faculty. This is hardly true. Renaudot called for freedom of practice for all properly trained medical men. A doctor of Montpellier, trained and certified, was as legitimately qualified to practice in Paris as any member of the sacrosanct Parisian faculty. As Renaudot argued, a doctoral degree was similar to a baptismal record, certifying one's faith anywhere in Christendom.[1] Renaudot was forced to fight corporatism by its own rules, on its own level. Yet the ultimate effect of his efforts would have been to destroy the legal precedence of the Parisian faculty and its autonomy as a nationwide licensing body. Leaving the doors to medical practice wide open, offering the floor of his academy to all opinions regardless of the reputation or allegiance of the speaker, seeking employment suitable to each unemployed rather than indiscriminately shutting him up in a *hôpital*— Renaudot defended these practices in a Paris where remaining detached from a corporation was almost a psychological impossibility.

Renaudot was no libertarian or leveller; he defended the values of order and stability as vehemently as did the Faculty of Medicine. Renaudot milked his influences and monopolies for all they were worth, yet his dependence upon the centralized state reflects more than simple self-interest. Long before he left Loudun, Renaudot had already become a Parisian. From his ideas on propaganda, national standards of medical practice, and aid to the poor, to his support of academic encyclopedian-

[1] *Remarques sur l'avertissement à Théophraste Renaudot . . .* , p. 23.

ism and the utopian hopes represented by the *Présence des absens*, unbridled confidence in Paris-centered institutions set the tone of his entire career. "Paris was the center of the world"[2] and the Bureau d'Adresse the "image and abridgement of the universal harmony which the Philosophers have so admired in the larger world."[3] Such rhetoric had long colored utopian and pansophic thought, but these were not empty phrases. Indeed, Renaudot's rhetoric and program were cut from the same cloth. France's problems cut through corporation and class, religion and region, and only a national monarchy, Renaudot believed, could adequately deal with them. For all of his accuracy in diagnosing social ills, Renaudot's prescriptions were perhaps premature. Traditional society might have been too weak to cope with new seventeenth century realities, but as his defeat in 1644 indicated, corporate values were still too strong to die.

La Rochefoucauld observed that it is easier to know man in general than one man in particular. With Renaudot the problem is compounded by the lack of information about a personal life separate from his public career. Indeed, these omissions tell us something of his total commitment to public work: he was a creation of the state he served, and hardly existed apart from it. His public life was that of a multidimensional man sensitive to the challenges of his age: an enterprising and clever entrepreneur, an innovative philanthropist, a dedicated servant of minister and king.

[2] *Présence des absens* (Paris: 1642), p. 3.
[3] *Renouvellement des Bureaux d'Adresse* (Paris: 1647), p. 26.

APPENDICES

BIBLIOGRAPHY

INDEX

APPENDIX A

Table des choses dont on peut donner & recevoir
advis au Bureau d'adresse (S.l.n.d.).

A

Abbregé des sciences, & briefves methodes de les apprendre.

Accademies, et personnes qui instruisent la Noblesse en toute sorte d'exercice, *Voyez, Arts.*

Addresses des chemins.

Advis pour le reglement & soulagement des pauvres, & pour toutes autres affaires.

Anatomies et dessections.

Animaux de toutes sortes, comme Dogues, & autres Chiens, Chatz d'Espagne, Singes, etc.

Antiques, medailles, vielles monnayes.

Argent à prester bailler et recevoir à rente, par correspondence de lettres de change ou autrement, et à changer en autres especes.

Artifices, inventions, raretez, secretz & curiositez licites à vendre, ou eschanger pour autres secretz.

Arts, sciences, & exercises à apprendre, comme Armes, Navigation, Artilerie, Escriture, Mathematiques: langues Françoise, Latine, Greque, Espagnole, et autres estrangeres: jeu de Luth, Danse, & autres disciplines.

Associations pour negocces.

Atteliers.

Ausmones à faire et recevoir sur bons certificats.

B

Baccalaureat, & autres degrez à obtenir.

Bains, estuves, douche.

Banque, Banquiers, & Agents en Cour de Rome.

Bastiments à donner à faire ou entreprende, & tous leurs materiaux, comme Ardoise, Bordeau; Brique, Chaux, Ciment, Pierre, Sable, Poutre, Soliveaux, Tuille, Menuiserie, Ferrure, etc. on se trouvent à bon conte.

Batteaux & autres vaisseaux à vendre, acheter, louer, & de renvoy.

Benefices à permuter ou donner à pension.

Bibliotheques.

Bled de tout sorte à vendre, & acheter en ville & aux champs.

Boeufs, Vaches, Brebes, Abeilles, & autres amenagements des champs.

Bouquets & fleurs en toutes saisons.

Boutiques souz des vefves: & franchises.

C

Carosses, Coches, Litieres, Charrettes, Chevaux, Muletez, et autres bestes de service à vendre, acheter, louer & de renvoy.

Chambres vides et garnies & meubles à louer.

Clerez de mestiers.

Commissions à exercer.

Compagnie à voyager.

Compagnons, & apprentifs de boutiques & mestiers, à placer.

Conditions de toutes sortes, comme Ausmoniers, & Chappellains, Escuyers, Pages, Gentils-hommes suivants.

    Secretaires.

    Maistres d'Hostel.

    Intendants.

    Gouverneurs, & Precepteurs d'Enfans.

    Lecteurs & Interpretes.

    Solliciteurs, au Parlement, Conseil, Etc.

    Clercs et copistes.

    Valets de chambre.

    Trompettes, Tambours, Fifves.

    Fauconniers.

    Sommeliers.

    Blanchisseurs.

    Fruitiers et Confituriers.

    Carossiers.

    Postillions.

    Palenfriers.

    Jardiniers.

    Portiers.

Concierges.

Laquais.

Aides de Cuisine, et autres.

Consultations pour maladies, & pour affaires.

Cours, leçons, disputes, conferences, et autres actes en Theologie, Medecine, Droit, philosophie & humanitez: Regens de classes.

Cuillette, et levee de fruits, & provision de maison à faire en gros ou en detail.

D

Distilation et autres preparations de remedes Chymiques, et dispensations de compositions celebres, & leux prix.

Droitz liquides & litigieux à poursuivre, faire payer et composer.

Deuils & pompes funebres à faire, & entre prendre.

E

Eaux de spa, & autres medicinales.

Estanges & rivieres à pescher, & marais à dessecher.

Estudes et practiques de Procureurs & Notaires à vendre, et acheter.

Experiences de la Medecine, agriculture, & autres.

F

Facteurs de marchands, & messagers.

Fermes fiefs, Terres Seigneuriales, & autres à prendre, et bailler à loyer ou à vendre, & eschanger.

Festins, nopces, & autres banquets à faire & entreprendre, Gibier et denrees de toutes sortes.

G

Gardes de malades, & d'accouchees: Matrones & sages femmes expertes.

Gazette de nouvelles etrangeres, & prix de marchandises.

Geneologies.

Gens cautionnez à employer au negoce: & autres à envoyer promptement pour affaires, à pied ou à cheval.

H

Habits, et ameublements à vendre, & louer.

Haras.

Heritages à vendre, acheter, louer, & eschanger.

Huissiers et sergents allants aux champs exploiter es mesmes lieux où on a affaire.

I

Images, figures, tableaux, pourtraiture, & taille douce.

Instruments de musique, & autres parties de mathematiques: & meubles curieux.

Inventaires et ventes publiques.

L

Logis jours et heures des Messagers, lettres & hardes à leur faire tenir.

Livres rares et manuscripts.

M

Machines, Modelles, & artifices, comme moulins de nouvelle invention, mouvements hydrauliques, & autres automates.

Maisons à louer, vendre acheter & eschanger en ville aux fauxbours, & aux champs.

Maistres qui cherchent des apprentis & compagnons.

Maistrises de lettres & de chefs-d'oeuvres de tous artz, & mestiers.

Maladies, leur remedes: lieux, personnes, meubles & aliments propres à les traitter.

Manoeuvres.

Marbe, Jaspe, Porpfyre.

Marchandises estoffes, & meubles de toutes sortes, à vendre acheter & harder.

Mariages.

Marine & ce qui en depend.

Memoire qu'on voudra laisser à la posterité de quelque chose.

Metaux, mineraux, & ce qui en depend.

Metayers, colons ou fermiers.

Meubles precieux & pieces de Cabinet.

Modes nouvelles.

Moulins à eau & à vent.

N

Noms et demeures de toutes les personnes de consideration comme
des Princes, & officiers de la Couronne, des Cours souveraines, &
subalternes, de la maison du Roy, estants en quartier ou n'y
estants point: des Theologiens, Medecins & Advocats fameaux, &
de toutes autres personnes de reputation, & qui excelleront en
leurs art, & profession: & accez vers eux.

Nouvelles qu'on voudre apprendre: & communication qu'on voudra avoir avec personnes dont on ne sçait la demeure.

O

Oculistes & Operateurs.

Offices à lever, vendre, acheter, eschanger & faire exercer.

Oyseaux de praye, & autres de toutes sortes, commes Aigles,
Eperviers, Paons, Poules de Barbarie, Faizants, Rossignols, &
autres.

Ordres.

P

Papier, de la Chine, jaspé et de toutes façons.

Parroisses, villages, villes, elections, Presidiaux, Bailliages, Sene-
chaussées, & autres jurisdictions de ce Royaume.

Pensions, & demy-pensions à tous prix.

Pierreries, bagues, joyaux & Orfevrerie.

Plan d'arbres, Arbrisseaux, Herbes, Fleurs, Graines, & oignons
rares.

Postes & Relais.

Q

Questions à resoudre.

R

Receptes à faire & bailler.

Recouverer ce qui est égaré.

Rentes sur le Roy, l'Hostel de Ville, & les particuliers à vendre, acheter, & eschanger.

Rouliers, Voituriers, Cochers, Batteliers.

S

Soldats à enroller pour le service du Roy.

T

Tapis, Tapisseries de haute lice, cuir doré & autres.

V

Voeux de Religion, & les conditions pour y entrer.

Y

Ypecras, maluoisie, vins excellentz, &c.

Trois milles personnes, placées en diverses conditions, & quatre fois autant qui, depuis son establissement, ont trouvé dans nostre Bureau, l'Addresse des commoditez contenues en ceste Table, luy serviront (mon Lecteur), de recommandation envers vous: s'il en faut encor à ceste institution, apres tant de titres, & la possession qu'elle a de la voix du peuple.

"l'Ouverture des Conferences du Bureau d'A-
dresse. Pour le premier Lundi du present mois de
Novembre 1634." *Seconde Centurie des Questions
traitées ez conferences du Bureau d'Adresse* (Paris:
Bureau d'Adresse, 1636).

Nos vacations se sont passées en la proposition et examen de
divers secrets et curiositez de quelque arts et sciences, dont je vous
toucherai sommairement aucunes en l'ordre auquel elles ont esté
proposées. La plupart desquelles ont esté trouvées veritables, au
rapport des personnes commises par la Compagnie à leur examen
et experience. Car ce lieu n'eust pas esté capable de contenir le
reste qu'on vous reserve aileurs.

La premiere, fut le moyen de descrire un Cercle de quel grandeur
qu'il soit, sans en connoitre le centre: encore mesmes que le centre
en fust inaccessible.

II. Le moyen de faire le vernis de la Chine noire et jaune doré.

III. Faire voir en un miroir plat les choses qui lui seront repre-
sentées sur la surface, et non enfoncées comme elles paroissent
d'ordinaire.

IV. Faire un miroir sphaerique qui repraesentera les figures en
leur vraye proportion, et non corrompues comme ez vulgaires.

V. Faire paroistre en un miroir concave une ou plusieurs figures
en l'air: fort illuminées.

VI. Faire raffraicher du vin promptement en Esté: voire glacer
l'eau ou il raffraischira.

VII. Dechiffrir tous chiffres communes et dechiffrables.

VIII. Donner l'invention d'un nombre presque infini de chiffres
qui ne se peuvent dechiffrer: comme entr'autres escrire avec un
seul poinct pour chacque lettre: avec deux livres, dans lesquels il
ne paroistra aucune marque extraordinaire, et autres.

IX. Escrire un chiffre que l'on pourra lire en deux langues
diverses.

X. Escrire sous un sens ouvert une autre signification caché, aussi ample que la premiere.

XI. Escrire sur un corps, qui ne perira point mesme au feu, auquel seul au contraire il se lira, et y faire response par mesme moyen, faisant disparoir les lettres quand on voudra, puis les faire retourner derechef.

XII. Faire une escriture ou impression, laquelle representera avec aussi peu de lettres que l'escriture ordinaire, toutes les proprietez de chaque chose.

XIII. Le moyen de donner quelque avis en six heures à cent lieuës d'ici, sans y employer les cloches ni le canon, ou tel autre moyen.

XIV. Le moyen de donner à l'instant avis de ce qui se fait à 50 lieuës et plus, de telle chose qu'on voudra, mesme de chose inopinée.

XV. Faire qu'une personne estant en son cabinet se fair entendre en cent divers endroits de son logis: et en recevoir response par mesme moyen sans bruit, et sans que ceux seront en sa compagnie s'en puisse apercevoir.

XVI. Monter et faire en une seule leçon les vrayes proportions du corps humain, aussi exactement qu'a fait Albert.

XVII. Enseigner aussi facilement le moyen de contretirer tous desseins, et de desseigner exactement tous les ordres des Colomnes selon leur vraye proportion.

XVIII. Le moyen de graver tres aisement à l'eau forte: mesme sans sçavoir hacher.

XIX. Calculer sans plumes ni jettons par un moyen qui ne se peut oublier.

XX. Apprendre la methode d'escrire en une heure, en retenant seulement trois lettres.

XXI. Conserver des fleurs, voire un jardin tout entier, tout le long de l'année.

XXII. L'art ou moyen d'apprendre tous les tours de passe-passe et subtilitez des charlattans: et par consequent cesser de les admirer.

XXIII. Faire voir deux corps solides actuellement froids, lesquels estans meslez ensemble s'eschaufferont d'eux mesmes à l'instant, en sorte qu'on n'y pourra plus toucher: et conserveront leur chaleur par plusieurs mois, et possible par plusieurs années.

234

XXIV. Montrer dans un instrument portatif en peinture mouvante et platte, en petit ou grand volume, tous les objets qui lui seront opposez.

XXV. Enseigner une lanque matrice de laquelle toutes les autres langues sont dialectes, et se peuvent apprendre par icelle: que le proposant soustient si facile, qu'il en montera toute la grammaire en six heures: mais il faut six mois pour apprendre la signification de tous ses mots.

XXVI. Enseigner à argumenter sans faillir en toute sorte de modes et figures à toutes personnes, en un quart d'heure.

XXVII. Montrer un secret, par le moyen duquel tout homme pourra prononcer toute langue estrangere aussi naivent que sa naturelle, fust elle du milieu de l'Asie, de l'Afrique et de l'Amerique, et luy habitent de l'Europe, ou de la terre Australe, ou au contraire: qui est un moyen de faire perdre leurs mauvais accens et prononciation, tant aux estrangers et regnicoles, qui les distinguent si fort les uns des autres.

XXVIII. Faire servir, sans chevilles, une solive rompuë en deux ou trois endroits.

XXIX. Perser à l'instant une porte avec une chandelle non allumée.

XXX. Faire porter trois cens pas un pistolet d'un pied et demi de long.

XXXI. Faire promptement quantité d'eau douce en plein mer.

XXXII. Mesurer la profondeur de la mer où sa sonde ne peut parvenir: ou bien là où elle est insensible.

XXXIII. Faire voir toutes les gentillesses et subtilitez qui se fond au jeu des chartes: comme faire venir à tel nombre qu'on voudra la charte que vous aurez pensée: dire à chacun de 15 personnes, qui auront retenu quinze couples des chartes; celle qu'il aura retenu, et plusieurs autres.

XXXIV. Tirer deux lignes, lesquelles prolongées à l'infini, s'approcheront tousjours et ne se rencontreront jamais.

XXXV. Faire une lumiere sans huile, cire, suif, gomme, et gresse à peu de fraiz, qui offencera moins la veue, pendant la lecture d'une nuit entiere, que la lumiere ordinaire durant un quart d'heure.

XXXVI. Faire des vitres au travers desquelles le Soleil ne penetre point, encore qui sa lumiere y passe.

XXXVII. Rendre lisibles les vieux characteres effecez.

XXXVIII. Se tenir sous les eaux l'espace de quelques heures sans tuyau.

XXXIX. Faire une aiguille non aimantée, qui tournera tousjours vers le Nord.

XL. Faire un feu sans matiere combustible, portatif en quelque lieu que ce soit, capable de cuire, et qui durera plusieurs centaines d'années; voire autant que le monde.

XLI. Faire l'arbe mineral, qui est un assemblage de metaux qui croissent en forme d'arbrisseau, dans un vaisseau de verre bien clos.

XLII. Convertir le fer, en acier et en cuivre: l'empescher de rouiller: et lui donner une trampe telle qu'une paire d'armes complette qui pesera des trois quarts moins que les ordinaires, resistera aux coups de mousquete.

XLIII. Acroistre tellement le pouls à un homme, qu'il paroisse avoir la fievre: et lui diminuer en sorte, qu'il paroisse moribund: le tout neantmoins sans prejudice de sa santé.

XLIV. Furent proposez presques infinis secrets pour la conservation de la santé et guerison des maladies, desquelles je vous reserver la deduction plus particuliere apres que les experiences en auront esté faites: n'y ayant aucun art ou science où la credulité soit moins excusable ni plus perilleuse lors qu'il s'agit de quelque effect extraordinaire, qu'en la Medecine: en laquelle plus j'apporte de circumspection et plus je promets de soin à faire valoir des choses certaines et dignes du public, avec le mesme zele que j'employe à publier tout ce qui le merite.

La Présence des absens (Paris: 1642), pp. 44-46.

DES TUMEURS

A ou a eu des bubes ou eleveures de petite vérole par tout les corps, ou aux parties marqués en la figure A, B, ou C, qui sont sorties peu ou en abondance, ou sont dispouies incontinent, des verrues plus larges ou estroites en leur racine, qu'en leur sommet, noirastre, blanchastre, rondes, longues.

A tumeur ou enfleur grande, mediocre ou petite, et de la grosseur de la moitié d'une lentille, d'un pois, d'une feve, noisette, noix, d'un oeuf de pigeon, de poule, d'oye, du poing, des deux poings, de la teste.

Qui a commancé depuis

ans					mois	jours			heures	
1	2	3	4	5	1	1	11	21	1	12
6	7	8	9	10	2	2	12	22	2	13
11	12	13	14	15	3	3	13	23	3	14
16	17	18	19	20	4	4	14	24	4	15
21	22	23	24	25	5	5	15	25	5	16
26	27	28	29	30	6	6	16	26	6	17
31	32	33	34	35	7	7	17	27	7	18
36	37	38	39	40	8	8	18	28	8	19
41	42	jusques	ou		9	9	19	29	9	20
environ					10	10	20	30	10	21
					11	ou environ			11	22
										23

En la partie du corps marquée en la figure A, B ou C.
Ceste tumeur est dure ou molle.
Sans doleur ou avec douleur.
Sans chaleur ou avec chaleur.
Rouge, jaunastre, pasle, livide, ou noire.
Venue en suite de quelque maladie, ou sans avoir esté malade.
Apres, ou sans cheute ou effort.

237

Remue, ou non remue par quand on l'a touché.

Este venue subitement, ou par succession de temps.

Paroist et disparoist de fois à autre: ou est toujours en mesme estat.

Est avec ou sans demangeaison.

Avec ou sans pustules ou bubes.

La marque du doigt y demeure quand on la presse, ou n'y demeure pas.

Aboutit ou non aboutit pas en pointe.

Bat ou non bat pas.

Est dure des le commancement, ou s'est endurcie apres l'application des remedes.

A des veines eflées tout à l'entour.

A fait escharre ou crouste.

Est avec ou sans epoinconnemens.

Est pesante.

Est transparante, et au travers laquelle on void la lumiere.

BIBLIOGRAPHY

I. Manuscript Sources

Bibliothèque de l'Arsenal, Paris
Rés. H. 8918

Bibliothèque Nationale, Paris
Série Fonds Français: Manuscripts 3840; 3854; 7484; Recueil de Dupré, police: 8068, 8069, 8083, 8085, 8110, 8116; Extrait des registres des paroisses: 8622; 9354; 10225; 14127; E. Renaudot, "Journal des principalles affaires de ma vie," 14348; 14462; 15648; 15770; 16744; Séguier: 17348, 17491; 18600; 18605; Collection Delamare: 21741, 21804; Archives de la Chambre Syndicale de la Librairie et l'Imprimerie de Paris: 21816, 21819, 21832; Collection Anisson-Duperron: 22076, 22084, 22106; 23045
Série Thoisy: Manuscript 148

Faculté de Médecine, Université de Paris
Commentarii Facultatis Medicinae, xiii (1636-1653)

II. Printed Sources

Théophraste Renaudot*
Medical

Description d'un médicament appellé Polychreston, Dispensé publiquement par Jacques Boisse Maistre Apotiquaire en la ville de Loudun, le 4. Decembre 1619. Avec le Harangue faite sur le subject par Théophraste Renaudot Docteur en Médecine, Conseiller & Médecin du Roy, devant Messieurs les Députéz des Eglises Réformées de ce Royaume assemblez à Loudun par permission de sa Majesté. Dédiée à Messieurs de l'Assemblée. (Loudun: Quentin Mareschal dit La-Barre, 1619). 40pp.

Discours sur le scelet, c'est à dire sur les os de l'homme. Faict le Mardy 7 jour de Janvier 1620. Par Théophraste Renaudot Docteur en Médecine, Conseiller et Médecin du Roy: en présence de Messieurs les Députez des Églises Réformées de

* Titles are listed chronologically by subject.

239

France et Souverainété de Béarn, assemblez à Loudun par permission de sa Majesté. Avec une Leçon Anatomique faicte en suitte sur le mesme scelet. Dédié à Messieurs de l'Assemblée. (Loudun: Quentin Mareschal, 1620). 101pp.

La Présence des absens, ou facile moyen de rendre present au Médecin l'estat d'un malade absent. Dressé par les Docteurs en Médecine Consultans charitablement À Paris pour les pauvres malades. Avec les figures du corps humain, et Table servant à ce dessein: Ensemble l'instruction pour s'en servir, mesmes par ceux qui ne sçavent point escrire. (Paris: Bureau d'Adresse, 1642). 60pp.

Belles-Lettres, History

Oraison funebre pour Monsieur de Sainte Marthe décedé à Loudun le 29 Mars MDCXXIII. Prononcée au Palais le Mercredi ensuivant 5. jour d'Avril en présance des Officiers & autres notables personnes dudit lieu. Par Jean Cesuet estudiant chez Théophraste Renaudot Doctor en Médecine Conseiller & Medecin du Roy. Dédiée à Monseigneur le President Chevallier. (Samur: B. Mignon, 1623). 26pp.

Éloge d'Armand Jean du Plessis, Cardinal de Richelieu. (Paris: 1627). 7pp.

Stances pour la Santé du Roy. À Monseigneur le Cardinal de Richelieu. (Paris: Jean Martin, 1627). 8pp.

Recit veritable de la vie et la mort du Mareschal de Gassion. (Orleans: Gilles Hotot et Gabriel Fremont, 1647). 16pp. Also published as No. 117 of *Recueil . . . de 1647*, 10 October 1647, pp. 897-908. Republished in: *Archives curieuses de l'histoire de France* (Paris: 1838), 2nd Series, VI, 38-55.

Bureau d'Adresse

Inventaire des adresses du Bureau de Rencontre, où chacun peut donner & recevoir avis de toutes les necessitez comoditez de la vie & société humaine. Par permission du Roy, contenue en ses Brevet, Arrests de son Conseil d'Estat, Déclaration,

Privilege, Confirmation, Arrest de sa Cour de Parlement, Sentences & jugements donnez en consequence. Dédié à Monseigneur le Commandeur de la Porte, par T. Renaudot, Médecin du Roy. (Paris: À l'Enseigne du Coq rue de la Calandre sortant au Marché neuf, ou l'un desdits Bureau d'adresse est étably, 1630). 36pp.

Table des choses dont on peut donner & recevoir advis au Bureau d'adresse. (S.l.n.d.). 1p. [1630].

Quinziesme Feuille du Bureau d'adresse, du premier septembre 1633. Republished in: *Variétés historiques et littéraires* (Édouard Fournier, ed. Paris: 1859), ix, 51-61.

"Ordonnance pour ceux qui arrivent dans Paris pour y chercher Maistre, et autres faits de Police 9 Decembre 1639," *Extraordinaire du 12 Decembre 1639,* 4pp.

"Ordonnance pour la défense faite à tous hostes de loger plus d'une nuit les estrangers et forains qui cherchent employ, sans avoir rapporté certificat du Bureau d'Adresse; et commandement aux artizans d'y aller chercher des compagnons et apprentifs," *Extraordinaire du 13 Mars 1640,* 4pp.

Le Renouvellement des Bureaux d'Adresse, à ce nouvel an MDCXLVII. *Avec une ample explication de leur utilitez et commoditez. Par Théophraste Renaudot Conseiller et Médecin du Roy, Historiographe de sa Majesté, Maistre et Intendant général des Bureaux d'Adresse de France.* (Paris: Bureau d'Adresse, 1647). 53pp.

Gazette, Nouvelles ordinaires, Relations, Extraordinaires

Recueil des Gazettes de l'année 1631. Dédié au Roy. Avec une préface servant à l'intelligence des choses qui y sont contenues. Et une Table alphabetique des matières. (Paris: Bureau d'Adresse, 1632). [Each *Gazette* is numbered individually: not until edition "F" does the date and place of publication appear on the last page ("4 juillet 1631, à Bureau d'Adresse. . . ."). The *Recueil* includes 32 weekly *Gazettes.*]

241

Recueil des Gazettes, Nouvelles, Relations et autres choses Memorables de toute l'Année 1632. Dédié au Roy. Par Théophraste Renaudot, Conseiller et Médecin de sa Majesté, Intendant Général des Bureaux d'Adresse en France (Paris: Bureau d'Adresse, 1633). 530pp. [Pages were numbered consecutively.]

Recueil des Gazettes, Nouvelles, et relations de toute l'année 1633. Dédié au Roy. . . . (Paris: Bureau d'Adresse, 1634). 532pp.

Recueil des Gazettes, Nouvelles, Relations, Extraordinaires et autres recits des choses avenues toute l'année 1634, dédié au Roy. . . . (Paris: Bureau d'Adresse, 1635). 596pp.

Recueil des Toutes les Gazettes, Nouvelles Ordinaires et Extraordinaires et autres Relations. Contenant le Récit des choses remarquables, avenues tout en ce Royaume qu'es pays estrangers, dont les nouvelles nous sont venues toute l'année 1635. Dédié au Roy. . . . (Paris: Bureau d'Adresse, 1636). 742pp.

Recueil de Toutes les Nouvelles ordinaires, extraordinaires, Gazettes et autres Relations. Contenant le récit des choses remarquables avenues tant en ce Royaume qu'es pays Estrangers, dont les Nouvelles nous sont venues tout l'année 1636. Avec les Édicts, Ordonnances, Déclarations, et Règlemens sur le fait des Armes, Justice et Police de ce Royaume, publiez toute ladite année dernière: Et autres pièces servantes à nostre Histoire. Par Théophraste Renaudot. . . . (Paris: Bureau d'Adresse, 1637). 836pp.

Recueil de . . . tout l'année 1637. . . . (Paris: Bureau d'Adresse, 1638). 808pp.

Recueil des Gazettes, Nouvelles, Relations, extraordinaires et autres récits des choses avenues toute l'année 1638. Par Théophraste Renaudot. . . . (Paris: Bureau d'Adresse, 1639). 772pp.

Recueil de toutes les nouvelles ordinaires, extraordinaires, Gazettes et autres Relations: contenant le récit des choses re-

marquables avenues tant en ce Royaume qu'aux pais Estrangers, dont les Nouvelles nous sont venues toute l'année 1639. Avec les Édits, Ordonnances, Déclarations et Règlements sur le fait des Armes, Justice et Police de ce Royaume, publié toute ladite année dernière: Et autres pièces servantes à nostre Histoire. Par Théophraste Renaudot. . . . (Paris: Bureau d'Adresse, 1640). 852pp.

Recueil des Gazettes, Nouvelles, Relations, Extraordinaires, et autres récits des choses avenues toute l'année 1640. Dédié à Monseigneur le Mareschal de la Mesleraye, Grand Maistre de l'Artellerie, etc., par Théophraste Renaudot. . . . (Paris: Bureau d'Adresse, 1641). 856pp.

Recueil . . . toute l'année 1641. Par Théophraste Renaudot. . . . (Paris: Bureau d'Adresse, 1642). 974pp. [Same title as above, but without dedication.]

Recueil des toutes les Gazettes, Nouvelles, Ordinaires, Extraordinaires et autres Relations: contenant le récit des choses remarquables avenues tant en ce Royaume qu'aux pais Estrangers, dont les Nouvelles nous sont venues toute l'année 1642. Avec les Edits, Ordonnances, Déclarations et Règlements sur le fait des Armes, Justice et Police de ce Royaume, publiez tout ladite année dernière: Et autres pièces servantes à nostre Histoire. Par Théophraste Renaudot. . . . (Paris: Bureau d'Adresse, 1643). 1216pp.

Recueil des Gazettes et Nouvelles, tant ordinaires que extraordinaires, et autres relations des choses avenues toute l'année 1643. Par Théophraste Renaudot. . . . (Paris: Bureau d'Adresse 1644). 1116pp.

Recueil . . . toute l'année 1644. Par Théophraste Renaudot. . . . (Paris: Bureau d'Adresse, 1645). 1064pp.

Recueil . . . toute l'année 1645. Par Théophraste Renaudot. . . . (Paris: Bureau d'Adresse, 1646). 1218pp.

Recueil des Gazettes, Nouvelles ordinaires et Extraordinaires: Relations et autres récits des choses avenues l'année 1646: Par

243

Théophraste Renaudot. . . . (Paris: Bureau d'Adresse, 1647). 1240pp.

Recueil . . . des choses avenues toute l'année 1647. Par Théophraste Renaudot. . . . (Paris: Bureau d'Adresse, 1648). 1290pp.

Recueil des Gazettes, Nouvelles ordinaires et extraordinaires, Relations, Actes et récits des choses avenues toute l'année 1648. Par Théophraste Renaudot. . . . (Paris: Bureau d'Adresse, 1649). 1768pp. [With the *Nouvelle* of 16 May 1648, the address of the Bureau d'Adresse ("rue de Calandre, qui sortent au Marché neuf") changed ("aux Galleries du Louvre, devant le rue St. Thomas").]

Recueil . . . toute l'année 1649. Par Théophraste Renaudot. . . . (Paris: Bureau d'Adresse, 1650). 1292pp.

Recueil . . . toute l'année 1650. Par Théophraste Renaudot. . . . (Paris: Bureau d'Adresse, 1651). 1720pp.

Recueil des Gazettes, Nouvelles ordinaires et extraordinaires, relations et Récits des choses avenues tant en ce Royaume qu'ailleurs toute l'année 1651. Imprimées et publiées par l'ordre de Mre Théophraste Renaudot. . . . (Paris: Bureau d'Adresse, 1652). 1516pp.

Recueil . . . toute l'année 1652. Imprimées et publiées par l'ordre de Mre Théophraste Renaudot. . . . (Paris: Bureau d'Adresse, 1653). 1200pp.

Recueil des Gazettes, Nouvelles ordinaires et extraordinaires, Relations et récits des choses avenues tant en ce Royaume qu'ailleurs toute l'année 1653. (Paris: Bureau d'Adresse, 1654). 1268pp. [Renaudot's name did not appear on the title page of this *Recueil*: he died on 25 October 1653.]

Academy

Première Centurie des Questions traitées ez Conférences du Bureau d'Adresse, depuis le 22. jour d'Aoust 1633. jusques au dernier Juillet 1634. Dédiée à monseigneur le Cardinal.

Avec une table des matières. (Paris: Bureau d'Adresse, 1634). 408pp.

Second edition. (Paris: Bureau d'Adresse, 1635).
Third edition. (Paris: Bureau d'Adresse, 1636).
Fourth edition. (Paris: Bureau d'Adresse, 1638).

Seconde Centurie des Questions traitées ez conférences du Bureau d'Adresse, depuis le 3. jour de Novembre 1634. jusques à l'11 Fevrier 1636. Dédiée à monseigneur le Chancellier. Avec une Table des Matières. (Paris: Bureau d'Adresse, 1636). 420pp.

Troisieme Centurie des Questions traictées aux Conférences du Bureau d'Adresse, depuis le 18 Fevrier 1636. jusques au 17. Janvier 1639. Dédiée à Monseigneur de Bautru. Avec un Table des Matières. (Paris: Bureau d'Adresse, 1639). 524pp.
Second edition. (Paris: Bureau d'Adresse, 1641).

Quatriesme Centurie des Questions traitées aux Conférences du Bureaux d'adresse, depuis le 24 Janvier 1639. jusques au 10 Juin 1641. Avec une Table des Matières. (Paris: Bureau d'Adresse, 1641). 460pp.

Cinquiesme et dernier tome du Recueil Général des Questions traitées es conférences du Bureau d'adresse, sur toutes sortes des Matières, Par les plus beaux Esprits de ce temps. Non encore mises au jour. (Paris: la veufve Guillaume Loyson, 1655). 2390pp. [Included conferences of 24 June 1641 through 1 September 1642. Edited by Eusèbe Renaudot.]

Recueil Général des Questions traictées es Conférences. . . . (Paris: Louis Chamhovdry, 1655-1656). 4 volumes.

Recueil Général des questions traitées es Conférences du Bureau d'Adresse, sur toutes sortes de Matières. Par les plus beaux Esprits de ce Temps. (Lyon: Antoine Valançol, 1666). [6 volumes, identical to earlier Paris editions.]

Recueil des Questions traitées es Conférences du Bureau d'Adresse. Par les plus beaux Esprits de ce Temps. Tome Septiesme et Dernier. (Paris: Jean Baptiste et Henry Loyson,

1670). [Included conferences of 24 June 1641 through 1 September 1642. Served as volume 7 of Lyon edition (Antoine Valançol: 1660).]

English translations:

A question whether there be nothing new? Being one of those questions handled in the weekly conferences of Monsieur Renaudot's Bureau d'addresses, at Paris. Translated into English, anno 1640. (London: Jasper Emery, at the Eagle and Child, in St. Paul's Churchyard, near St. Augustin's gate, s.d.). Reprinted in: *The Harleian Miscellany* (London: 1809), II, 35-37.

A question of the cock; and whether his crowing affrights the lion? Being one of those questions handled in the weekly conferences of Monsieur Renaudot's Bureau d'addresses, at Paris. Translated into English anno 1640. Reprinted in: *The Harleian Miscellany* (London: 1808), I, 439-41.

A General Collection of Discourses of the Virtuosi of France, upon questions of all sorts of philosophy, and other Natural Knowledge. Made in the assembly of the Beaux Esprits at Paris, by the most ingenius persons of that nation. Render'd into English by G. Havers, gent. (London: T. Dring and J. Starkey, 1664). [Included conferences 1-100 (22 August 1633 through 31 July 1634).]

Mercure françois

Le vingt-deuxiesme tome du Mercure François, ou Suitte de l'histoire de nostre temps, sous la Règne du Très-Christien Roy de France et de Navarre, Louys XIII. Es années 1637 et 1638. (Paris: Olivier de Varennes, 1641). 596pp.

Le vingt-troisiesme tome du Mercure François, . . . Es années 1639 et 1640. (Paris: Olivier de Varennes, 1646). 819pp.

Le vingt-quatriesme tome du Mercure François . . . sous le règne du Très-Chrestien Roy de France et de Navarre Louis XIII jusqu'à sa mort. Es années 1641, 1642, et 1643. (Paris: Olivier de Varennes, 1647). 1105pp.

Tome première de l'Histoire de Nostre Temps, sous le Règne du Très-Chrestien Roy de France et de Navarre Louys XIV es années 1643 et 1644. Ou Tome Vingt-cinquiesme du Mercure François, es années 1643 et 1644. (Paris: Jean Henault, 1648). 787pp.

Litigation Material

Lettres du Roy en forme de Chartre. Contenans le privilege octroyé par Sa Majesté à Théophraste Renaudot, l'un de ses Conseillers et Médecins ordinaires, Maistre et Intendant Général des Bureaux d'Adresse de ce Royaume; et à ses enfans, successors, et ayans droit de lieu, de faire, imprimer, faire imprimer, et vendre par qui et où bon semblera les Gazettes, Nouvelles, et Récits de tout ce qui s'est passé tant dedans que dehors le Royaume, Conférance, prix courant des marchandises et autres impressions desdits Bureaux, à perpetuité et tant que les dites Gazettes, Nouvelles et autres impressions auront cours en cedit Royaume; et ce exclusivement à toutes autres personnes: En suite des Déclarations, Lettres et Arrests de Conseil, nagueres donnez sur le fait desdits impressions. (S.l.n.d.). 16pp.

"Si l'establissements des Monts-de-piété est nécessaire en France," *Extraordinaire*, 13 March 1636. 8pp.

"Replique aux nouvelles objections contre les Monts-de-piété," *Extraordinaire*, 25 March 1637. 4pp.

"Arrest du Conseil, Commission et Brevet de Sa Majesté, pour l'achat, troque et vente au Bureau d'Adresse de toutes choses licites: en attendant l'establissement des Monts-de-piété," *Extraordinaire*, 9 April 1637. 4pp.

"Extrait des Registres des Requestes ordinaires de l'Hostel du Roy," *Extraordinaire*, 24 August 1637. 4pp.

"Lettres patentes portantes attribution et connoissance souveraine aux Requestes de l'Hostel, de l'Establissement des Bureaux d'Adresse par toute la France, circonstances et dependances d'iceux 30 Septembre 1639," *Extraordinaire*, 3 Octobre 1639. 4pp.

Requete de Théophraste Renaudot, addressée au Conseil du Roy, pour que son proces contre la Faculté de Médecine de Paris ne soit pas porté devant le Parlement. (S.l., 1640). 1p.

Factum de l'instance de Théophraste Renaudot . . . défendeur au principal, appelant d'une sentance du Lieutenanct Civil, donné par defaut, et demandeur en Lettres Patentes du septième Decembre, et défendeur. Contre les Doyen et Docteurs de l'Escole en Médecine de Paris intimez, défendeurs ausdits Lettres, et opposans à l'execution du Committitur obtenu sur l'entérinement d'icelles. (S.l.n.d.). 7pp.

Factum du procez d'entre maistre Théophraste Renaudot . . . demandeur en Requeste présentée au Conseil privé du Roy le 30 Octobre 1640. Contre les Doyen et Docteurs en Médecine de la Faculté de Paris, défendeurs: sans que les qualitez puissant prejudicier. (S.l.n.d.). 20pp.

Les Consultations charitables pour les malades. Dédiées à Monseigneur de Noyers, Secretaire d'Estat. (Paris: Bureau d'Adresse, 1640). 12pp. [Another edition appeared in the *Recueil* of 1640 as *Extraordinaire*, 7 November 1640.]

Response de Théophraste Renaudot . . . au Libelle fait contre les Consultations charitables pour les pauvres malades. (Paris: Bureau d'Adresse, 1641). 91pp.

Remarques sur l'avertissement à Monsieur Théophraste Renaudot, Portées à son Autheur par Maschurat Compagnon Imprimeur. (Paris, 1641). 46pp.

"Arrests du Conseil donnez en faveur des Consultations Charitables pour les pauvres malades, entre Me. Théophraste Renaudot et les autres Docteurs en Médecine Consultans avec luy d'une part et les Doyen et Docteurs de l'Eschole de Médecine de Paris, d'autre," *Extraordinaire*, 25 July 1641. 8pp.

Le Grand-Mercy de Maschurat, compagnon d'Imprimerie. À l'Autheur de l'Avertissement à Monsieur Renaudot. (S.l.n.d.).

27pp. [Virtually identical to *Remarques sur l'avertissement à Monsieur T. R.*]

Extrait des registres du Conseil Privé du Roy (30 Octobre 1640). Suivi par d'un autre arrêt (14 Juin 1641). (S.l.n.d.). 4pp.

"La confirmation des Lettres Patentes et Arrests défendans l'impression des Gazettes et Nouvelles," *Extraordinaire*, 4 Septembre 1643. 8pp.

Requeste présentée à la Reyne par Théophraste Renaudot en faveur des pauvres malades de ce Royaume. (S.l.n.d.). 8 pp. Also appeared in *Réponse à l'examen de la request présentée à la Reyne.*

Factum du procez, d'entre Théophraste Renaudot, demandeur en rapport d'arrest: Et les Médecins de l'Eschole de Paris, deffendeurs. (Paris, 1643). 8pp.

Response à l'examen de la Requeste présentée à la Reine par Mr. Théophraste Renaudot, Portée à son autheur par Maschurat Compagnon Imprimeur. (Paris, 1644). 75pp.

Factum, touchant les Monts-de-piété. (S.l.n.d.). 2p.

Plaise à Nosseigneurs du Conseil en l'Instance pour Théophraste Renaudot Demandeur, d'une part: Contre Thomas Desprez, Nicolas Thibaut sa caution, François Colas, Magdelaine Cuvellier ayant les droits cedez d'Elisabeth le Moine, Estienne de Beaufort et Consors Défendeurs d'autre part. (S.l.n.d.). 3pp.

Response au Factum des Maistres et Gardes des six Corps des Marchands de la Ville de Paris, Opposans. Par Mr. Théophraste Renaudot . . . Demandeur et poursuivant la vérification des Lettres Patentes du mois d'Octobre 1643, pour la continuation des Vents à grâce et pures et simples. (S.l.n.d.). 32pp. [Also appeared in *Factum, où il est montré . . . par T. R. . . .*]

Défenses et raisons pour la continuation des Vents à Grâce et pures et simples, par lesquelles les personnes pauvres et incom-

249

modées trouvent à l'instant argent sur leurs meubles moins nécessaires. Ou Response que met et baille par devant vous Nosseigneurs de Parlement, Mre Théophraste Renaudot . . . *Demandeur en Lettres Patentes par luy obtenues de sa Majesté au mois d'Octobre 1643, et Défendeur.* (Paris, 1647). 11pp.

Factum, où il est montré que le seul et plus prompt moyen de bannir l'usure de la France, est l'entérinement des Lettres Patentes, obtenues par Théophraste Renaudot . . . *En suite duquel Factum est celui des six Corps des Marchands de Paris, Opposans audit entérinement. Avec sa Responce. Faite par l'impetrant desdites Lettres, article par article.* (Paris: Bureau d'Adresse, 1650). 12pp.

Raisons convainquantes de la nécessité qu'il y a en France, d'establir les Vents à grâce et pures et simples, entérinant les Lettres patentes données au mois d'Octobre 1643. (S.l.n.d.). 4pp.

Mazarinades

La prise de Charenton par les troupes du Roy commandées par Son Altesse Royale. (S. Germain en Laye: 12 February 1649). 8pp.

La prise par assaut de la ville de Quillebeve en Normandie. Avec la réduction en l'obeissance du Roy, de celle de Ponteau-de-mer, en la mesme Province: par le Comte d'Harcourt. (S. Germain en Laye: 21 February 1649). 8pp.

La prise de la ville et chasteau de Brie-Comte Robert. (S. Germain en Laye: 3 March 1649). 8pp.

Le siege mis devant le Ponteau de Mer: par l'ordre de Duc de Longueville. Que le Gouverneur et les habitans du lieu ont fait lever. Le Te Deum chanté pour la ratification de la paix avec l'Empire: Et ce qui s'est n'agueres passé à la Cour. (S. Germain en Laye: 10 March 1649).

La paix en France. (S. Germain en Laye: 14 March 1649). 8pp.

250

La prise du chasteau de Neufbourg. (S. Germain en Laye: 16 March 1649). 4pp.

La Déplorable Mort de Charles I, Roy de la Grand'Bretagne. (S. Germain en Laye: 18 March 1649). 8pp.

La Déclaration du Roy pour la paix, Donnée au mois de Mars et vérifiée en Parlement le premier d'Avril, 1649. (S. Germain en Laye: 1 April 1649). 12pp.

Miscellaneous

Catolicon François, ou Plainctes de deux Chasteaux, raportées par Renaudot, Maistre du Bureau d'Adresse. (S.l., 1636). 159pp. [Apocryphally attributed to Renaudot.]

"Requeste présentée au Roy, par Théophraste Renaudot, l'un des Médecins de Sa Majesté, . . . Sur le sujet des Gazettes et Nouvelles," *Extraordinaire,* 21 September, 1640. 4pp.

Response de Théophraste Renaudot . . . à l'autheur des libelles intitulez Avis du Gazetier de Cologne à celui de Paris: Response des Peuples de Flandre au Donneur d'Avis François, et Réfutation du Correctif des Ingrediens, etc. (Paris: Bureau d'Adresse, 1648). 176pp.

"l'Apologie du Bureau d'Adresse contre ceux qui se plaignent de ce qu'il ne leur peut plus donner gratuitement les Gazettes," *Extraordinaire,* 9 June 1651, 12pp.

"l'Avertissement au Lecteur," *Extraordinaire,* 10 August 1651. 12pp.

Contemporary Printed Sources: Memoires and Letters

Aubéry, le sieur. *l'Histoire du Cardinal-Duc de Richelieu.* (Cologne: Pierre du Marteau, 1666). [Paris: 1660].

Bachot, Estienne. *Apologie ou Défense pour la saignée contre ses Calomniateurs: avec une réponse au Libelle intitulé Examen ou Raisonnments sur l'Usage de la Saignée.* (Paris: S. Cramoisy, 1646).

251

Blegny, Nicolas de. *Le livre commode, contenant les addresses de la ville de Paris, et le trésor des almanachs pour l'année bissextile 1692.* . . . (Paris: la veuve de Denis Nion, 1692). Also published by Édouard Fournier in 1878 edition (Paris: Elzevirienne).

Bodin, Jean. *Six livres de la république.* (Paris: Jacques de Puis, 1583).

Campanella, Tommaso. *La cité du soleil.* (Paris: Lavasseur, s.d.). Originally published as *Civitas Solis.* (Paris: Dionys Houssaye, 1637).

Cardan, Jerome. *The Book of My Life* (*De vita propria liber*). Trans. and ed., Jean Stoner. (New York: E. P. Dutton, 1930).

Carneau, Étienne. *La Stimmimachie, ou le grand combat des médecins modernes touchant l'usage de l'Antimoine. Poeme historicomique dédié à Messieurs les Médecins de la Faculté de Paris. Par le sieur C.C.* (Paris: Jean Pasle, 1656).

Chartier, I. *La science du plomb sacré des sages, ou de l'Antimoine, où sont décrites ses rares et particulières Vertus, Puissances, et Qualitez. Par I. Chartier, Escuyer, Conseiller, et Médecin ordinaire du Roy, et son Professeur en Médecine au Collège Royale de France, Docteur Regent en la Faculté de Médecine de Paris.* (Paris: I. de Senleeque et F. le Cointe, 1651).

Le Commerce des nouvelles restably, ou le courrier arresté par le Gazette (Paris, 1649).

Corps des marchands, Paris. *Factum, pour les maistres et Gardes des six Corps des Marchands de la Ville de Paris, deffendeurs. Contre Maistre Théophraste Renaudot, demandeur, et poursuivant la vérification des Lettres Patentes par luy obtenues au mois d'Octobre 1641. Pour l'establissement des Ventes à grâces, et pures et simples* (Paris: 1644).

―――. *Causes d'opposition que mettent pardevant vous Nosseigneurs tenans la Cour de Parlement à Paris, les Maistres et Gardes des six Corps des Marchands de cette ville de Paris, deffendeurs et opposans. Contre Mr Théophraste Renaudot, demandeur et poursuivant la vérification des Lettres patentes par luy obtenues au mois d'Octobre 1643, pour l'establissement des Vents à grâces et pures et simples.* 28 November 1647.

Courrier françois (Paris: Rolin de la Haye, 1649). [Contains 12 issues of 8 pages each.]

Faculté de Médecine, Université de Paris. *Statuts de la Faculté de Médecine* (1598). Published by M. Thèry, *Histoire de l'éducation en France.* (Paris: 1858), II, 372-88.

———. *La Défense de la Faculté de Médecine de Paris, contre son Calumniateur. Dédiée à Monseigneur l'Eminentissime Cardinal Duc de Richelieu* (Paris, 1641). [Attributed to René Moreau.]

———. *Advertissement à Théophraste Renaudot, contenant les Mémoires pour justifier les Anciens droicts et privilèges de la Faculté de Médecine de Paris* (Paris, 1641). [Attributed to Guy Patin.]

———. *Requête présentée au prévôt de Paris par les Doyen et les Docteurs de la Faculté de Médecine de Paris contre Théophraste Renaudot* (Paris, 1643).

———. *Examen de la Requeste présentée à la Reine par le Gazettier* (Paris: 4 Novembre, 1643).

———. *Arrest de la Cour de Parlement, pour les Doyen et Docteurs Regens de la Faculté de Médecine de Paris, contre Théophraste Renaudot, Gazettier, soy disant Médecin du Roy, et de l'Université de Montpellier, les Docteurs en Médecine dudit Montpellier, et d'autres Universitez ses Adherans, et les Chancelier, Professeurs et Docteurs Regens en ladite Faculté de, Médecine de Montpellier, intervenus en cause avec luy. Prononcé en l'Audience de la Grand Chambre, le Mardy premier jour de Mars l'an 1644. Avec les Plaidoyers de Monsieur Talon, Advocat Général, et des Advocats des Parties* (Paris: Claude Merlot, 1644).

———. *Magistri Michaelis de la Vigne, Vernonaei, Doctoris Medici, et Medicae Facultatis Parisiensis Decani, Orationes Duae, quarum prior Habita Est apud Dom. Propraetorem Urbanum, die IX. Decembris, MDCXLIII. Posterior in frequenti, Senatu Calendis Martiis, anno Domini MDCXLIV. Adversus Theophrastum Renaudot, Gazettarium, Medicum Monspeliensem, et omnes Medicos extraneos, Lutetiae Parisiorum Medicinam illicite factitantes* (Paris: Claudium Morlot, 1644).

253

Furetière, Antoine. *Le roman bourgeois* (Amsterdam: David Martier, 1714 [Paris: 1666]).

Gerbier, Balthazar. *Exposition du chevalier Balthazar Gerbier à messieurs les docteurs en Théologie de la Faculté à Paris, sur l'establissement des monts-de-piété* (Paris: François Preuveray, 1644). Reprinted in: *Archives curieuses de l'histoire de France* (Paris: 1838), 2nd Series, VI, 233-42.

————. *Remonstrance très-humble du Chevalier Balthazar Gerbier et ses associez, à monseigneur l'illustrissime Archevesque de Paris, touchant le Mont-de-Piété, et quelques mauvais bruits que nombre d'usuriers sement contre ce pieux, utile et nécessaire establissement.* (Paris: François Pomeray, 1643). Reprinted in: *Archives curieuses de l'histoire de France* (Paris: 1838), 2nd Series, VI, 215-26.

Germain, Claude. *Orthodoxe ou l'Abus de l'Antimoine, dialogue très-nécessaire pour détromper ceux qui donnent ou prennent le Vin et Pouldre Émetique . . .* (Paris: Thomas Blaize, 1652).

Godefroy, Théodore. *Le Cérémonial François: ou Description des Cérémonies, rangs et séances observées aux couronnements, entrées et enterrements des roys et roynes de France* (Paris: Cramoisy, 1649 [1619]).

Hartlib, Samuel. *A Further Discovery of the Office of Publick Address for Accomodations* (London: 1648). Published in *Harleian Miscellany*, VI (1810), 14-27.

d'Hozier Louis-Pierre. *Armorial général ou registres de la noblesse de France* (Paris: 1738-1768).

Laffemas, Barthelemy de. *Le mérite du travail et labeur, dédié aux Chefs de la Police. Faict par B de L., valet de Chambre du Roy, natif de Beau-Semblant en Dauphiné* (Paris: Pierre Pantonnier, 1602).

————. *Recueil présenté au Roy, de ce qui se passé en l'assemblée du Commerce au Palais à Paris. Faict par Laffemas Controlleur général dudit Commerce* (Paris: Pantonnier, 1604).

Laffemas, Isaac de. *L'Histoire du Commerce de France, enrichie des plus notables antiquitez du traffic des pais estranges* (Paris: Toussaincts du Bray, 1606).

Lis et Fais. (S.l.n.d.).

Loret, J. *La muze historique: ou recueil des lettres en vers contenant les nouvelles du temps écrites à son altesse de Longueville, depuis Duchesse de Nemours* (Paris: 1650-1665). Eds. J. Ravenel and E. V. de la Pelouze (Paris: P. Jannet, 1857).

Machiavelli, Niccolò. *The Prince and the Discourses*. Trans., Luigi Ricci and Christian E. Detmold. Introd., Max Lerner (New York: Modern Library, 1940).

Martin, Jean. *Nouvelles ordinaires des divert endroicts* (Paris, 1631-1632).

Mayerne, Louis Turquet, Sieur de. *Apologie contre les détracteurs des livres de la monarchie aristodemocratique* (S.l., 1617).

———. *Epistre au Roy. Présentée à sa Majesté au mois d'octobre 1591* (Tours: Jamet Mettayer, 1592).

———. *La monarchie aristodémocratique, ou le gouvernement composé et meslé de trois formes de légitimes républiques* (Paris: 1611).

———. *Traicté des négoces et traffiques, ou contracts qui se font en choses meubles. Règlements et administration du Bureau, ou Chambre politique des marchans* (Paris: 1599).

Mazarin, Jules. *Lettres pendant son ministère*. Ed., A. Chéruel (Paris: Imprimerie Nationale, 1872-1906).

Mazarinades. *Choix de Mazarinades*. Ed., Celestin Moreau (Paris: J. Renouard, 1853).

———. See Théophraste Renaudot.

Mémoire concernant les pauvres qu'on appelle enfermez, dédié à Monseigneur Messire Henry de Gondy, Éveque de Paris, Conseiller du Roy en ses Conseils d'Estat et privé, et maistre de l'Oratoire de Sa Majesté (Paris, 1617). Published in: *Archives curieuses de l'histoire de France*, ed., Petitot, 1st Series, xv, 241-70.

Mersenne, Marin. *Correspondance*. Eds., Paul Tannery, Cornelius de Waard, and René Pintard (Paris: Presses Universitaires de France, 1945-1967).

Montaigne, Michel de. *Essais* (Paris: Imprimerie Nationale, 1962).

Montchrétien, Antoyne de. *Traicté de l'Oeconomie politique. Dédié au Roy et à la Reyne Mère du Roy* (S.l., 1614).

Montpellier, Université de Médecine. *Matricule de l'Université de Médecine de Montpellier 1503-1599*. Ed., Marcel Gouron (Geneva: E. Droz, 1957).

Moreau, René. See Faculté de Médecine, Université de Paris.

Morgues, Mathieu de. *l'Ambassadeur chimerique, ou les chercheurs de duppes du Cardinal de Richelieu. Reveue et augmentée par l'autheur* (S.l., 1643).

————. *Diverses pièces pour la défense de la Royne Mère du Roy très-Chrestien Louys XIII faites et reveues par Messire Mathieu du Morgues Sieur de S. Germain, Conseiller et Prédicateur ordinaire du Roy Très-Chrestien, et Conseiller Prédicateur, et premier Aumosnier de la Royne Mère de Sa Majesté* (S.l., 1643). [Includes "Jugement sur la preface et diverses pièces que le Cardinal de Richelieu pretend de faire servir à l'histoire de son crédit," pp. 613-705.]

Naudé, Gabriel. *Jugement de tout ce qui a esté imprimé contre le Cardinal Mazarin, depuis le sixième Janvier, jusques à la Déclaration du premier Avril mil six cens quarante-neuf* (S.l. n.d.).

Patin, Guy. *Lettres de Gui Patin: nouvelle édition augmentée de lettres inédites, précedée d'une notice biographique accompagnée de remarques scientifiques, historiques, philosophiques et littéraires.* Ed., J-H. Reveillé-Parise (Paris: J-B. Baillière, 1846). 3 volumes.

————. *Lettres 1630-1672.* Ed., Paul Triaire (Paris: H. Champion, 1907). [Only first volume published: last letter published was dated 23 March 1649.]

————. *Le nez pourry de Théophraste Renaudot, grand gazettier de France et espion de Mazarin: Appellé dans les Chroniques 'Nebulo Hebdomadarius, de patria Diabolorum,' Avec sa vie infame et bouquine, récompensée d'une Vérole Euripienne, ses usures; la décadance de ses Monts-de-piété, et la ruine de tous ses fourneaux et alambics (excepte celle de sa Conférence, rétablie depuis quinze jours) par la perte de son Procez contre les Docteurs de la Faculté de Médecine de Paris.* (S.l.n.d.).

————. See Faculté de Médecine, Université de Paris.

Perreau, Jacques. *Rabbat-Joye de l'Antimoine triomphant, ou Examen de l'Antimoine Justifié de M. Eusèbe Renaudot, etc.* (Paris: Simon Moinet, 1654).

Planis Campy, David de. *Bouquet Composé des plus belles fleurs chimiques, ou Ajencement des préparations, et experiences es plus rares secrets, et Médicamens Pharmaco-Chimiques; prins des Mineraux, Animaux, et Végétaux. Le tout par une méthode très-facile, et non commune aux Chimiques ordinaires. Par D. de P.C., dit l'Edelphe, Chirurgien du Roy* (Paris: Pierre Billaine, 1629).

Platter, Thomas d.J. *Beschreibung der Reisen durch Frankreich, Spanien, England und die Niederlande (1595-1600).* Ed., Ruth Keiser (Basel: Schwabe, 1968).

Pommeray, François. See Jean Martin.

Ramus, Pierre. *Advertissements sur la réformation de l'Université de Paris, au Roy* (Paris: André Wechel, 1562).

———. *Dialectique de Pierre de la Ramée* (Paris: André Wechel, 1555).

Rapine, Florimand. *Recueil très-exact et curieux de tout ce qui s'est fait et passé de singulier et mémorable en l'Assemblée générale des Estats tenues à Paris en l'année 1614 et particulièrement en chacune séance du tiers Ordre. Avec le Cahier dudit Ordre, et autres pièces concernans le mesme sujet. Dédié à Monseigneur le Premier President, Garde des Sceaux de France* (Paris, 1651).

Renaudot, Eusèbe. *l'Antimoine Justifié et l'Antimoine triomphant: ou Discours apologetique faisant voir que le Poudre et le Vin Émetique et les autres remèdes tirés de l'antimoine ne sont point vénéneux, mais souverains pour guerir la pluspart des maladies, qui y sont exactement expliquées* (Paris: Jean Henault, 1653).

———. *Cinquiesme et dernier tome du Recueil Général des Questions traittées es conférences du Bureau d'Adresse, sur toutes sortes des Matières, Par les plus beaux Esprits de ce temps. Non encore mises au jour* (Paris: veufe Guillaume Loyson, 1655). [Includes sessions 296 (24 June 1641) through 345 (1 September 1642).]

Renaudot, Eusèbe. *Recueil des Questions traitées es Conférences du Bureau d'Adresse. Par les beaux Esprits de ce Temps. Tome Septiesme et Dernier* (Paris: Jean Baptiste et Henry Loyson, 1670). [Serves as volume VII of 1666 Lyon edition of *Recueil Général* (listed under Théophraste Renaudot). Includes session 296 (24 June 1641) through 345 (1 September 1642).]

———. See Théophraste Renaudot.

Renaudot, Isaac. See Eusèbe Renaudot.

Richelieu, Armand Jean de Plessis, Cardinal de. *Lettres, instructions diplomatiques et papiers d'état.* Ed., M. Avenel (Paris: Imprimerie Imperiale, 1853-1867; Imprimerie Nationale, 1874-1877). 8 Volumes.

———. *Testament politique.* Ed., L. André (Paris: R. Laffont, 1947).

Richesource, I.D.S. Escuyer Sieur de. *La première partie des Conférences Academiques et Oratoires, Accompagnées de leurs résolutions. Dans lesquelles on voit le plus bel usage des maxims de la Philosophie et des preceptes de l'Eloquence. Dédiée à Monseigneur Foucquet procurer général, Sur-Intendant des Finances et Ministre d'Estat* (Paris, 1661).

Riolan, Jean *fils. Curieuses recherches sur les Escholes en Médecine, de Paris, et de Montpellier, Nécessaire d'estre sçeues, pour la conservation de la Vie: Par un Ancien Docteur en Médecine de la Faculté de Paris* (Paris: Gaspar Meturas, 1651).

Sainte Marthe, Scévole de. *Éloges des hommes illustres qui depuis un siècle ont fleuri en France dans la profession des lettres ...* (Paris, 1644). [Trans. from 1616 original Latin edn. by Guillaume Colletet.]

Sarasin, Jean François. *Oeuvres.* Ed., Paul Festugière (Paris: Champion, 1926). 2 volumes.

Savot, Louis. *Le Livre de Galien de l'Art de guerir par la Saignée, traduit du Grec. Ensemble un Discours dedié à Messieurs les Médecins de Paris sur les causes par lesquelles on ne saigne pas encore tant aillieurs qu'à Paris, et pourquoy quelques Médecins mesme ont détracté de cette pratique de Paris* (Paris: Pierre Metayer, 1603).

Sennerti, Danielis. *Operum.* Paris: Apud Societatem, 1641.

258

Sorel, Charles. *Discours sur l'Académie Françoise, establie pour la correction et l'embellissement du Langage: pour sçavoir si elle est de quelque utilité aux Particuliers et au Public. Et où l'on void les Raisons de part et d'autre sans desquisement* (Paris: Guillaume de Luyne, 1654).

———. *Rôle des presentations faictes au Grand Jour de l'Éloquence françoise. Première assize le 13 mars 1634* (S.l.n.d.). Published in: *Variétés historique et littéraires,* ed., Édouard Fournier (Paris: 1855), pp. 127-40.

Tallemant des Réaux, Gédeon. *Historiettes.* Ed., Antoine Adam (Paris: Gallimard, 1960).

Trincant, Louis. *Abrégé des antiquitez de Loudun et pais du Loudunois.* Ed., Roger Drouault (Loudun: A. Roiffe, 1894 [1626]).

Vendosme, Louis. See Jean Martin.

Vigne, Michel de la. See Faculté de Médecine, Université de Paris.

Vives, Juan Luis. "De subventione pauperum," ed., F. R. Salter, *Some Early Tracts on Poor Relief* (London: Methuen, 1926).

La Voyage de Théophraste Renaudot Gazettier à la Cour (S.l.n.d.).

III. Secondary Studies

Adam, Antoine. *Histoire de la littérature française au XVIIᵉ siècle: l'époque d'Henri IV et de Louis XIII* (Paris: Domat, 1948).

Anderson, Fulton H. *Francis Bacon: His Career and Thought* (Los Angeles: University of Southern California Press, 1962).

André, Louis. See É. Bourgeois.

Ariès, Philippe. *Centuries of Childhood: A Social History of Family Life* (New York: Random House, 1965 [1960]).

Armstrong, Elizabeth. *Robert Estienne, Royal Printer. An Historical Study of the Elder Stephanus* (London: Cambridge University Press, 1954).

Ascoli, Georges. *La Grande Bretagne devant l'opinion française au XVIIᵉ siècle* (Paris: J. Camber, 1930).

d'Avenel, G. *Richelieu et la monarchie absolue* (Paris: Plon, 1884-1890). 4 volumes.

Avril, Pierre. *Les origines de la distinction des établissements d'utilité publique* (Paris: A. Rousseau, 1900).

Baron, Hans. "Franciscan Poverty and Civic Wealth as Factors in the Rise of Humanistic Thought," *Speculum*, XIII (1938), 1-37.

Bégué, André. *Les consultations charitables de Théophraste Renaudot* (Paris: J-B. Baillière, 1899).

Blaize, A. *Des monts-de-piété et des banques de prêt sur gages en France et dans les divers états de l'Europe* (Paris: Pagnerre, 1856 [1843]).

Bloch, Marc. *Les rois thaumaturges: étude sur le caractère surnaturel attribué à la puissance royale particulièrement en France et en Angleterre* (Paris: A. Colin, 1961 [1923]).

Bonnefont, Gaston. *Un docteur d'autrefois* (Limoges, 1893).

————. *Un oublié, Théophraste Renaudot: créateur de la presse, de la publicité, des dispensaires, des monts-de-piété* (Limoges, 1899).

Boulet, Marguerite. See F. Dahl.

Bouralière, M. de la. "Une lettre inédite de Théophraste Renaudot," *Bulletin de la Société des Antiquaires de l'Ouest* (1884), 307-12.

Bourgeois, Émile, and Louis André. *Les sources de l'histoire de France: XVIIe siècle (1610-1715).* Vol. IV: Journaux et pamphlets (Paris: A. Picard, 1924).

Brown, Harcourt. *Scientific Organizations in Seventeenth Century France (1620-1680)* (Baltimore: Johns Hopkins Press, 1934).

Butterfield, Herbert. *The Origins of Modern Science 1300-1800* (New York: Colliers, 1962 [1957]).

Cahen, Leon. "Les idées charitables à Paris au XVIIe et au XVIIIe siècles, d'après les règlements des compagnies charitables," *Revue d'histoire moderne et contemporaine*, II (1900), 5-22.

Caillet, Jules. *De l'administration en France sous le ministère du Cardinal de Richelieu* (Paris: Didot, 1857).

Campbell, Mildred. " 'Of People Either Too Few or Too Many': the Conflict of Opinion on Population and Its Relation to Emigration," *Conflict in Stuart England: Essays in Honour of Wallace Notestein*, eds., W. A. Aiken and B. D. Henning (London: Jonathan Cape, 1960), pp. 169-202.

Candille, Marcel. "Évolution des principes d'assistance hospitalière," *La revue administrative* (July 1954), 371-76.

Cauchie, Maurice. "Le rôle des poètes dans la seconde querelle de l'antimoine 1651-1656," *Revue des sciences modernes* (1955), 401-06.

Chalumeau, R. P. "l'Assistance aux malades pauvres au XVIIe siècle," *Dix-septième siècle*, Nos. 90-91 (1971), 75-86.

Chancerel, Robert. *Les apothecaires et l'ancienne faculté de médecine de Paris* (Dijon, 1892).

Chauchat, A. M. *La curieuse et grande figure de Théophraste Renaudot* (Paris: Hachette, 1939).

Chereau, Achille. "Théophraste Renaudot," *l'Union médicale*, 3rd Series, (Paris, 1878).

Chevalier, A. G. "l'École de médecine de Montpellier," *Revue Ciba*, Basel (May 1959).

Chevalier, L. *Classes laborieuses et classes dangereuses à Paris pendant la première moitié du XIXe siècle* (Paris: Plon, 1958).

Chill, Emanuel. "Religion and Mendicity in Seventeenth-Century France," *International Review of Social History*, VII (1962), 400-25.

Church, William F. "Cardinal Richelieu and the Social Estates of the Realm," *Album Helen Maud Cam* (Louvain: 1961), II, pp. 261-270.

Clark, G. N. *Science and Social Welfare in the Age of Newton.* Oxford: Clarendon Press, 1949.

Coornaert, Émile. *Les compagnonnages en France du moyen âge à nos jours* (Paris: Éditions Ouvrières, 1966).

————. *Les corporations en France avant 1789* (Paris: Gallimard, 1941).

Corlieu, Auguste. *l'Ancienne faculté de médecine de Paris* (Paris: Delahaye, 1877).

————. *Centenaire de la faculté de médecine de Paris (1794-1894)* (Paris: Imprimerie Nationale, 1896).

————. *Les chirurgiens de l'Hôtel-Dieu de Paris du XVe au XIXe siècle* (Paris, 1901).

————. *l'Église Saint-Côme et le collège de chirurgie* (Paris, 1901).

————. *l'Enseignement au collège de chirurgie, depuis son origines jusqu'à la Révolution française* (Paris, 1890).

————. *Généalogie de Renaudot* (S.l.n.d.).

Corlieu, Auguste. *l'Hôpital des cliniques de la faculté de médecine de Paris* (Paris: Delahaye, 1878).

Dahl, Folke, Fanny Petibon and Marguerite Boulet. "Les débuts de la presse française," *Acta Bibliothecae Gotoburgensis* (Goteborg and Paris, 1951).

Dainville, François de. *La géographie des humanistes: les Jesuites et l'éducation de la société française* (Paris: Beauchesne, 1940).

Dangon, Georges. "Théophraste Renaudot, médecin et gazetier," *Le courrier graphique*, Paris (March 1947), 11-24.

Darricou, R. "l'Action charitable d'une reine de France: Anne de Autriche," *Dix-septième siècle*, Nos. 90-91 (1971), 111-25.

Daumard, Adeline. *La bourgeoisie parisienne de 1815 à 1848* (Paris: S.E.V.P.E.N., 1963).

Davis, Natalie Zemon. "Poor Relief, Humanism, and Heresy: the Case of Lyon," *Studies in Medieval and Renaissance History,* v (1968), 217-75.

———. "A Trade Union in Sixteenth-Century France," *Economic History Review*, 2nd series, xix (1966), 48-69.

Debus, Allen G. *The English Paracelsians* (New York: Franklin Watts, 1966).

Delaroche, Pierre. *Une épidemie de peste à Loudun en 1632* (Bordeaux: Delmas, 1936).

Delavaud, L. *Quelques collaborateurs de Richelieu* (Paris, 1915). *Rapports et notices sur l'édition des mémoires du Cardinal Richelieu*, Vol. ii, fascicules iv and v.

Deloche, Maximin. *Autour de la plume de Richelieu* (Paris, 1920).

———. *La maison du Cardinal Richelieu* (Paris: H. Champion, 1912).

Denounain, J-J. "Les problèmes de l'honnête homme vers 1635: 'Religio medici' et les Conférences du Bureau d'Adresse," *Études anglaises*, xviii (1965), 235-57.

Dewhurst, Kenneth. *John Locke (1632-1704) Physician and Philospher: A Medical Biography with an Edition of the Medical Notes in His Journals* (London: Wellcome Historical Medical Library, 1963).

Deyon, Pierre. "À propos du pauperisme au milieu du XVIIᵉ siècle: peinture et charité chrétienne," *Annales*, xxii (1967), 137-53.

Dreux du Radier, M. *Bibliothèque historique et critique du Poitou* (Paris: Ganeau, 1754).

Drouault, Roger. "Notes inédites sur la famille de Théophraste Renaudot," *Revue poitevine*, 1892.

———. *Recherches sur les établissements hospitaliers du Loudunais* (Loudun: A. Roiffe, 1897).

Dumoulin, Maurice, "La construction de l'Île Saint-Louis," *Études de topographie parisienne*, III (1931), 1-288.

Dumoustier de la Fond. *Essais sur l'histoire de la ville de Loudun* (Poitiers: Michel-Vincent Chevrier, 1778).

Duplantier, Raymond. "La vie tormentée et l'oeuvre laborieuse de Théophraste Renaudot," *Bulletin de la Société des Antiquaires de l'Ouest* (1947), 292-331.

Eisenstein, Elizabeth L. "The Advent of Printing and the Problem of the Renaissance," *Past and Present*, No. 45 (1969), 19-90.

———. "The Advent of Printing in Current Historical Literature: Notes and Comments on an Elusive Transformation," *American Historical Review*, LXXV (1970), 727-43.

Émery, Michel. *Renaudot et l'introduction de la médication chimique* (Montpellier: Hamelin, 1888).

Estivals, Robert. *Le dépôt légal sous l'ancien régime* (Paris: M. Rivière, 1961).

Evans, Wilfred Hugo. *l'Historien Mézeray et la conception de l'histoire en France au XVIIᵉ siècle* (Paris: J. Gamber, 1930).

Falk, Henri. *Les privilèges de librairie sous l'ancien régime* (Paris, 1906).

Fauvelle, René. *Les étudiants en médecine de Paris sous le Grand Roi* (Paris: Steinheil, 1899).

Febvre, Lucien. *Le problème de l'incroyance au XVIᵉ siècle: la réligion de Rabelais* (Paris: A. Michel, 1962 [1942]).

———. and Henri-Jean Martin. *l'Apparition du livre* (Paris: A. Michel, 1958).

Feillet, Alphonse. *La misère au temps de la Fronde et St. Vincent de Paul, ou un chapitre de l'histoire du paupérisme en France* (Paris: Didie, 1862).

Fosseyeux, Marcel. "La taxe des pauvres au XVIᵉ siècle," *Revue d'histoire de l'Église de France*, XX (1934), 407-32.

Foucault, Michel. *Madness and Civilization: A History of Insanity in the Age of Reason* (New York: Random House, 1965 [1961]).

———. *Naissance de la clinique* (Paris: Presses Universitaires de France, 1963).

———. *The Order of Things: An Archaeology of the Human Sciences* (New York: Random House, 1970 [1966]).

Fournier, Édouard. *Les écrivains sur le trône: rois et princes journalistes depuis Louis XIII jusqu'à Napoleon* (Paris, 1865).

Frank, Joseph. *The Beginnings of the English Newspaper 1620-1660.* (Cambridge: Harvard University Press, 1961).

Friedrich, Carl J. *The Age of the Baroque 1610-1660* (New York: Harper, 1952).

Funck-Brentano, Franz. "l'Imprimerie à Paris en 1645," *Revue des études historiques* (1902), 483-86.

Geremek, Bronislaw. *Le salariat dans l'artisanat parisien aux XIIIe –XVe siècle: étude sur le marché de la main d'oeuvre au moyen âge* (Paris: Mouton, 1968 [1962]).

Germain, A. *l'Université de Montpellier* (Montpellier: 1879-1886).

Ghinato, P. Alberto, O.F.M. *Monte di pietà e monti frumentari di Amelia: origine e antichi statuti* (Rome: Edizioni Francescane, 1956).

Gilbert, Neal W. *Renaissance Concepts of Method* (New York: Columbia University Press, 1960).

Gilles de la Tourette, Georges. "Un essai de faculté libre au XVIIe siècle: Théophraste Renaudot, fondateur du journalisme et des consultations charitables," *Revue scientifique*, xlix (April 1892), 449-56.

———. *Théophraste Renaudot, d'après des documents inédits* (Paris: Plon, 1884).

———. *La vie et les oeuvres de Théophraste Renaudot* (Paris, 1892).

Goubert, Pierre. *Beauvais et le Beauvaisis* (Paris: S.E.V.P.E.N., 1960).

Grand-Mesnil, Marie-Noële. *Mazarin, la Fronde et la presse 1647-1649* (Paris: A. Colin, 1967).

Granel, François. "l'Empreinte montpellieraine de Théophraste Renaudot," *Monspelliensis Hippocrates*, 19 (1963), 13-24.

de Granges de Surgères, le Marquis. *Répertoire historique et biographique de la Gazette de France depuis l'origine jusqu'à la Révolution (1631-1790)* (Paris: Henri Leclerc, 1902-1906).

Grasset, (?). *Conference . . . sur Théophraste Renaudot, docteur en 1606 de la faculté de médecine de Montpellier, sa vie et ses oeuvres* (Montpellier: 1892).

Gray, Hanna H. "Renaissance Humanism: The Pursuit of Eloquence," *Renaissance Essays*. Eds., P. O. Kristeller and P. P. Weiner (New York: Harper, 1968), pp. 199-217. Originally published in *Journal of the History of Ideas*, xxiv (1963).

Griffet, H., S.J. *Histoire du règne de Louis XIII* (Paris: Librairie associés, 1758). Preface by P. Daniel.

Gutton, J-P. "À l'aube du XVIIᵉ siècle: idées nouvelles sur les pauvres," *Cahiers d'histoire*, x (1965), 87-97.

Haag, Eugène. *La France protestante* (Paris: Cherbuliez, 1858). Vol. viii: Article "Renaudot."

Hahn, André and Pauli Dumaître. *Histoire de la médecine et du livre médical* (Paris: Olivier Perrin, 1962).

Hamy, E-T. "La famille de Guy de la Brosse," *Bulletin du Muséum d'Histoire Naturelle*, vi (1900), 13-16.

Hanotaux, Gabriel. *Histoire du Cardinal de Richelieu* (Paris: Plon, 1896-1947). 6 volumes.

Harsin, Paul. *Crédit public et banque d'état en France du XVIIᵉ et XVIIIᵉ siècle* (Paris: Droz, 1933).

Hatin, Eugene. *À propos de Théophraste Renaudot: l'histoire, la fantaisie et la fatalité* (Paris: 1884).

———. *Bibliographie historique et critique de la presse périodique française, ou catalogue systematique et raisonné de tous les écrits périodiques, de quelque valeur publiés ou ayant circulé en France depuis l'origine du journal jusqu'à nos jours* (Paris: Firmin-Didot, 1866).

———. *Histoire du journal en France* (Paris: Havard, 1846).

———. *Histoire politique et littéraire de la presse en France* (Paris: Poulet-Malassis, 1859-1861). 8 volumes.

———. *La maison du grand-coq* (Paris: 1885).

Hatin, Eugene. *Manuel théorique et pratique de la liberté de la presse, 1500-1868* (Paris: Pagnerre, 1868).

———. *Théophraste Renaudot et ses "innocentes inventions"* (Poitiers: H. Oudin, 1883).

Hauser, Henri. "Les compagnonnages d'arts et métiers à Dijon aux XVIIᵉ et XVIIIᵉ siècles," *Revue bourguignonne,* xvii (1907), 1-220.

———. *Ouvriers du temps passé (XVᵉ et XVIᵉ siècles)* (Paris: Falcan, 1898).

———. *La pensée et l'action économiques du Cardinal Richelieu* (Paris: Presses Universitaires de France, 1944).

Hawley, Grace Agnes. *John Evelyn and the Advancement of Learning* (New York: Columbia University Press, 1962).

Hayden, J. Michael. "Deputies and *qualités*: The Estates General of 1614," *French Historical Studies,* iii (1964), 507-24.

Heilbroner, Robert L. *The Great Ascent: The Struggle for Economic Development in Our Time* (New York: Harper, 1963).

Hexter, J. H. "The Education of the Aristocracy in the Renaissance," *Reappraisals in History* (Evanston: Northwestern University Press, 1961), pp. 45-70. Originally published in *Journal of Modern History* (March 1950).

Hill, Christopher. "William Perkins and the Poor," *Puritans and Revolution: The English Revolution of the Seventeenth Century* (New York: Schocken, 1964). Originally published in *Past and Present,* ii (1957).

Holmes, Catherine E. *l'Éloquence judiciare de 1620 à 1660. Reflet des problèmes sociaux, religieux et politiques de l'époque* (Paris: A. G. Nizet, 1967).

Houghton, Walter E., Jr. "The English Virtuoso in the Seventeenth Century," *Journal of the History of Ideas,* iii (1942), 51-73, 190-219.

———. "The History of Trades: Its Relation to Seventeenth Century Thought as Seen in Bacon, Petty, Evelyn, and Boyle," *Journal of the History of Ideas,* ii (1941), 33-60.

Huxley, Aldous. *The Devils of Loudun* (New York: Harper and Row, 1965 [1952]).

Imbert, Jean. "Les prescriptions hospitalières du Concile de Trent et leur diffusion en France," *Revue d'histoire de l'Église de France*, XLII (1956), 5-28.

Inauguration de la statue de Théophraste Renaudot (1586-1653) fondateur de journalisme et des consultations charitables pour les pauvres malades, 4 juin 1893 (Paris: 1893).

Inauguration des statues de Théophraste Renaudot, ses principales oeuvres, la Gazette jusqu'en 1893 (Paris: 1893).

Jaryc, Marc. "Studies of 1935-1942 on the History of the Periodic Press," *Journal of Modern History*, XV (1943), 127-41.

Jones, Richard Foster. *Ancients and Moderns: A Study of the Rise of the Scientific Movement in Seventeenth Century England* (Berkeley: University of California Press, 1965 [1959]).

Jordan, Wilbur K. *Men of Substance: A Study of the Thought of Two English Revolutionaries, Henry Parker and Henry Robinson* (Chicago: University of Chicago Press, 1942).

———. *Philanthropy in England 1480-1660: A Study of the Changing Pattern of English Social Aspirations* (London: George Allen and Unwin, 1959).

Jourdain, Charles M. G. *Histoire de l'Université de Paris au XVIIe et XVIIIe siècles* (Paris: Hachette, 1862-1866).

Kerviler, René. *Guillaume Bautru, Comte de Serrant* (Paris: Menu, 1876).

———. *La presse politique sous Richelieu et l'académicien Jean de Sirmond 1589-1649* (Paris: Baur, 1876).

Kingdon, Robert M. "Social Welfare in Calvin's Geneva," *American Historical Review*, LXXVI (1971), 50-69.

Knachel, Philip A. *England and the Fronde: The Impact of the English Civil War and Revolution in France* (Ithaca: Cornell University Press, 1967).

Koyré, Alexandre. "La Renaissance: les sciences exactes," *Histoire générale des sciences*, ed., René Taton (Paris: Presses Universitaires de France, 1958), Vol. II, 91-107.

Krieger, Étienne. *Une grande querelle médicale: histoire thérapeutique de l'antimoine* (Paris, 1878).

Kuhn, Thomas S. *The Copernican Revolution: Planetary Astronomy in the Development of Western Thought* (New York: Modern Library, 1959 [1957]).

267

Lapeyre, Henri. *Une famille de marchands: les Ruiz* (Paris: Armand Colin, 1955).

Larrieu, Felix. *Gui Patin: sa vie, son oeuvre, sa thérapeutique* (Paris: 1889).

Lastic, Vicomte, Saint-Jal. "Théophraste Renaudot," *Revue poitevine* (1873), 45-50, 106-11, 138-42, 169-77, 206-12.

Lathuillère, Roger. *La préciosité: étude historique et linguistique* (Geneva: Droz, 1966).

Lecoq, Marcel. *l'Assistance par le travail en France* (Paris: V. Girard, 1900).

Legué, Gabriel, *Urbain Grandier et les possédées de Loudun* (Paris: 1880).

LeLong, P. Jacques. *Bibliothèque historique de la France* (Paris: Gabriel Martin, 1719).

Lenoble, Robert. *Mersenne, ou la naissance du mécanisme* (Paris: 1943).

Lepreux, H. "Une enquête sur l'imprimerie de Paris en 1644," *Bibliographe moderne*, xiv (1910), 5-36.

————. "Une statistique des imprimeurs et libraires en 1625," *Revue des bibliothèques*, xxi (1911), 404-09.

Lerosy, A. *Loudun, histoire civile et religieuse* (Loudun: Librairie Blanchard, 1908).

Lewis, W. H. *The Splendid Century: Life in the France of Louis XIV* (New York: Doubleday Anchor, 1957 [1953]).

Ligou, D. *Le Protestantisme en France de 1598 à 1715* (Paris: S.E.D.E.S., 1968).

Livois, René de. *Histoire de la presse française*, Vol. 1: "Des origines à 1881" (Lausanne: 1965).

Lorris, Pierre Georges. *La Fronde* (Paris: A. Michel, 1961).

Lousse, E. *La société d'ancien régime: organization et réprésentation corporatives* (Louvain: 1943).

Lublinskaya, A. D. *French Absolutism: The Crucial Phase, 1620-1629* (New York: Cambridge University Press, 1968).

Mandrou, Robert. *De la culture populaire aux XVIIe et XVIIIe siècles: la bibliothèque bleue de Troyes* (Paris: Stock, 1964).

————. *La France aux XVIIe et XVIIIe siècles* (Paris: Presses Universitaires de France, 1967).

————. *Introduction à la France moderne: essai de psychologie historique 1500-1640* (Paris: A. Michel, 1961).

————. *Magistrats et sorciers en France au XVIIᵉ siècle* (Paris: Plon, 1968).

Manevy, Raymond. *La presse française de Renaudot à Rochefort* (Paris: J. Foret, 1958).

Martin, Henri-Jean. "Ce qu'on lisait à Paris au XVIᵉ siècle," *Bulletin d'Humanisme et Renaissance*, XXI (1959), 222-30. English trans. in *French Humanism 1470-1600*, ed., Werner L. Gundersheimer (New York: Harper and Row, 1969).

————. "l'Édition parisienne au XVIIᵉ siècle, quelques aspects économiques," *Annales*, VII (1952), 303-18.

————. "Un grand éditeur parisien au XVIIᵉ siècle: Sebastien Cramoisy," *Gutenberg-Jahrbuch* (1967), 179-88.

————. *Livre, pouvoirs et société à Paris au XVIIᵉ siècle (1598-1701)* (Geneva: Droz, 1969).

————. "Un projet de réforme de l'imprimerie parisienne en 1645," *Humanisme actif: mélanges d'art et de littérature offerts à Julien Cain* (Paris: Hermann, 1968).

————. See Lucien Febvre.

Mauro, Frederic. *Le XVIᵉ siècle européen: aspects économiques* (Paris: Presses Universitaires de France, 1966).

Mellottée, Paul. *Histoire économique de l'imprimerie*, Vol. I: *l'Imprimerie sous l'ancien régime 1439-1789* (Paris: 1905).

Merbaum, Richard. "The Role and Goal of Science in the Life and Works of Marin Mersenne," Master's thesis, Department of History, New York University, 1968.

Metzger, Hélène. *Les doctrines chimiques en France du début du XVIIᵉ à la fin du XVIIIᵉ siècle* (Paris: 1923).

Millepierres, François. "Théophraste Renaudot," *Revue de Paris*, No. 11 (Novembre 1964), 32-39.

————. *La vie quotidienne des médecins au temps de Molière* (Paris: Hachette, 1964).

Mitton, Ferdinand. *La presse française des origines à la Révolution* (Paris: Guy le Prat, 1945).

Mollat, Michel. "La notion de pauvreté au moyen âge: position de problèmes," *Revue d'histoire de l'Église de France*, LII (1966), 6-24.

Mols, Roger, S. J. *Introduction à la démographie historique des villes d'Europe du XIVe au XVIIIe siècle* (Louvain: Recueil de travaux d'histoire et de philologie, 1954-1956).

Monnier, Alexandre. *Histoire de l'assistance publique dans les temps anciens et modernes* (Paris: Guillaumin, 1866).

Moreau, Celestin. *Bibliographie des Mazarinades* (Paris: Renouard, 1850-1851). 3 volumes.

Mousnier, Roland. "Le Conseil du Roi de la mort de Henri III au gouvernement personnel de Louis XIV," *Études d'histoire moderne et contemporaine* (1947-1948), 29-67.

———. *Les XVIe et XVIIe siècles* (Paris: Presses Universitaires de France, 1965 [1954]).

———. *État et société en France aux XVIIe et XVIIIe siècles* (Paris: Centre de documentation universitaire, 1969).

———. "Études sur la population de la France au XVIIe siècle," *Dix-septième siècle* (1952), 527-42.

———. "Paris, capitale politique au moyen âge et dans les temps modernes," *Colloques. Cahiers et civilizations* (1962), 39-80.

———. "Quelques raisons de la Fronde: les causes des journées révolutionaires parisiennes de 1648," *Dix-septième siècle* (1949), 33-78.

———. *La venalité des offices sous Henri IV et Louis XIII* (Rouen: Maugard, 1945).

Nelson, Benjamin N. *The Idea of Usury: From Tribal Brotherhood to Universal Otherhood* (Chicago: University of Chicago Press, 1969 [1949]).

Nouvelle biographie générale (Paris: Firmin-Didot, 1862-1866). 46 volumes.

O'Connell, D. P. *Richelieu* (New York: World Publishing, 1968).

Olivier-Martin, Fr. *l'Organization corporative de la France d'ancien régime* (Paris: Librairie du Recueil Sirey, 1938).

Ong, Walter J., S.J. *Ramus, Method and the Decay of Dialogue: From the Art of Discourse to the Art of Reason* (Cambridge: Harvard University Press, 1958).

Pagès, Georges. "Essai sur l'évolution des institutions administratives en France du commencement du XVIe siècle à la fin du XVIIe," *Revue d'histoire moderne* (1932), 8-57.

Pannetier, Odette. et al. *La vie de Théophraste Renaudot* (Paris: Gallimard, 1929).

Pattison, Mark. *Isaac Causabon* (Oxford: Clarendon Press, 1892).

Paultre, Christian. *De la répression de la mendacité et du vagabondage en France sous l'ancien régime* (Paris: Larose, 1906).

Pellisson-Fontanier, Paul. *Histoire de l'Académie Française, depuis son établissement jusqu'à 1652* (Paris: J-B. Coignard, 1729).

Petibon, Fanny. See F. Dahl.

Pigelet, Jacques. *Organization intérieure de la presse périodique française* (Orleans: 1909).

Pintard, René. *La Mothe le Vayer, Gassendi, Guy Patin: études de bibliographie et de critique suivies de textes inédits de Guy Patin* (Paris: Boivin, 1943).

———. *Le libertinage érudit dans la première moitié du XVIIe siècle* (Paris: Boivin, 1943).

Pottinger, David T. *The French Book Trade in the Ancien Regime 1500-1791* (Cambridge: Harvard University Press, 1958).

Pound, J. F. "An Elizabethan Census of the Poor: The Treatment of Vagrancy in Norwich, 1570-1580," *University of Birmingham Historical Journal*, VIII (1962), 134-62.

Purver, Margery. *The Royal Society: Concept and Creation* (Cambridge: M.I.T. Press, 1967).

Quemada, Bernard. *Introduction à l'étude du vocabulaire médical 1600-1710* (Besançon: Université de Besançon, 1955).

Ranum, Orest E. *Paris in the Age of Absolutism* (New York: John Wiley, 1968).

———. *Richelieu and the Councillors of Louis XIII* (Oxford: Clarendon Press, 1963).

Raynaud, Maurice. *Les médecins au temps de Molière* (Paris: Didier, 1862).

Revillot, M. *Un maître des conférences au milieu du XVIIe siècle: Jean de Soudier de Richesource* (Montpellier: 1881).

Reyna, Ferdinando. *Des origins du ballet* (Paris: A. Tallone, 1955).

Rice, James V. *Gabriel Naudé* (Baltimore: Johns Hopkins Press, 1939).

271

Richard, Guy. "Un aspect particulier de la politique économique et sociale de la monarchie au XVIIe siècle: Richelieu, Colbert, la noblesse et le commerce," *Dix-septième siècle*, No. 49 (1960), 11-41.

Richardson, Lula M. "The Conferences of Théophraste Renaudot: An Episode in the Quarrel of the Ancients and the Moderns," *Modern Language Notes* (May 1933), 312-16.

Rigal, Jeanne. *La communauté des maîtres-chirurgiens jurés de Paris au XVIIe et au XVIIIe siècle* (Paris: Vigot, 1936).

Rossi, Paolo. *Francis Bacon: From Magic to Science* (Chicago: University of Chicago Press, 1968 [1957]).

Rothkrug, Lionel. *Opposition to Louis XIV: The Political and Social Origins of the French Enlightenment* (Princeton: Princeton University Press, 1965).

Rothrock, George A. "Officials and King's Men: A Note on the Possibilities of Royal Control in the Estates General," *French Historical Studies*, II (1962), 504-10.

Rousselet, Albin. *Théophraste Renaudot, fondateur des policliniques* (Paris: 1892).

Roy, Émile, *La vie et les oeuvres de Charles Sorel, Sieur de Souvigny 1602-1674* (Paris: Hachette, 1891).

Santillana, Giorgio de. *The Crime of Galileo* (Chicago: University of Chicago Press, 1955).

Seguin, Jean-Pierre. *l'Information en France avant la périodique: 517 canards imprimés entre 1529 et 1631* (Paris: Maisonneuve et Larose, 1964).

———. *l'Information en France, de Louis XII à Henri II* (Geneva: E. Droz, 1961).

Snyders, Georges. *La pédagogie en France aux XVIIe et XVIIIe siècles* (Paris: Presses Universitaires de France, 1965).

Solomon, Howard M. "The Innocent Inventions of Théophraste Renaudot: Public Welfare, Science, and Propaganda in Seventeenth Century France." Ph.D. dissertation, Department of History, Northwestern University, 1969.

Spinka, Matthew. *John Amos Comenius, That Incomparable Moravian* (Chicago: University of Chicago Press, 1943).

St. Leon, Martin. *Les compagnonnages* (Paris: A. Colin, 1901).

Stauffenegger, R. "Réforme, richesse, et pauvreté," *Revue d'histoire de l'Église de France*, LII (1966), 47-58.

Tapié, Victor L. *La France de Louis XIII et de Richelieu* (Paris: Flammarion, 1967).

Taton, René, ed. *Histoire générale des sciences*. Vol. II: "La Science Moderne, de 1450 à 1800" (Paris: Presses Universitaires de France, 1958).

———. *Les origines de l'Académie Royale des Sciences* (Paris: 1965).

"Théophraste Renaudot et les petites affiches et avis divers à Lyon," *Bulletin historique et archeologique du diocèse de Lyon*, No. 1 (1930), 92-94.

Thèry, M. *Histoire de l'éducation en France* (Paris: 1858).

Thuau, Étienne. *Raison d'État et pensée politique à l'époque de Richelieu* (Paris: A. Colin, 1966).

Tierney, Brian. *Medieval Poor Law: A Sketch of Canonical Theory and Its Application in England* (Berkeley: University of California Press, 1959).

Treves, Paolo. "The Title of Campanella's 'City of the Sun,'" *Journal of the Warbourg and Courtauld Institutes*, III, (1939-1940), 248-51.

Trevor-Roper, H. R. "Three Foreigners: The Philosophers of the Puritan Revolution," *The Crisis of the Seventeenth Century: Religion, the Reformation, and Social Change* (New York: Harper and Row, 1968), pp. 237-93.

Triare, Paul. "Richelieu et Guy Patin," *La France médicale* (1905), 21-24.

Turnbull, George Henry. *Samuel Hartlib: A Sketch of His Life and His Relations to J. A. Comenius* (London: Oxford University Press, 1920).

———. *Hartlib, Dury and Comenius: Gleanings from Hartlib's Papers* (London: University Press of Liverpool, 1947).

Vaillé, Eugène. *Histoire générale des postes françaises*. Vol. III: "De la réforme de Louis XIII à la surintendance générale des postes (1630-1668)" (Paris: Presses Universitaires de France, 1950).

Varin-d'Ainvelle, M. *La presse en France: genèse et évolution de ses fonctions psycho-sociales* (Paris: Presses Universitaires de France, 1965).

Venard, Marc. *Bourgeois et paysans au XVIIe siècle: recherche sur le rôle des bourgeois parisiens dans la vie agricole au XVIIe siècle* (Paris: S.E.V.P.E.N., 1957).

Weill, Georges. *Le journal, origines, évolution et la rôle de la presse périodique* (Paris: Renaissance du Livre, 1934).

Wolf, John B. *Louis XIV* (New York: W. W. Norton, 1968).

Yates, Frances A. *The Art of Memory* (Chicago: University of Chicago Press, 1966).

―――. *The French Academy of the Sixteenth Century* (London: University of London Press, 1947).

―――. *Giordano Bruno and the Hermetic Tradition* (Chicago: University of Chicago Press, 1964).

Zeller, Gaston. "l'Administration monarchique avant les intendants: parlements et gouverneurs," *Revue historique* (1947), 180-216.

―――. "Une notion de caractère historico-sociale: la dérogeance," *Cahiers internationaux de sociologie* (1947), 40-74.

INDEX

Abyssinia, 151. *See also* Ethiopia
Académie Française, 62, 66, 67, 91, 95, 99, 204, 217
Académie Gazetique, 96
Académie Royale de Poesie et de Musique, 61-62
academies, xiv, 53, 61, 63, 91. *See also* Renaissance academies
Academy of Paris, 177. *See also* Faculty of Medicine
Acadia, 144
Actus Triumphalis, 9
administration, 165, 195, 196, 196n, 197-98. *See also* royal administration
aeolipyle, 74
Affiches, 116
Africa, 158n
air, 72
Aire, 135
Albigensians, 7
alchemy, 174, 181. *See also* chemical medicine, hermeticism
alembics, 174
"Alep in Syrie," 156
Alexander, 125
Amelia, 48n
Amiens, 133
Amsterdam, 107, 113
anatomy, 7, 163
Anjou, 132
Anne of Austria, 130, 141, 186-87, 198-99, 202, 205, 206, 207. *See also Gazette*, Louis XIII
annual, 105, 106-07, 108
antidotes, 79
Antimoine justifié, 219
antimony, 170-74, 219-20. *See also* chemical medicine
Antwerp, 157
Apelles, 125

Apologie du Bureau d'Adresse, 212
apothecaries, 80, 166-67, 169. *See also* antimony, Faculty of Medicine, Théophraste Renaudot
Aquaviva, Cardinal, 51
Arab medicine, 179, 181-82. *See also* antimony, chemical medicine
Aragon, 143
Archbishop of Canterbury, 160
Archbishop of Paris, 162n
Aristotle, 70-71, 70n, 71n, 87
Armorial général, 151
arms, 53
aromatic waters, 169
Arsenal, 72
artillery, 53
Assemblies of Notables, 98
astrology, 81-82
astronomers, 62
astronomy, 70, 106
Aubéry, 145-46
Aumônier de France, 195
Avertissement à Théophraste Renaudot, 180-81
Avignon, 51, 166

Babylon, 157
baccalaureate, 163
Bacon, Francis, xiv, 66, 74-75, 87
Balkan principalities, 158
ballet, 57, 57n, 125. *See also Gazette*
Ballet des Improvistes, 140
Baltic Sea, 144
Balzac, J. L. Guez de, 111
ban et arrière-ban, 132
banks, 53
Bapaume, 135
barbers, 10, 167, 168. *See also* surgeons

281